The Otogibōko

A Collection of Ghost Stories of Old Japan

A COMPLETE TRANSLATION OF THE OTOGIBŌKO

Translated and annotated by

Yoshiko Dykstra

Kanji Press

HONOLULU

This publication is printed on acid-free paper and
meets the guidelines for permanence and durability
of the Council of Library Resources.

Print-ready copy prepared by Kanji Press.

DISTRIBUTED BY

UNIVERSITY OF HAWAI'I PRESS
2840 Kolowalu Street
Honolulu, Hawai'i 96822
www.uhpress.hawaii.edu

CONTENTS

INTRODUCTION TO THE OTOGIBŌKO

This volume is a translation of the entire *Otogibōko*,[1] which was published in 1666. *Otogibōko* is a collection of supernatural tales comprising sixty-eight stories in thirteen chapters. Its author, Asai Ryōi,[2] is widely regarded as the finest writer of *kanazōshi*[3] produced in Japan between 1600 and 1682.

I use the reading *otogibōko* instead of *togibōko*. The term *otogi*[4] or *togi* is related to a group of storytellers called *otogishū*[5] or *togishū*, who were hired by feudal lords. Over time their stories created a new genre called *otogizōshi*[6] in the Muromachi period (1392–1573). A *bōko*[7] customarily was placed near a child's pillow to ward off evil spirits and was buried with a dead child as a companion.

In the eighty years prior to Ihara Saikaku,[8] abundant *kanazōshi* writings were produced, including essays, Buddhist *setsuwa* tales, travelogues, and records of famous scenic places. These *kanazōshi* cover a wide range of didactic and informative topics written in

---

1. 伽婢子, *A Doll for Entertainment*.
2. 浅井了意 (d. 1691).
3. 仮名草子, prose literature. For a study of Edo literature, including *kanazōshi* and *ukiyozōshi,* see Haruo Shirane, ed., *Early Modern Japanese Literature,* Columbia University Press (2002): 21–169.
4. 御伽, entertainment.
5. 御伽衆.
6. お伽草子, booklets for entertainment.
7. 婢子, a toy or a doll in the likeness of a child.
8. 1642– 1693.

easy-to-read kana mixed with some kanji characters. They attracted a large audience of samurai, merchants, and city-dwellers throughout the Edo period.[9] During these eighty years, the *kanazōshi* genre underwent notable changes. In the early period, *kanazōshi* maintained a medieval aesthetic exclusive to a small group of readers, including aristocrats, upper-class samurai, merchants, and wealthy medical doctors, as well as certain *otogishū* like *renga*[10] masters and storytellers. In other words, at that time *kanizōshi* was a form of mental exercise or play among the intelligentsia.

The best-selling *Kiyomizu monogatari*,[11] by Asayama Irin'an, appeared in 1638. It sold two to three thousand copies in Kyoto and in the rural areas. The work compares Buddhism's propagation of belief in future liberation from karma with Confucianism's pragmatic approach to daily life in the present world, with its useful lessons on the relationships between ruler and subject, parent and child, husband and wife, and friends. The question and answer format in *Kiyomizu monogatari* set forth easily accessible explanations and examples of the Confucian ideas that were promoted by the Tokugawa shogunate. The work answered the questions and needs of contemporary readers, including the masterless samurai. It was a guide for living under the new Tokugawa regime and system. By that time, the pool of *kanazōshi* authors had become more diversified. Many writers were without patrons, working as sorts of scholarly *rōnin*. The audience for *kanazōshi* mushroomed as the development of the movable-type press made written works inexpensive to print. The popularity of *kanazōshi* peaked between 1658 and 1672, with Asai Ryōi becoming the genre's best-selling author. He produced many works, starting with *Kanninki*,[12] followed by *Ukiyo monogatari*[13] and *Otogibōko*.

Asai was fifty years old when he began to write *kanazōshi*. He became the resident priest of Shōganji, a temple in Kyoto, when he was over sixty years of age. His aim in *Otogibōko* was to educate people in the correct Way. *Otogibōko* is full of didactic tales interspersed with

....

9. 1600–1868.

10. Linked verse.

11. 清水物語.

12. 堪忍記, *Forbearance Records*.

13. 浮世物語, *Tales of the Floating World*.

tales of ghosts and the supernatural—all strongly colored with Buddhist morality. After he became popular as a *kanazōshi* writer, Asai returned to seeking the Way in his capacity as a priest. As he grew older, he wrote commentaries to Buddhist texts, such as *Zen'aku ingakyō jikikai*[14] and *Amidakyō kobu*,[15] and preached until the very end of his life.

Prior to *Otogibōko*, some Chinese supernatural tales like those in *Sentōshinwa*[16] and a similar Korean version, *Kingōshinwa*,[17] were known in Japan. *Sentōshinwa*[18] was imported to Japan before 1482.[19] The majority of *Otogibōko's* sixty-five stories are from Chinese and Korean sources. The collection's most famous tale in English translation is "Botan no tōrō."[20] This tale shows the efficacy of recitation of *The Lotus Sutra* for appeasing and saving the protagonist's disturbed soul.

Asai adapted these foreign tales to his *Otogibōko* by changing place names and qualities of characters from the original Chinese works. Sometimes Asai only kept the original tale's framework and created his own narrative. For example, "The Plum Blossom Spirit"[21] tells the tale of a young samurai and the spirit of the plum blossoms. Asai changes the original Chinese Dragon Palace into Kaizenji, a temple in Ina District of Shin Province. His introduction of *waka*[22] makes the tale sound more elegant, along the lines of Heian *monogatari*.[23] The tale's historical context of the Takeda clan's attack on the Murakami clan[24] provides a setting that was familiar to contemporary Japanese readers. At the end, the young samurai protagonist dies on the battlefield, feeling his life has been futile after losing his beloved. The tale conveys the Buddhist teaching of the impermanence of life. Similar to his reference

....

14. 善悪因果経直解, *Commentary on the Karma Sutra of Good and Bad.*

15. 阿弥陀経鼓吹, *Inspiration of the Amida Sutra.*

16. 剪灯新話 (Chinese: *Jian deng xin hua*), *New Tales under the Lamplight*, by Qu You, 1387.

17. 金鰲新話. See *Kingōshinwa*, Ajia Bunkasha, 1973.

18. Abbreviated as *SS* in the footnotes of the translated tales.

19. See Hanada Fujio in *Otogibōko, Shinnihonkoten bungaku taikei*, Iwanami, shoten, 2001, p. 500.

20. "The Peony Lantern." *Otogibōko* (hereafter *OT*), 3-3.

21. *OT*, 12-1.

22. A form of courtly poetry.

23. Romantic fiction.

24. The attack is described in *Kōyōgunkan*, 5.

to the Takeda attack on the Murakami, Asai inserts other historical details, often related to the Ōnin War,[25] to make the stories more familiar and accessible to his readers.

As mentioned in the two prefaces to *Otogibōko* (one in Japanese and the other in *kanbun*), Asai did not write these stories to educate people who already had the benefit of education. Instead, the goal of his stories was to guide young innocent children to the correct Way. Thus, *Otogibōko* is an apt title for the collection.

In many of *Otogibōko*'s stories, the simple life of a happy and easygoing young man is turned upside down after meeting a ghost or spirit in the form of a beautiful woman. His life becomes more complicated as the story progresses and his difficulties lead him to think more deeply and understand the true meaning of life. His personality matures and he decides to renounce ordinary life because he realizes its futility. The story ends with him becoming a Buddhist ascetic in order to be delivered from his sad and distressing situation, or with his untimely death. Here again, we see the author's *hōben*[26] in guiding unknowing young people to the correct Way. In the case of "*Botan no tōrō*," the timeless theme of a man's fatal attraction to an enchanting female warns the reader about the menacing power of human longing and love, especially when it is bound up with carnal desire.

"The Courtesan Miyagino"[27] expresses another Buddhist principle. Miyagino dies toward the end of the story, but there is a possibility that she is reborn as a child of the Takakura family. This development embodies the Buddhist idea of karmic rebirth, thereby creating hope for Miyagino's heartbroken husband.

A few stories in *Otogibōko*, such as "A Lump of Lice,"[28] are unrelated to religious teachings or historical incidents. Instead they inform the reader about medicinal herbs used to cure unusual ailments. This non-Buddhist tale suggests Asai's interest in systems of Chinese herbal medicine[29] that recently had been introduced.

....

25. 1467–1477.

26. 方便, skillful means.

27. *OT,* 6-3.

28. *OT,* 13-6.

29. E.g., *honzō kōmoku* 本草綱目.

After translating the entire collection, I have come to believe that *Otogibōko*'s fantastic tales of ghosts and the supernatural are a form of *hōben*. Buddhist priests used this technique to teach uneducated people about the futility of life, and to guide them to the right Way. Although Asai Ryōi was a renowned writer of *kanazōshi*, after he returned to his priestly calling, writing *kanazōshi* became nothing more than a skillful means of *shujōsaido*.[30]

Some words used in the translation require further explanation. *Chigiru*,[31] the word for male and female protagonists making a pledge, typically connotes a purely mental relationship, but it also can refer to sexual intercourse. If one's soul is unsettled after death, it returns to this life as a *yūrei*.[32] Funeral rites are performed to appease such a disturbed soul, as in "A Pledge in a Changed Life."[33] I translate *yōkai*[34] as a demonic being, something strange and mysterious that adversely affects humans. I translate *kai*[35] as something extraordinary, frightening, supernatural, and unfathomable. Thus, the *kaidan*[36] stories in *Otogibōko* anticipate later *kaidan* collections, such as *Ugetsu monogatari* by Ueda Akinari.[37]

In this book I supply kanji for names, titles of books, and terms when necessary. Macrons are omitted for well-known terms and place names such as Tokyo, Osaka, and Kyoto. The pinyin system is used for romanization of Chinese names and terms. I use Japanese readings for most Chinese place names, titles of books, and personal names, like "Lady Ri" for "Lady Li." I also use modern Japanese readings for the romanization of Japanese names and terms, including *waka* poems: "i" for "hi," "wa" for "ha," "o" for "uo." Family and given names are interchangeably used. Some poems are identified with similar ones

30. 衆生済度, delivering others. For my conclusion, refer to Emoto Yutaka, *Otogiboko*, Kyōikusha, p. 45.
31. 契る
32. 幽霊, ghost or spirit.
33. See *OT*, 11-3, 25.
34. 妖怪.
35. 怪.
36. 怪談, ghost tales.
37. 1734–1809.

found in anthologies like *Shin shūiwakashū* and *Shinshūishū*.[38] This information is placed in the footnotes. The present illustrated text is based on the text owned by Kokuritsu Kokkai Toshokan, the National Diet Library.

My deep appreciation goes to Dr. Michael Cooper, former editor of *Monumenta Nipponica*, who read this translation and spent hours helping to improve some of my *waka* translations. I am grateful for the efforts and enthusiasm of Stephanie Chun of the University of Hawai'i Press, Dr. Lise McKean, and Gregory Foster, who edited my entire manuscript, and Julie Chun of the University of Hawai'i Press for managing the project and designing the book. Finally, this book is dedicated to my late husband, Dr. Andrew H. Dykstra, who always encouraged and supported my translation of classical Japanese literature.

38. 新拾遺和歌集, compiled in 1363.

PREFACE TO *OTOGIBŌKO* (KANA)

The holy men[1] teach by preaching the immutable way of the human world, rectify themselves through virtuous deeds, and discipline their minds by setting forth the reason and logic [of this life]. The countries under heaven follow their example and they are models for laypeople.

Although they do not usually talk about anything strange like demonic powers,[2] they may speak [of them] and show examples when the situation demands. Therefore, the *Eki*[3] mentions a dragon fighting in a field, the *Sho* records a pheasant crying in a pot, the *Shunjū* shows troublesome bandits, and the *Shi* contains chapters of folk songs and *Tei*-style poems.[4] Thus, these [Chinese classics] have been handed down to later generations as models. Moreover, the Buddhist writings teach us the karmic law of the three generations of past, present, and future; warn us of the karma of transmigrations of the Four Lives;[5] and show and preach to us about a variety of mysterious powers.[6]

1. *Seijin* 聖人, "holy men," those admired in the Confucian classics, including Confucius himself.
2. *Kairikiranshin* 怪力乱神, strange powers and disturbed gods.
3. The following four writings belong to the Chinese classics: *Ekikyō* 易経, *Shokyō* 書経, *Shunjū* 春秋, and *Shikyō* 詩経.
4. The *Tei* style of poetry includes lewd poems about men and women affected by demonic powers.
5. *Shishō* 四生, "the four forms of birth," including mammals and egg-bearing animals.
6. *Jintsū* 神通 and *henge* 変化 are here translated together as "mysterious powers." *Henge* refers to transformations, such as Bodhisattva Kannon changing into a human.

Now Shinto,[7] "the Way of the gods," shows us the wonderful and mysterious spirits in stones, earth, grass, and trees. So these Three Teachings [Confucian, Buddhist, and Shinto] teach us something mysterious, strange, extraordinary,[8] and impressive. These teachings are not at all in vain. They take the role of go-between to guide us in the Ways.

The writings of holy and wise men from the past as well as the various Chinese classics are so abundant that they reach to the eaves. Why do writings from the past and present in Japan fill five carts?[9] [Tales] like *Yamato monogatari* by Former Emperor Hanayama,[10] *Shūi mongatari* by Grand Councilor Uji,[11] and others like *Taketori monogatari*,[12] and the chapter about Toshikage in *Utsubo monogatari*,[13] contain so many mysterious and strange stories that we cannot count them on our fingers.

But this *Otogibōko* was compiled and narrated in recent times, not in the distant past. It is not meant to please scholars, but to entertain young girls so that they may be awakened, rectify themselves, and be helped to advance in the correct way. People in olden times would have hated those who cherish what they saw while not believing what they heard.

Everything in heaven and earth, including the Five Ways of Yin-Yang,[14] is so vast, immeasurable, mysteriously profound, and unfathomable. Do not doubt what you hear even when you don't see it with your eyes. This is written in the first month of the sixth year of Kanbun [1666].

—Shoshi[15] Hyōsuishi Shōun[16]

....

7. *Shintō* or *shindō* 神道, "the Way of the gods," is a traditional set of religious concepts and practices indigenous to Japan. It contrasts with Buddhism, Confucianism, and Christianity, which originated outside of Japan.

8. *Kaii* 怪異, something extraordinary or unfathomable, and therefore fearsome and frightening to people.

9. The expression *gosha ni tsumu* 五車に積む means 殿, abundant.

10. Emperor Hanayama, the sixty-fifth emperor of Japan, is popularly believed to have written *Yamato monogatari* 大和物語 in 951.

11. *Ujishūi monogatari* 宇治拾遺物語.

12. 竹取物語, the first *monogatari* (fiction) literature of Japan.

13. *Utsubo monogatari* 宇津保物語, written in the middle of the Heian period, contains the first chapter in which something fantastic about Toshikage is narrated.

14. *nyōgogyō* 陰陽五行, referring to all the phenomena in this world.

15. *Shoshi* or *shoji* 処士, those who were not serving in the government.

16. Hyōsuishi Shōun 瓢水子松雲 is the pen name of Asai Ryōi, the author.

PREFACE TO *OTOGIBŌKO* (KANBUN)[1]

Otogibōko is a collection of mysterious stories by Shōun that were originally written on scrolls. The language is so beautiful that readers will be completely impressed by its fanciful style. In the *Analects of Confucius*, mysteries such as spirits like gods and demons[2] are not talked about. Does [*Otogibōko*] deserve the insult that it cheats its readers? No, that is not so. Gentlemen aiming to attain the Way by investigating the origin of things, selecting words, and accumulating [merit from] good deeds and virtue have names that remain eternal. In contrast, common folk do not know how to read the classics; their ears are not able to hear great teachings while their bodies are incapable of maintaining proper conduct. Thus day after day, they remain in a vulgar, secular condition. When they hear something great and intelligent, they become confused and withdraw, muttering. Various sutras and writings have broad and profound meanings, but [to ignorant common folk] it is just like beating drums before a group of the deaf. What is the use?

Otogibōko inspires new things and explains difficult things with ease. It pleases common people by its humor. The book awakens the sleepy and makes the tired feel refreshed. This is what common people like and understand. [The book] strongly warns against lustful relationships between men and women and wants to reason about the mysteries of ghosts and spirits. Even if it is not fitting for the gentleman's

1. Chinese writing that is annotated so it can be read in Japanese.

2. *Kaijin* 怪神.

way, [the book] only wishes to provide a means [for presenting] ethical guidance to common people.

[This is written in] the latter part of the first month of the sixth year of Kanbun [1666].

—Unshō[3]

---

3. Unidentified. Possibly another pen name of the author.

THE *OTOGIBŌKO*

1-1   The Beam of the Dragon Palace

Spanning east to west, Seta Bridge in Gō Province[1] was the greatest bridge in the eastern provinces. To the west of the [bridge], Shiga[2] and Karasaki[3] were seen in the north and the ferryboats of Yamada[4] and Yabase.[5] [Here] one could enjoy watching boats sailing[6] to Shiozu[7] and Kaizu.[8] From the south, Ishiyama Temple,[9] where a bell was rung every evening, was visible, as well as Iwama Temple,[10] accessible from the mountains. To the east of the bridge, facing north, lay Shina Village, famous for the lotus flowers that bloomed in the middle of the sixth month. It was a joy to smell their fragrance, which filled the air and kept visitors' hearts from becoming soiled and muddy.[11] To the south, Mount Tanakami[12] appeared in the shadow of the setting sun. [Here] the sounds of cicadas cooled the heat of summer. The road to Ise continued behind the bridge; before it, the lake flowed to the Uji river, where it emerged as the Shishitobi rapids.[13]

There was a cave called Hotarudani[14] north of the bridge. Nearby, several million *koku*[15] of fireflies appeared on the surface of the lake

....

1. The bridge spans Seta 瀬田 River in Ōtsu-shi. It was believed that below the bridge one could travel to the Dragon Palace.

2. 滋賀; in Shiga-sato, Otsu-shi. Shiga-ken is known as an *utamakura* 歌枕, poetic spot.

3. 辛崎; in Otsu-shi.

4. 山田: present-day Kita Yamada-cho, Kusatsu-shi.

5. 矢橋: present-day Yabase-cho, Kusatsu-shi.

6. The boats loaded in Tsuruga traveled to the Kinai area.

7. 塩津; in present-day Nishiasai-cho, Ika-gun. Shiozu was an important transportation point between the Kinai 畿内 and Hokuriku 北陸 areas.

8. 海津; in present-day Makino-cho, Takashima-gun. Kaizu is about 7.5 *ri*, or 19 miles, from Tsuruga.

9. 石山寺; located to the west of Seta Bridge, Ishiyama Temple is sacred for the Kannon faith.

10. 岩間寺; in Uchihata-cho, Otsu-shi, Shiga-ken.

11. Lotus blossoms, grown in the mud, keep visitors' hearts from muddy secular delusions.

12. 田上山; in Otsu-shi, Tanakami is known as an *utamakura*.

13. Shishitobi 鹿飛: deer jumping. The name comes from a saying that deer could jump from one spot to another in the narrow parts of the lake.

14. 蛍谷; in present-day Hotarudani, Otsu-shi, Hotarudani is known for fireflies (*Tōkaidō meishoki* 東海道名所記, 5).

15. One *koku* 石, or *goku*, equals 180 liters.

from the fourth month to the middle of the fifth. Some gathered into balls, others formed circles and rings like carriage wheels. They flew up to the clouds and plummeted onto the lake to disperse. During the rains of the fifth month, they shone radiantly like pomegranate [seeds], reflecting the light. It was a sight not to be ignored, and numerous spectators, secular and non-secular alike, came and composed poems, talking and writing at length about the fireflies.

A small shrine was located on the beach southeast of the bridge. Once Tawara Tōda Hidesato[16] traveled to the Dragon Palace [from there] and destroyed a huge centipede on Mount Mikami,[17] returning with a roll of silk, a straw bag, a pot, and a hanging bell.[18] The bell was donated to Mii Temple and is celebrated to this day.

In the Eishō era,[19] during the reign of Emperor Gokashiwabara,[20] Makami Akina[21] lived in Matsumoto in Shiga District.[22] He had been a student at court,[23] but since retiring from that position to avoid worldly affairs, he spent peaceful days and months in [Matsumoto]. One evening, two men dressed in hunting clothes and *eboshi* hats visited him. Kneeling in his garden, they announced, "We have come to invite you to the Dragon Palace at the bottom of the sea."

Surprised, Makami asked, "How would we travel there? The human world and the Dragon Palace are far apart. I heard there was a way [to get there] in the old days, but it has since disappeared." The messengers replied, "A fine horse with a saddle is waiting for you outside the gate. If you ride the horse, you will have no trouble, no matter how high the waves or how deep the water." Makami, still skeptical, stood up and went outside, where he was greeted by a strong, black horse standing

---

16. 俵藤太秀郷; Tōda defeated Taira Masakado 平将門 in 940 and was appointed a governor of Shimotsuke Province.

17. The mountain in Shiga-ken is also called Mukadeyama 百足山, based on the Tawara Tōda legend.

18. The story of Tawara Tōda, the centipede, and the Dragon Palace gifts is in *Taiheiki,* 太平記 15.

19. 1504–1521.

20. 後柏原 (r. 1500–1526).

21. Makami 真上 is unidentified, but Akina 阿祇奈 may come from Agina 阿芸奈, a name that appears in the Emperor Kōgen 孝元 (r. 214–158 B.C.) entry in the *Kojiki* 古事記.

22. Present-day Matsumoto, Ōtsu-shi, Shiga-ken.

23. *Monjōshō* 文章生: a student mainly of Chinese history and literature.

eleven feet high[24] with a saddle trimmed in gold, stirrups decorated with *raden* blue shells, and a silver bit. A score of attendants in white[25] stood [by the horse]. As soon as they helped Makami mount, the horse rose and flew into the sky with two escorts riding ahead.

When Makami looked down, he saw nothing but clouds of waves and rising spray. After a while, he arrived at the gate of the Dragon Palace, which was carefully guarded by men with spears and long swords. They wore helmets of shrimp, crab, turban, and clam shells and tied their helmet strings tightly [under their chins].[26] As soon as they saw Makami, they all kneeled and touched their heads to the ground in respect. The two escorts went through the gate, and soon two officials dressed in green came out to lead Makami inside. He saw the three Chinese characters for "Ganjinmon"[27] in a frame above the gate. After walking for half a *chō*,[28] Makami ascended steps to the front hall of the palace, where he saw the Dragon King sitting. The king wore a crown decorated with a five-colored cloud and a flying snow sword at his waist and held a *shaku*[29] in his hand. He rose and led Makami to a white jade seat in the hall. Bowing deeply, Makami introduced himself: "I am a humble subject from the great country of Japan. I will decay and perish like a plant. How can I receive courtesy fit for a high-ranking guest from a divine king who lowers himself [by treating me so highly]?"

The king replied, "I have heard of you for a long time and now I see your noble face. There is no use declining my offer." The king urged Makami to take the seat offered him and took his own, which was decorated with the seven jewels[30] and faced south.[31]After a while, an announcement was made: "Honorable guests have arrived." The

....

24. *Takenanaki* 長七寸; the starting height measurement of a horse was four *shaku* (four feet); inches were added: *hitoki* 一寸, *futaki* 二寸, and so on.

25. Low-ranking officers dressed in white hunting clothes.

26. *Kabuto no o o shimeru* 甲の緒をしめる: to tie one's helmet tightly. The expression is used to indicate firm determination.

27. 含仁門: Gate of Including Mercy.

28. One *chō* is about 109 meters.

29. 笏: a long, wooden spatula-shaped object held in the right hand on formal occasions.

30. *Shichihō* 七宝: usually includes gold, silver, lapis lazuli, *hari* (glass), emeralds, red coral, and *karketana* stones.

31. Rulers traditionally sat facing south.

king rose from his seat and descended the stairs to welcome three new guests, who appeared very noble, unlike anyone in this world. Wearing jeweled crowns and straightening their brocade sleeves, they solemnly emerged from a litter decorated with the seven jewels. They quietly climbed the steps and took their places. Makami left his seat and hid himself, crouching by a gold screen.

When everyone was seated, the king said to his recently arrived guests, "I have invited a student from the human world. Please see for yourself." The king called to Makami, who emerged and bowed to the guests, who returned the courtesy. When they urged, "Please take your seat next to the king," Makami declined, saying, "I am a humble subject. How can I take a nobleman's place?" The three guests replied, "Although the human world and the Dragon Palace are far apart and the way between them has been severed, our divine king has no doubt been thinking of humans and has invited you [here] because you are an unusual man. You needn't be so modest and decline the seat offered you. Quickly, take your seat." Makami did so, and the king continued:

"I have built a new palace. The director of woodworking and the head of palace carpenters conferred and built a jade foundation, a beam resembling a rainbow,[32] cloud-like ridgepoles, and beautifully decorated pillars. Everything is finished except for a commemorative message on the top beam. I had heard that Akinagimi of Makami [in Japan] was a man celebrated for his virtue and learning. So I invited him from that distant place. I would be happy if he were to write a verse on the beam for me."

Two boys of twelve or thirteen years appeared, wearing the *karawa* hairstyle.[33] One of them held an ink stone of green jade, which contained ink made from sacred *akaza* plant ashes,[34] safflower,[35] and civet, as well as a writing brush made from a spotted bamboo[36] stem and

---

32. *Niji no utsubari* 虹のうつばり is a beam arched like a rainbow.

33. *Karawa* 唐輪 is a Chinese hairstyle for children; the hair is divided into two to make two loops at the top of the head.

34. The young leaves of the *akaza* plant are edible, and the ashes of the plant were used as a dye.

35. Safflower was mixed with ink to make it shiny

36. *Hanchiku* 班竹.

rhinoceros hair. The other offered Makami a piece of *kōjin*[37] silk, three meters long. Makami declined at first but eventually dipped the brush in the ink and wrote:

"There is a great sea dividing heaven and earth. Among the living creatures in the sea, the god of the sea, the Dragon King,[38] is most distinguished. His virtues have long benefitted his world. How could anyone overlook his blessings? Therefore, everyone prays to the god by burning incense and holding lights [candles]. Seeing a flying dragon is very auspicious, and we follow its mysterious traces.[39]

"On this day, a jade palace was newly built with brilliant decorations. The poles and pillars are adorned with crystal and coral, and the top beam with yellow amber and blue-green stones. Jade screens reflect the blue clouds of the mountains. When we open the jade doors, white mist from a [nearby] cave rises and surrounds us. Under the high sky and deep in the ground, [the Dragon King] has calmed the eight thousand *ri* of the southern sea and the five hundred of the northern sea while controlling the rain and wind. By ascending to the sky and descending to the springs, he realizes the wishes of his people. By hiding and revealing himself, he assists the higher emperor with his mercy. His power has been known from ancient times to the present, and his virtues extend even to the sand and pebbles. Black turtles and red carp leap to celebrate [the king], and the echoes in the woods and mountains gather to rejoice. Here I have composed poems to write on the decorated beam:

A new palace was built deep in the sea of Japan.
All water creatures follow the Dragon King's virtues.
Their singing voices honor the king, resounding like the wind.
The sea and river gods come to pay homage[40] to their sovereign.

osamareru
michi zo shirukeki

....

37. 鮫人: the inhabitants of the southern sea. The relationship between *kōjin* and silk is unclear, but here the text suggests that silk made by *kōjin* is rare and expensive.

38. *Watatsumi* 竜神.

39. The sentences suggest an homage to the Dragon King.

40. *Chōsō* 朝宗: a ceremony for worshiping the sovereign held in spring and autumn.

tatsunomiya no
yo wa hisakata no
tsukiji to o shiru

The king,
Knowing how to rule,
His reign in the Dragon Palace
Lasts forever,
Never to cease.

"I humbly hope that my writing on the top beam causes hundreds of fortunes and thousands of joys to spread widely. This jeweled palace will bring peace and comfort while the sea will be calm, and the reign [of the king] will be limitless like that of the sun and the moon in the sky."

At this, the Dragon King was greatly pleased and showed Makami's writing to the three guests, who all admired it. Soon a feast celebrating the completion of the top beam was held and the king said to Makami, "Being human, you may not realize that one of my guests is the deity of the sea, one the deity of rivers, and one the deity of deep pools. They have befriended you. I hope you will enjoy yourself freely at this feast." Saying this, the king circulated sake cups among his guests and urged them to drink.

Before long, more than a score of twenty-year-old ladies appeared. They sang and danced elegantly like snowflakes in the wind. Their facial features were otherworldly and their figures were very gentle and elegant; flowers adorned their jade hair ornaments. They wore thin white silk garments with sleeves. Their singing voices echoed in the clouds. They danced for a while and then retired.

The ladies were followed by more than ten children—lovely as *hina* dolls—wearing the *binzura* hairstyle[41] and dressed in embroidered *hitatare* robes over brocade *hakama* skirts. They danced about, holding flowers and turning their sleeves. It was most interesting to see that their clear singing voices, harmonizing well with the stringed instruments, rose high enough to brush the dust off the top beam.

After this performance, the king was overjoyed. The sake cups

---

41. Made by dividing the hair into two parts and looping them by the ears.

were washed and a new bottle placed before Makami. Then the king began to play a jade flute and sang the song "Kaikokugin." After he finished singing, he asked, "Is there any one here who can entertain my guests?" A creature humbly came forward, a crab spirit who called himself Kakukaishi. He sang:

"I hide myself behind rocks in the valley. In the autumn, when the *katsura* fruits are ripe, charmed by the clear moon and the cool winds, I venture out to the rivers and swim in the sea. My tummy is tinged yellow and my shell is round and hard. With my eyes looking skyward and my eight legs crossed, I make young women laugh, while my taste softens a warrior's harsh expression. Donning armor and holding a spear, I roll my eyes, foam at the mouth, and am called Buchōkōshi, Prince with No Intestines."

Kakukaishi danced *tsunate no mai*[42] by stepping forward and backward and running right and left while other crab spirits beat time. Everyone had a good laugh. Next, someone calling himself Master Gen ran out, beating time by turning his sleeves and extending his neck. This was a turtle spirit. He sang:

....
42. Unidentified. Because *tsunate* 綱手 refers to rope used to pull a boat, the dance probably imitates drawing a boat.

"I hide myself in the *medogi* thicket[43] and play among the lotus leaves. I float with letters on my back and can predict the future when caught in a [fisherman's] net.[44] My shell can tell fortunes[45] and my breast harbors a warrior's spirit. I become a world treasure [because I can see the future] and teach the Way. Hiding my six elements (head, tail, two hands, and two feet), I enjoy the longevity of a thousand years. My breath is like a thread and I enjoy life, dragging my tail.[46] I dance the Blue Sea."[47]

Master Gen danced, moving his head, craning his neck, and straining his eyes while raising his feet, keeping them in the air for a while, then drawing them in slowly. Everyone at the party roared with laughter, holding their stomachs while raising and lowering their heads.

Shrimps, clams, echoes from the mountains and woods, and various fishes followed, displaying their talents for the entertainment of all. Everyone had enough to drink, and eventually the three guests rose from their seats and thanked the king, who saw them off at the bottom of the steps.

Makami, too, straightened his sleeves and turned to the king. "I enjoyed myself very much. I hope you will show me every building in the Dragon Palace."

"That is easily done." Saying this, the king stepped down into the garden. Suddenly Makami was surrounded by clouds. The king had summoned a cloud official: the spirit of a large clam with a large nose and mouth, who wore a helmet of seven circles.[48]

Rounding his lips, the official blew into the sky, and everything became flat: There were no rocks or mountains. Clouds and mist were cleared away over several scores of *ri*. Jade trees lined the garden, which was covered with gold sand. Five-colored blossoms bloomed on the trees, and four-colored lotus flowers opened in the pool, releasing a delicate

---

43. *Medohagi* is a kind of *hagi* plant that belongs to the bean family; it grows to 1.5 meters high.

44. According to an old legend, a divine turtle, caught in a fisherman's net, told the country's fortune at the time of Emperor Yuan of the Song (*Shiki* 史記).

45. Ancient Chinese read their fortunes in the cracks of turtle shells.

46. The expression suggests an informal lifestyle, e.g., leaving court to live freely among the poor.

47. *Seigaiha* 青海波 is regarded as the most elegant of *gagaku* music pieces. The dancers dress in blue costumes with a wave design.

48. *Nanawata* 七曲: many circular layers.

fragrance. Accompanying the official along a gold gallery, Makami saw another garden, its ground covered in lapis lazuli, and an edifice made of crystal and *hari* glass[49] that was decorated with precious stones.[50] He thought he would have a commanding view from the top of the building but was unable to reach the first floor. "Common men cannot climb to [the first] floor," the official explained, "only those with divine powers." They ascended another tower where Makami saw something round like a mirror that was very shiny; the glare blinded him. The official said, "This is called the *denbo* mirror of the Electric Mother. Moving it slightly will create enough lightning to dazzle the world."

Next, Makami saw many drums, small and large. When he tried one of them, the official warned, "If you beat a single drum very lightly, it will thunder in every mountain, river, valley, and plain. Some people will lose their lives [because of the sound], and others will survive but lose their hearing. This is the small drum of Raikō, the Thunder Lord."

Makami spied something like a bellows beside him. He tried squeezing it, but the official stopped him, saying, "This leather bag belongs to Sōfū, the Wind Guard. If you squeeze it hard, there will be landslides with rocks flying into the sky, and people's houses will be blown away in all directions." There was a water jar with something like a broom for a lid. Makami tried stirring the water in the jar with it, but again the official stopped him. "This jar belongs to the Flood-Rain Master. If you soak this broom in the jar and shake it vigorously, it causes heavy rainfall and floods in the human world where the mountains and land meet the sea."

Makami asked the official, "Where is the officer who controls all of these things?"

"The Thunder Lord, the Electric Mother, the Wind Guard, and the Flood-Rain Master are extremely unruly, so they are usually kept in prison, where they cannot move as they like. When they are released to assume their roles, they all gather here. Since rain, wind, thunder, and lightning must have limits, if they overdo it, they are punished."

[Thinking it] impossible to see every building in the Dragon Palace, Makami returned to the king, who entertained him in various ways before offering him two strands of pearls on a lapis lazuli tray and

---

49. *Hari* 玻璃, a kind of glass; one of the seven jewels.

50. *Tama* 珠; also translated as "pearl."

two *hiki*[51] of thin silk that resembled ice[52] as farewell gifts. The king bid farewell to Makami on the steps and sent the cloud official with him as his escort. Makami closed his eyes and felt as if he were running in the sky. Finally, he arrived at the shrine of the Dragon King, east of Seta Bridge.

Makami took the pearls and silk home as treasures. Later he lived in obscurity, practicing the Way. No one knew what later became of him.[53]

1-2   One Hundred Ryō[54] of Gold

Heiji Ayano of Hirano in Kawachi Province[55] was an earnest and virtuous man. His close friend, Gennai Yuri, was immature and thoughtless. Gennai served Matsunaga Nagayoshi.[56] He was promoted to *daikan*[57] and moved to Yamato Province[58] with his wife, children, and elderly mother. Weighed down by expenses, Gennai borrowed one hundred *ryō* of gold from Heiji. Being good friends, they did not exchange any promissory notes or pledges.

....

51. One *hiki* equals 6.24 meters.

52. *Kōri no kinu* 氷の絹: ice silk. In the text, silk is often identified with ice. Here the sheen of the silk is compared to that of ice.

53. This story, based on *Sentōshinwa* (hereafter, *SS*) 1-1 (水宮慶会録), introduces Tawara Tōda and the Dragon Palace legend with auspicious descriptions of places near Seta Bridge, the entrance to the Dragon Palace. With its passages commemorating the construction of a new building in the palace, it is a fitting start to this collection.

54. One gold *ryō* 両 coin equaled 4 *monme* 匁 and 4 *bu* 分 in the Edo period. One *monme* was 3.75 grams. One *bu* was a quarter of a *monme*. One gold *ryō* equaled 60 *monme* in silver and 4 *kan* 貫 in copper. One *kaneitsūhō* 寛永通宝 coin of copper or iron in the Edo period equaled 1 *mon* 文.

55. Kawachi no kuni 河内国 is in present-day Yamanoi-cho, Kashiwara-shi, Osaka-fu.

56. Matsunaga Nagayoshi could be Matsunaga Hisahide 松永久秀, or Matsunaga Danjō 弾正, (1510–1577), a subject of Miyoshi Nagayoshi 三好長慶 (1522–1564). Matsunaga later defeated Miyoshi, caused the death of Ashikaga Yoshiteru 足利義輝 (the thirteenth shogun of the Muromachi shogunate, 1536–1565), and was defeated by Oda Nobunaga 織田信長 (1534–1582). Matsunaga was an elder of Miyoshi who administered for him as a *shugodai* 守護代. For the relationship between Matsunaga and Miyoshi, see *Korōgun monogatari* 古老軍物語, 6.

57. 代官: local administrators responsible for collecting taxes for their *daimyō* lord, among other things.

58. Washū 和州, or Yamato no kuni 大和国, present-day Nara-ken.

Meanwhile, the Hosokawa and the Miyoshi families[59] began feuding, which caused disturbances in the provinces of Kawachi and Tsu.[60] [During the upheaval] Heiji lost all his assets and was left with no means of surviving even a single day. Things quieted down during the Kōji,[61] when Miyoshi was in the capital, Kyoto. Miyoshi's elder, Matsunaga, built a castle in Washū[62] Province and greatly exploited the people, including the peasants.

Heiji took his family to Washū and went to see Gennai [who was serving Matsunaga]. Matsunaga's castle was impressive, with many workers. Heiji arrived unkempt and haggard, looking scarcely like his previous self. He rented a house in the vicinity for his wife and children.

When Heiji saw Gennai, he explained his circumstances. Gennai did not remember his friend at first, but after hearing details about their old village and Heiji's name, he finally recalled their friendship. Truly surprised, he urged Heiji to have some sake, never mentioning a word about his debt. Heiji returned home empty handed.

At home his wife complained, "We have been wandering around, dependent on Gennai's consideration. How dare you return home after drinking sake and without a word about the one hundred *ryō* of gold! If things continue as they are, we will starve to death by the roadside." Heiji agreed and impatiently waited for morning, when he hurried off to see Gennai.

After Gennai heard Heiji's explanation, he said, "Truly, I haven't forgotten the money I borrowed from you. How can I ignore my debt? Bring the promissory note and I will return the entire sum." Heiji replied, "Because we come from the same village and have been friends for a long time, I lent you the money without a note or pledge. Since then I have been robbed of my assets and have lost everything. If I had the money [you owe me], I could settle my affairs and feed my wife and children. Please help me and return the money."

....

59. The feud between Hosokawa Harumoto 細川晴元 (1514–1563) and his subject Miyoshi Nagayoshi involved the shogun and divided the shogunate. The fighting reached various places in Settsu 摂津 (partly Osaka and Hyogo-ken) and Kawachi (the eastern part of Osaka). Miyoshi emerged victorious in 1562.

60. Tsunokuni 津の国, or Settsu, was located in the Osaka area.

61. 1555–1558.

62. In 1560 Matsunaga built Tamonjō Castle, located in present-day Hōren-chō, Nara-shi (*Korōgun monogatari*, 6).

Laughing, Gennai insisted, "I cannot return any money without a note. When you bring it to me, I will repay my debt." Saying this, he sent Heiji home. Six months passed; it was now the twelfth month. [Heiji] had barely made it through the year, and he had no means to survive New Year's. Without food or clothing, his wife and children could do nothing but cry. Heiji was unbearably sad, seeing them starving in the freezing cold, so he again visited Gennai and tearfully begged him, "I have saved not a *sen*[63] and have no rice to cook. My wife and children will die of cold and starvation. I am not asking for the entire sum of the debt, but if you can let me have enough to help my family for New Year's, I would be most grateful."

Gennai replied, "Although I feel very sorry for you, my income is limited; I cannot return all your money now. But tomorrow, I will prepare two *koku* of rice and two *kan*[64] of *zeni* for you [and bring them to you], which should be enough for New Year's." At this, Heiji was overjoyed. When he reached home, he said to his family, "Tomorrow, we will be blessed. Let us wait [until then] and [for now] comfort ourselves for our past miseries." His family, too, was greatly pleased and could hardly wait for morning.

When the next day arrived, Heiji told one of his children to go outside the gate and watch the passers-by, saying, "If you see anyone carrying rice and money, let me know." Soon the child returned. "I see someone carrying a rice bag on his back," he reported. Heiji quickly went out, but the man carrying the rice passed him without a glance. Thinking he may have overlooked his house, Heiji stopped him and inquired, "I wonder if your rice is for Heiji Ayano." The man answered, "No, this is from the castle to pay for some fish."

After some time had passed, the child ran into the house, saying, "I see someone carrying money." Heiji ran out and saw the man pass by, ignoring his house. He asked him, "Isn't the money you're carrying for Heiji, from Master Yuri Gennai?" The man replied, "No, this is to cover the cost of the *yahagi*[65] ordered by Yuge Saburō."[66] Heiji felt most ashamed.

....

63. *Sen* 銭, or *zeni*: money in general. Around 1567, when this story takes place, 100 *sen* coins could buy 1.3 *to* 斗 of rice (*Dokushibiyō* 読史備要). One *to* equals 18 liters.

64. See *OT*, 1-2, n.1.

65. 矢矧: fletching.

66. 弓削三郎; Yuge instigated the downfall of Matsunaga Danjō (*Korōgunki*, 6; *Honchō shōgunki* 本朝将軍記, 12).

Many people passed Heiji's house carrying rice and money to pre-pare for New Year's. He stopped each of them to inquire, but none had been sent to him from Gennai. Thus he passed the whole day waiting in vain. When the street was empty, Heiji finally went inside. With no oil to light the lamps, his wife and children spent the night crying [in the dark], again with no means to obtain rice or firewood.

Heiji thought, "It is most regrettable that Gennai has betrayed me after making such a firm promise. I will kill him and settle this." Heiji sharpened his sword and quietly went to Gennai's house. But then he reflected, "It is true that Gennai wronged me, but his elderly mother, wife, and children are not guilty. If I kill him, his family will be left with no means to survive. Indeed, someone has wronged me, but I will not harm others. If the Heavenly Way exists, I should be blessed." Thinking this, Heiji returned home. He barely managed to get through New Year's by selling his sword and kimono.

One morning, Heiji left home and went to visit the Kannon of Hatsuse[67] to pray for his future. Traveling deep into the mountains, he came to a pool and accidentally fell in. As soon as he fell, the wa-ter in the pool parted to reveal a road. Heiji continued on the road for about two *chō* before coming to a *rōmon*.[68] On the second story of the structure, there was a sign that read "Seiseikan" "Pure Hall". When Heiji passed through the gate into the compound, he saw nothing but old pine trees, which had quietly stood for many years crossing their branches. He went to the end of a gallery and looked near the steps to the hall but saw no one to address. He heard only a bell in the distance, harmonizing with the sound of handbells.[69] Hungry and tired, Heiji fell asleep, resting his head on a foundation stone.

In time an old man with long eyebrows, dressed in a hat and shoes and carrying a white stick, appeared. He laughed at Heiji, saying, "We haven't seen each other for a long time. Do you remember the old

....

67. The eleven-faced Kannon in Hase Temple, located in present-day Hatsuse, Sakurai-shi, Nara, has been worshipped since the Heian period. For more stories of the Kannon of Hase Temple, see Yoshiko Dykstra, "Tales of the Compassionate Kannon: The *Hasedera Kannon genki*," *Monumenta Nipponica* 31 (1976): 113–143.

68. 楼門· a two-storied gate structure

69. A priest rings a *shinrei* 振鈴 bell while practicing the Way.

days?" Heiji sat up and knelt,[70] replying, "This is my first time visiting here. How should I know the old days?"

"Indeed. Being consumed by hunger and exhaustion, you must have forgotten." Saying this, the old man took out a pear and a jujube[71] fruit from his robe and gave them to Heiji. After eating them, Heiji felt a coolness in his chest and a freshness in his heart—as if seeing the moon in a sky clear of fog and clouds. He felt the dark illusions [in his mind] disappear and he remembered the past[72] as if it were yesterday. The old man continued, "Once you controlled the neighboring villages of Hatsuse. You always visited Kannon with deep faith and offered flowers and candles. However, you abused the peasants with heavy taxation,[73] showing them no mercy. You should have fallen into the bad realms,[74] but your misfortune was reversed, and you were reborn as a human being, thanks to the great mercy of Kannon. You enjoyed wealth for a while, but now you are poor because of your past bad karma.[75] When you were angry at Gennai, you thought of doing something wicked. Evil demons immediately began following you and were going to destroy your family. But as soon as you changed your mind, the demons left thanks to the Japanese deities[76] and the lucky god.[77] The results of good and bad deeds are like shadows following forms and sounds following voices. Hereafter, no matter what, refrain from evil and practice good." Thus the old man instructed him.

Thinking the old man was not of the human world but from a sacred place, Heiji asked him about the present time: "The world now is like entangled threads; many lords are like bees fighting. No one knows who will win or lose. Will you please tell me the future?"

The old man replied, "Now the people's minds and hearts are

....

70. Heiji got up from his sleeping position and quickly knelt down before the old man to show his respect.

71. These fruits were considered a sage's medicines.

72. I.e., his previous life.

73. The tax included military duties as well as extra labor.

74. A person moves through the six realms (hell, the realms of hungry ghosts, of animals, of *ashura*, of humans, and heaven) according to his sins or merits; *akushu* 悪趣 are the three lowest realms.

75. *Gōkan* 業感; the present results of one's good and bad deeds in a previous life.

76. *Shinmei* 神明.

77. *Fukujin* 福神.

like those of dogs and wolves. One rises to kill and attack others to make them obey his family and clan. Because of this, the king's way[78] is diminished and imperial power is greatly reduced. The way of the three-five rites[79] is ignored and war is frequent in the five-seven areas.[80] Subjects betray their lords, sons their fathers, and brothers become enemies. When lowly men of good fortune climb to higher stations, they succomb [to arrogance], and once they lose their powers of restraint, they destroy great families of higher status. Killing one's son-in-law and his child invites uneasiness among close relations, and the people will never rest easy." Thus the old man explained the results of good and bad deeds by recounting what had happened to many celebrated men in the present time as if reflecting their circumstances clearly in a mirror.

Heiji asked the old man about Gennai: "Yuri Gennai has not yet returned what he owes me. He boasts of his power and prestige. I wonder if his end will also come soon."

The old man replied, "His lord has committed a great mistake by abusing the people and indulging in profits. Both the Myōshū deities[81] and the divine spirits hate him. His tally of luck and longevity [in the Land after Death][82] has been eliminated. Soon his hands and feet will be handcuffed and shackled, and his neck tied with a rope while his flesh is left to rot and his bones scattered. Because Gennai has been serving him, he has also committed unspeakable wrongdoings, like ignoring his debt to you. All that he has accumulated and protected for himself was taken from another. Look and see; within three years, his wealth will be gone while misfortune visits him. You should take heed. Living near him is dangerous and Kyoto will not remain quiet. Quickly

---

78. *Ōhō* 王法.

79. *Sankō-gojō* 三綱五常. *Sankō* (three strings or ties) involves a lord, a father, and a man: a lord relates to his subject; a father to his son; a man to a woman. *Gojō* (five consistencies or rites) are always (*jō*) present in human relationships: *jin* 仁 (benevolence); *gi* 義 (righteousness); *rei* 礼 (courtesy); *chi* 智 (wisdom); and *shin* 信 (faith).

80. *Goki-shichidō* 五畿七道. *Goki* are the five provinces of Yamato, Yamashiro, Kawachi, Izumi, and Settsu. *Shichidō* are the seven highways of Tōkaidō, Tōsandō, Hokurikudō, San'indō, San'yōdō, Nankaidō, and Seikaidō. Thus the expression means "throughout Japan."

81. *Myōshū* 冥衆: various deities such as *deva* kings, demon kings, and King Yama (Enma) of hell.

82. *Fukuju no fuda* 福寿の籍: the wooden tally or tablet in the Land after Death that records a person's lifespan and fortune based on his conduct in this life.

return home and move to Kasatori[83] Valley, deep in Yamashina." Saying this, the old man gave him ten *ryō* of gold, taught him the way home, and sent him on his way.

When Heiji had walked about one *chō*, he found himself outside a cave behind a mountain. Nearly thirty days had passed since he had left home, and his wife and children were overjoyed to see him. Soon afterward he and his family moved to Kasatori Valley. He became a merchant, supporting his family by cutting and selling firewood. His family felt much safer and spent peaceful days there.

Meanwhile, in the year of Kanoe-Horse of Eiroku,[84] Matsunaga betrayed Oda and was defeated.[85] Gennai was caught and killed. All that he had was taken by his enemy. When people heard of these events [years later], they realized they had occurred within three years [of Heiji's arrival in Yamashina]. It was said that Heiji's descendants were still living there.[86]

2-1   A Hermitage by the Totsu River

Nagatsugu made a living by selling medicinal herbs in Sakai in Izumi.[87] Long afflicted with scabs, he went to the Totsu River hot spring in Ki Province.[88] His scabs were gone in a fortnight—most likely due to the efficacy of [the spring water]. One day Nagatsugu reflected, "I have heard of many medicinal plants, carrots and lily roots,[89] growing deep in the Totsu River hot spring. Maybe I should go and look for them." So he left his servant at an inn, went deep into the mountains, and lost his way. While descending a valley, he saw a beautiful basket flowing

....

83. The area near the upper Kasatori River in present-day Uji-shi, Kyoto-fu.

84. Eiroku 13; 1570.

85. Matsunaga betrayed Oda Nobunaga in 1573 and was pardoned. In 1577 he again plotted against Nobunaga and finally committed suicide (*Korōgun monogatari*, 6; *Kōyōgunkan* 甲陽軍艦, 2).

86. This tale is based on *SS*, 1-2 (三山福地志). Asai used the story of the rise and fall of Matsunaga Danjō as background and reframed the story into a Buddhist one involving the Hasedera Kannon.

87. Present-day Sakai-shi, Osaka-fu.

88. This could be the Totsu river 十津川 in Wa Province, Nara-ken. The river flows by present-day Totsugawa Village, Yoshino-gun.

89. Decocted Korean carrots and lily roots were used to increase energy.

down a stream. "Maybe there is a village somewhere upstream," he reasoned, continuing up along the stream.

Meanwhile the sun was about to set; birds called loudly to each
other as they hurried to their nests. After Nagatsugu had traveled about
ten *chō*, he came to a gate curved out of rock. Stepping inside, he saw
five or six scores of houses with thatched roofs, all in a line. Their stone
walls were green with moss, their bamboo doors stood lonesome,[90]
and the *kabuki* crossbars[91] on their gates were ornately covered with
vines. Dogs were barking in the yards, and roosters were crowing on
the roofs. The village appeared to be a comfortable place to live, with
mulberry and hemp plants growing profusely. It did not look shabby
and neglected at all; there were neat piles of *shiishiba*[92] firewood and
rice mixed with hulled millet laid out [on straw mats] to dry.

The men of the village were dressed in old-fashioned clothing:
eboshi hats, *hakama* skirts, and *suhō* robes. Their quiet manner of
walking was elegant and respectable. Seeing Nagatsugu resting, they
were surprised and asked him guardedly, "Who are you, wandering
into this village? This is not a place widely known to outsiders."

Nagatsugu explained how he came to be in their village. An old
man in formal attire, wearing *emogi* shoes, carrying an *akagi* stick,[93]
and calling himself Third Rank Chūjō,[94] spoke: "This place is deep
in the mountains and surrounded by steep rocks. Wolves and bears
are rampant and foxes and tree spirits abound. The sun is already set.
Leaving you here would be like ignoring someone about to drown. Follow me. I will let you stay with me." The old man led Nagatsugu to his
home.

The house was clean and the old man's male and female servants
were courteous. After Nagatsugu was led to a room and took a seat
near a lit candle, he asked his host, "This is an unusual village. How
have you come to live here?" The old man, knitting his brows, replied,
"This is where refugees from the secular world live. If you insist on

....

90. The door was rarely used, which suggests there were few visitors.

91. *Kabuki* 冠木: a horizontal pole supported by two poles; a gate-like structure.

92. The dried branches of the *shii* 椎 tree were used for firewood.

93. The dried stem of the *akagi* plant is strong enough to use as a walking stick.

94. *Chūjō* 中将: middle captain. For the translation of official ranks and titles, see George
Sansom, *A History of Japan*, vol. 1 (Stanford: Stanford University Press, 1958), 67–109.

hearing our tale, I may have to tell you something sad."

Nagatsugu persisted, so the old man began his story: "We have lived here since the downfall of the Heike clan, whose members sank in the western sea.[95] I am the first son of Daifu Minister Shigemori[96] of Komatsu and am called Third Rank Chūjō Koremori.[97] My grandfather, who was Grand Minister Nyūdō Kiyomori [1118–1182], was an unpopular, wicked man who was guilty of many wrongdoings. My father, the minister, died early, and my uncle Munemori [1147–1185] took power, but he was also guilty of inhumanity. Many people in my family indulged in luxury, glory, and arrogance, which brought about the ruin of our clan.

"At that time, Yoritomo [1147–1199], a military assistant commander, gathered his followers and loyal subjects and raised an army in a northeastern province. He also urged Kanja Yoshinaka [d. 1184], who hailed from one of the northern provinces, to rebel against the imperial court. The Genji clan rose up like bees and spread out like ants to attack us in various provinces. We fought back in vain. Finally, we were expelled from the capital by the Kiso clan, and we fled to Ichinotani in Settsu Province,[98] where we had peace for a while until Kurō Yoshitsune [1159–1189] attacked us. [During the battle] many of our allies, including Michimori [d. age 30] and Atsumori [1169–1184], lost their lives. All who witnessed these events lost their souls and were chilled in their hearts. Could anyone hearing of such sadness ever forget our tragedies, even after he was reborn?

"Some of us constructed a castle in Susaki in Yashima,[99] and we confined ourselves there. A few missed their homes beyond the clouds while others missed their wives and children. While our bodies were in Yashima, our hearts were in the capital. Everything seemed futile: To each other we would remark, 'There is no hope in our future.' In my desperation, I summoned three men who had served me for a long

....

95. Refers to the last battle of the Heike against the Genji in 1185, which took place at Dannoura Beach in present-day Shimonoseki-shi, Yamaguchi-ken. For the downfall of the Heike clan, see Paul Varley, *Warriors of Japan* (Honolulu: University of Hawai'i Press, 1994), 78–115.

96. Taira Shigemori 平重盛 (1138–1179) was the first son of Kiyomori. A *daifu* 内府 was an official under the Minister of the Left and Right.

97. Chūjō Koremori 中将 維盛.

98. Present-day Ichinotani-cho, Suma-ku, Kobe-shi.

99. Present-day Takamatsu-shi, Kagawa-ken.

time and were familiar with traveling by boat. They were a samurai, Yosahyōe Shigekage;[100] a young boy, Ishidōmaru;[101] and a *toneri*, Takesato.[102] We quietly left Yashima by boat and arrived at Yūki Beach in Awa,[103] where I composed a poem:

oriori wa
shiranu uraji no
moshiogusa[104]
kaki[105] *oku ato o*
katmi to mo miyo

From time to time,
At a strange seaside
Regard the seaweeds
Gathered for salt
As my keepsake.

"Shigekage replied:

waga omoi
sora fuku kaze ni
tagufuashi
katabuku tsuki ni
utsuru yūgure

My thoughts compared
To the wind
Blowing in the sky
The evening is reflected

----

100. 与三兵衛重影; a son of Kageyasu, who was a subject of Taira Shigemori. After his father died, he was brought up by Koremori and changed his name to Shigekage (*Genpeisuiseiki* 源平盛衰記, 40; *Heike monogatari* 平家物語, 10).

101. 石童丸; he had served Koremori since he was eight years old.

102. 武里. *Toneri* 舎人: a nobleman's servant.

103. Present-day Yuki-cho, Kaibe-gun, Tokushima-ken.

104. 藻塩草: a seaweed used for making salt.

105. 掻き; from *kakiatsumeru* (to gather) but also *kaki* 書き (to write).

On the slanting moon.

"Wiping away his tears, Ishidōmaru recited his poem:

tamaboko[106] *no*
michi yuki kanete
noru fune ni
kokoro wa itodo
akogare[107] *ni keri*

Unable to continue
Our way
We go on board
My heart longs
So much for something.[108]

"We continued our journey by boat, passing the beaches at Waka and Fukiage[109] in Ki Province before finally landing at Yura Port.[110] We looked back toward the old capital that we greatly missed. Our party soon visited Mount Kōya,[111] where we saw Takiguchi Tokiyori Nyūdō,[112] who guided us to various temples. Planning to visit Kumano, we started off from the Santō Ford[113] and Fujishiro.[114] We went to

....

106. 玉鉾; a *makura-kotoba* 枕詞 (pillow word). This is a poetic diction placed before a noun to enhance its meaning. Here it relates to the word that follows, *michi yuki* (going away or going on a trip).

107. *Akogare* あこがれ: to long or yearn for.

108. The young boy yearns for something unknown in the future, which contrasts with the sad tone of the poems by the two older men.

109. Both Waka 和歌 (Wakayama-shi) and Fukiage 吹上 (the area from the Ki River to Mount Zōga) beaches are known as "poetic spots."

110. Present-day Yura-cho, Hidaka-gun, Wakayama-ken.

111. 高野山; along with Kongobuji Temple, the headquarters of the Shingon sect.

112. 滝口時頼入道; a subject of Taira Shigemori, Tokiyori fell in love with Yokobue. After her death, he went to Mount Kōya to take the tonsure.

113. Present-day Sandonaka, Wakayama-shi.

114. Present-day Fujishiro, Nankai-shi.

Chisato Beach,[115] Kaburazaka,[116] Kokinomori,[117] Fukiage, and Waka.
We passed Iwashiro Shrine[118] and rested by the Iwata river,[119] where
[Koremori] composed a poem:

iwatagawa
chikai no fune[120] *ni*
sao sashite
shizumu waga mi mo
ukabi nuru kana

Iwata River
Rowing the boat
Of the pledge
My sinking body
Is going to float.

"After that, we visited the main, new, and Nachi shrines.[121] We soon
left Hamanomiya[122] by boat and landed [on an island where] we shaved
off the bark of a pine tree on the beach and wrote the following:[123]

Gonnosuke Chūjō of the third rank, Taira Koremori, left the
battleground and went into the water on the twenty-eighth
day of the third month in the first era of Genryaku at the age of

....

115. Present-day Nanbu-cho, Hidaka-gun, the location of Chisato-ōji Shrine.

116. Present-day Kabusaka Pass (蕪坂峠), between Arita-shi and Shimotsu-cho, Kaisō-gun.

117. Unidentified.

118. The shrine is in present-day Nishi-iwashiro, Nanbu-cho, Hidaka-gun. Visitors to Kumano
used to write their names and dedicate poems on a board before the worshiping hall of
the shrine.

119. Refers to the middle stream of the Tomita river in Nishimuro-gun.

120. 誓の舟: the boat of the pledge, i.e., the boat of the Buddha's pledge to save sentient
beings. The poem suggests that the poet, after visiting so many sacred places, would be
saved by the Buddha.

121. Kumano-hongū-taisha 熊野本大社 (Hongū-cho, Higshimuro-gun) is one of the three
Kumano shrines (熊野三山), together with the new and Nachi shrines.

122. The party left Hamanomiya (present-day Katsuura-cho, Nachi, Higashimuro-gun) and
arrived at Kaneshima (金島), where they recorded their names (*Genpeiseisuiki*, 40).

123. In *Genpeiseisuiki*, 40, the ages of Shigekage and Ishidōmaru are not given. The *Kugebunin*
公家補任 states that Koremori was twenty-five years old when he died.

twenty-seven with Shigekage, who was the same age, and with Ishidōmaru, who was eighteen.

umarete wa
tsui ni shini chōu
kotonomi zo
sadame naki yoni
sadameari keru[124]

Once
I was born
Finally I die
That is the fatal fact
In this transient world.

"That is what I wrote, telling the world that we had committed suicide. But we have been hiding in these mountains.[125] Soon we sought Sadayoshi,[126] a governor of Higo, who told us, 'After the downfall of the Heike clan, many were drowned in the sea of Dannoura. Our allies hiding in the capital were all killed. There were no survivors.'

"Hearing his story, we thought we were fortunate to be alive and consoled ourselves in the midst of our grief. We began to cultivate the land here and gather firewood. We have been nourishing our hearts and minds peacefully and purifying our souls by admiring nature.[127] Watching cherry blossoms, we think of the arrival of spring, and seeing the fallen leaves, we know the autumn is coming. We count the moons and know the end of each month when no moon appears. The families and descendants of Sadayoshi, Shigekage, and Ishidōmaru presently living in this village. I wonder if Yoritomo has taken over the world. Please let us know."

....

124. The poem appears in *Genpeiseisuiki*, 40.

125. *Genpeiseisuiki*, 40, mentions that Koremori's suicide was erroneous and that he was alive and living in Nachi.

126. A son of Taira Iesada was thought to be missing but suddenly visited Utsunomiya Asatsugu (recorded in the entry of the seventh month of 1185, *Azumakagami* 吾妻鑑, 4.)

127. *Seifūrōgetsu* 清風朗月: to appreciate the pure wind and bright moon.

Nagatsugu was greatly astonished by the old man's story. He courteously touched his forehead to the ground, saying, "I did not know you were a man of such high rank. I thought you were just a villager. Please excuse my ignorance."

The old man reassured him: "No, no. I am not so at all. Well, well." They were then joined by Sadayoshi, Shigekage, and Ishidōmaru. They all appeared to be sixty years of age. Sadayoshi said to Nagatsugu, "Now that we are all relaxed and familiar with each other, please let us hear about the changes in the world."

So Nagatsugu began: "I will start with what I have heard. Since the Heike clan came to an end in the western sea, Yoritomo[128] controlled the world for a while, but soon died of illness. Kabakanja Yorinori [d. 1193] and Kurōhangan Yoshitsune [d. 1189] were killed by Yoritomo. Yoriie [1182–1204], a son of Yoritomo, took power but died of illness and left no heir. So the second son of Yoritomo [Sanetomo, 1192–1291],[129] who was the younger brother of Yoriie, assumed the shogunate. Zenji Kugyō [1200–1219], a son of Yoriie's mistress, was appointed *betto* administrator of Hachiman Shrine in Tsurugaoka.[130] Meanwhile, the Wada, Hatakeyama, and Kajiwara clans were defeated. Sanetomo was killed[131] by Zenji Kugyō one night while visiting Hachiman Shrine. After that, Hōjō Yoshitoki [1163–1224] took over. The Hōjō went on to control the shogunate for nine generations.

"Nyūdō Sōkan Takatoki [1303–1333],[132] a governor of Sagami, caused a great disturbance, and Nitta Yoshisada [d. 1338][133] took over the

---

128. Yoritomo fell from a horse, became ill, and died in 1199. For the war between the Heike and the Genji, see *Genpeiseisuki*, 39, 40; *Honchō shōgunki*, 10; and Varley, *Warriors of Japan*, 78–158.

129. 源実朝; the third Kamakura shogun, Sanetomo, was the second son of Yoritomo; his mother was Hōjō Masako. He was a celebrated poet, and his sudden death at the hands of his nephew Zenji Kugyō made him a tragic hero. His poetic work includes an anthology, the *Kinyōwakashū* 金葉和歌集.

130. 鶴岡八幡宮; in present-day Yukinoshita, Kamakura-shi.

131. The murder took place on the twenty-seventh day of the first month in 1291. Zenji was also killed after the death of Sanetomo on the same night.

132. 高時入道宗鑑; the fourteenth Kamakura shogunate *shikken* 執権 administrator; Takatoki killed himself when the Nitta attacked the shogunate.

133. After Nitta Yoshisada 新田義貞 defeated the Kamakura shogunate, he sided against Ashikaga Takauji and finally killed himself in 1338. For more about the Nitta and the Ashikaga, see Varley, *Warriors of Japan*, 199–205.

Kamakura shogunate. Ashikaga Takauji [1305–1358][134] fought against Nitta and finally defeated Nitta Yoshisada. His son, Ashikaga Yoshinori [1330–1367], was appointed Kyoto Lord,[135] and his second son, Motouji [1340–1367], Kamakura Lord. The world was quiet for some time, but the way of the emperors[136] had greatly declined. Power and prestige were with the warrior class. Later, the Kyoto and Kamakura lords began feuding, and the *shikken* controller of the Kamakura shogunate was driven away by the Uesugi clan.[137] Meanwhile, the Kyoto Lord lost his power, and many warrior lords in various provinces rebelled. The country plunged into great confusion and local battles were incessant.[138]

"Matsunaga Danjō [1510–1577], a subject of Shuridaibu Miyoshi

....

134. The first Muromachi (Ashikaga) shogun.

135. *Kyō no kubō* 京の公方.

136. *Ōdō* 王道: the imperial way; i.e., the controlling power of emperors.

137. Refers to the *kantō kanrei* 関東管領 of the Uesugi clan, who traditionally took the position. A *kanrei* administrator was placed in Kamakura by the Ashikaga shogunate to supervise administration in the east. It was the equivalent of the *shikken* of the Kamakura shogunate in Kamakura.

138. See *Honchō shōgunki*, 10. For the rise of the local lords and their domains, see Sansom, *A History of Japan*.

[1522–1564], controlled Nankai and Kinai; Imagawa Yoshimoto [1519–1560], the Suruga-Enshu areas; Provincial Governor Minamoto Tomonori [1528–1576], Seishū Province; Takeda Harunobu [1521–1575], the Kō-Shin provinces; Hōjō Ujiyasu [1515–1571], the eight provinces in Kantō; and Satake Yoshishige [1547–1612], the Hitachi area. Ashina Moritaka [d. 1517] controlled Aizu, while Nagao Kagetora [1530–1578], ruled Echigo. Asakura Yoshikage [1533–1573] protected his Echizen domain. The Hatakeyamas[139] were in Kawachi. Sue, a governor of Owari [d. 1555], usurped Nagato of Suō, and Mōri Motonari [1497–1571] rose in Aki while Amako Yoshihisa [1566–1610] spread his power to Izumo, Oki, Iwami, and Hōki. The Ōtomo [Sōrin, 1530–1587] were in Bungo, and the Ryūzōji [Takanobu, 1529–1584] were in Hizen. The Asai [Nagamasa, 1545–1573] and the Sasaki were in Gō Province. The Oda clan was in Owari, the Saitō [Dosan, d. 1556] in Mino, and the Tsutsui in Yamato. Many more warrior lords acquired power in local areas, kept their armies, fought at village boundaries, and attacked and robbed each other's territory.

"During the 374 years since the second year of Juei [1183]—from the time Emperor Antoku went into the western sea to the present, the second year of Kōji [1556]—we have had twenty-six emperors, three generations of [Minamoto] since Yoritomo in Kamakura, and nine generations of Hōjō. After twelve generations of Ashikaga shoguns, we now have the thirteenth Ashikaga shogun, Yoshiteru."[140]

Hearing Nagatsugu's story, his host could not stop his tears. The night had deepened. Everything was quiet on the mountain except the wind blowing through the trees near the eaves. In his heart and mind, Nagatsugu felt cool and purified. His host offered him something more to drink. Soon dawn broke: Red clouds appeared on the mountain's shoulders, and birds sounded more clearly. Finally, Nagatsugu rose to start his journey home. He courteously bowed to his host to take his leave. The old man said to him, "We are neither hermits nor ghosts. Spending so many years [here] has been unexpectedly fortunate for us. Please do not say [anything about us] to the world when you return home." He recited a poem:

....

139. 畠山; one of the three *kanrei* families of the Ashikaga shogunate.
140. Ashikaga Yoshifuji changed his name to Yoshiteru 義輝 in 1554.

miyamabe no
tsuki wa mukashi no
tsuki nagara
haruka ni kawaru
hito no yo no naka

The moon
In this deep mountain
Remains the same as in the past
But how much the human world
Has changed!

The old man bid him farewell and went inside. After Nagatsugu stepped through the rock gate, he placed a bamboo branch at every *chō* to mark his way. He eventually reached his home near the Totsu river. The following spring, he went back into the mountains with food and drink. But all he saw was decayed pine trees, high rocks, and pampas grass growing in abundance. Similarly, woodcutters in the area noted only the faint sound of birds, and grass gatherers the sight of valley streams. Unable to find the [way to the village]—his bamboo markers having disappeared—Nagatsugu returned home. The village may have been a hermitage for those who had attained the Way. No one ever discovered its whereabouts.[141]

2-2   The Red Sash

A rich man named Chōhachi of Hamada lived in the port of Tsuruga[142] in Echizen Province. He had two daughters. His neighbor was also wealthy, the merchant Higaki Heita, who had once served as a samurai under Governor Wakabayashi Nagakado.[143] Heita had a son, Heiji. Heiji and Hamada's older daughter were the same age and had played together since they were young. Higaki thought of Hamada's daughter as his son's future bride and proposed the marriage using a proper

....

141. This story, based on *SS*, 2-2 (天台鵬訪隠録), was rewritten as a Japanese historical tale using materials from *Genpeiseisuiki*, 39, 40; and *Honchō shōgunki*, 10.

142. Present-day Tsuruga-shi, Fukui-ken.

143. Wakabayashi Kuröemon joined the Ikkō sect and fought against Nobunaga; see *Shinchōki* 信長記, 8.

go-between. Hamada immediately accepted the proposal and offered sake and food as betrothal gifts. In turn, Higaki presented the older Hamada daughter with a red sash.[144]

Meanwhile, some Asakura men rebelled in the fall of 1575.[145] They guarded the forts and fortresses in Itadori, Kinometōge, Hachifuse, Imajō, Hiuchi, Suizu, and Ryūmonji Temple.[146] Governor Wakabayashi also guarded the new castle at Kawano. Their enemies were Lord Oda Nobunaga and his son, Nobutada. Nobunaga's eighty thousand soldiers arrived at Tsuruga and Kinoshita Tōkichirō was ordered to surround the new castle.[147] Because of his connection to Governor Wakabayashi, Higaki immediately closed his house in Tsuruga and went to Kyoto to stay with relations. The Higaki hid themselves in Kyoto for five years, during which time they sent no news to Tsuruga.

Hamada's older daughter was now nineteen years old. She was a beautiful girl and had several marriage proposals, but she refused them all, saying, "Since I was young, I was promised to Heiji. Even though he has forsaken me, I have no intention of accepting any other man's proposal. Besides, it would be a shame if Heiji were still alive and returned home [to find me married]."

The daughter rarely left her room. Always and in everything she did, her thoughts were of Heiji; she missed him so much she secretly shed tears. Finally, weak from loneliness, she became ill and was confined to bed. Six months later, she passed away. Her parents' grief was beyond description. They tearfully buried her at a temple at Oshio. But before the burial, the mother stroked her daughter's forehead, saying, "This is the sash that your future husband gave you. It's of no use to anyone here. Why don't you take it to the next world and always keep

---

144. *Shinku no uchiobi* 真紅の撃帯; the *uchiobi*, or *nagoyaobi*, was made by pounding (*uchi*) the sash material with a pallet (*hera*). It was very popular among young women of the Edo period.

145. Refers to the Ikkōikki 一向一揆, a religious revolt involving members of the Ikkō sect of the Pure Land school.

146. Itadori, present-day Gifu-ken, is close to the boundary of Fukui-ken. Kinometōge and Hachifuse are in present-day Fukushima-shi; Imajō is located in the central part of present-day Fukui-ken; Hiuchi was a castle in the northern region; and Suizu is in Tsuruga-shi. Ryūmonji Temple (of the Sōtō sect) was a castle at the time; it is in present-day Fukui-ken. The new castle at Kawano, to the north of Tsuruga, faced the sea.

147. For Hideyoshi (Kinoshita Tōkichirō) and Asakura, see Okanoya Shigeru, *Meishōgenkōroku*, II, *Nyūton puresu*, 201–203.

it with you." She put the sash around her daughter's waist.

A month later, Heiji returned to Tsuruga alone. Hamada invited him to his home and asked, "What happened?" Heiji explained, "Lord Nobunaga brought his eighty thousand soldiers to Tsuruga while Governor Wakabayashi guarded the new castle at Kawano. My father was afraid of being drawn into the conflict because of his former ties to the governor. So we immediately fled to Kyoto to stay with our relations and hid ourselves there. Meanwhile, my parents died, but I could not forget the promise I had made to your daughter. So I have returned alone."

Hearing this, Hamada and his wife tearfully replied, "After you left, our daughter missed you so much she fell ill and finally passed away early last month. She must have been so sad and lonely because she had no news from you for such a long time. Please look at this. She wrote a poem on the lid of her *suzuri* writing box." Heiji took the box in his hands and read the poem written on the lid:

semete yawa
ka o dani nioe
ume no hana
shiranu yamaji no
okuni sakutomo

The plum blossoms
Opening in the inner part
Of a strange mountain path
At least send the scent
Of their blossoms [to me].[148]

Reading the poem, Heiji became immensely sad and he regretted neglecting the girl. He went to the *jibutsudo*[149] and prayed, reciting Amida Buddha's name before her memorial tablet and offering flowers and incense. Her parents followed him and addressed the tablet: "Here are the offerings from your beloved Heiji. Receive them now." When

....

148. The poem is a gentle rebuff: Plum blossoms blooming on a remote mountain send me more news with just their fragrance than you. *Kaori* (fragrance or scent) is suggested by *tayori* (news), while *ume* (plum blossom) represents the girl's wish for Heiji.

149. A private hall where a devotee keeps his principal image.

they fell prostrate from sorrow, Heiji and the rest of the household wept and raised their voices in grief. It was indeed a sad sight.

After a while, the father and mother said to Heiji, "You must feel helpless since you have been left alone after your parents' departure. Even though our daughter is dead, we don't regard you as a stranger. Please stay with us until you find your way." They allowed Heiji to reside with them and later built a separate place for him behind their own home.

On the day of the *chuin*[150] service, forty-nine days after the daughter's death, the Hamada family went to her grave at Oshio while Heiji stayed behind to look after the house. They returned at sunset and Heiji received them at the gate. After everyone had gone inside, he noticed something had fallen out of the carriage of the Hamada's sixteen-year-old younger daughter. Heiji cautiously picked it up and found it was the red sash [that he had given to the older sister]. He clutched it to his bosom and returned to his room. That evening he sat alone by the candlelight, deep in thought.

Later that night, Heiji heard someone knocking at the side door.[151] When he opened it, the younger sister slipped in. She said to him, "I have been grieving for my older sister. Did you pick up the red sash I dropped outside my carriage this evening? Because of a deep karmic link in our previous lives, I have come to exchange a marriage pledge with you."

At this Heiji was most confused and surprised. "I don't think we have such a link. Because of your parents' generosity, I have been well treated here. Doing something [that may be seen as] improper, without their knowledge, is utterly impossible. If they discover this, what would I do? Please leave here immediately." Heiji tried in vain to reason with her. The younger sister became greatly distressed and retorted, "My father wants you to stay here as my future husband. If you ignore my sincere feelings in coming here tonight in secret, I will commit suicide. That will make you regret your decision, and I will hate you even after I am reborn in the next life." Heiji was so overwhelmed by her words that he finally consented. The younger sister stayed with him until dawn.

The younger sister visited him every night and left at dawn. Heiji

---

150. A memorial service held every seven days after death.

151. *Tsumado* 妻戸; mainly used to go out to the yard and garden.

began to relent and was no longer fearful of guards[152] [discovering their affair]. He grew more relaxed and gave in to his irresistible desire for her.

Thus they spent the next thirty days. Then one night the sister said to Heiji, "No one has discovered us yet. But an affair like this cannot remain hidden for long and, when it is revealed, we will have trouble. Will you take me somewhere else, a place where we can continue to enjoy ourselves?" Heiji, unable to ignore his strong feelings for her, agreed and took her to the port of Mikuni,[153] where his father's former servant was living. After hearing Heiji's story, the servant willingly looked after them.

About a year passed before the younger sister declared, "We have come here against my parents' wishes. But a year has passed, and they must be worrying about us. Now they may forgive us. Let us return home."

Heiji again agreed to her request and took her back to Tsuruga. Leaving her in the boat, he went alone to see her parents. When he saw them, he apologized, saying, "Despite your great kindness, I have behaved improperly. But some time has passed, so I hope you are no longer angry with us. I have brought your daughter home today. Will you please forgive us?"

"What are you talking about?" demanded Hamada, who looked very confused. Heiji explained everything in detail and took out the red sash. Seeing it, the surprised Hamada said, "This is the very sash given to my deceased daughter by your family as a betrothal gift. It was put in the coffin with her when she was buried. Besides, our younger daughter is presently ill in bed. How could she run away with you?"

Heiji insisted that he had left the younger daughter with the boat. Someone sent to verify his story returned saying there was no one but a boatman in the boat. While the confused parents were still wondering what had happened, their younger daughter suddenly got up from her bed. She spoke gibberish at first and then said [to them], "I was engaged to Heiji but left this life early and became a mistress of the [grave] mound. But because my relationship with him has not ended, I am appearing to you like this. Please make my younger sister his wife. Then she will recover from her illness. This is exactly what I wish. If

---

152. A reference to an old love poem by Ariwara Narihira (825–880) in *Kokinshū* 古今集, 3, and *Isomonogatari* 伊勢物語, 5 dan. The old poem used *sekimori* 防人 (barrier guard).

153. Present-day Mikuni-chō, Sakai-gun, Fukui-ken.

my wish is not fulfilled, I will take my sister with me and make her my companion in the Land after Death."

Everyone was most surprised and examined the girl closely. She looked just like the younger sister, but in voice and manner of speaking she resembled the older sister. Her father questioned her, saying, "But you have already left this world. Why are you still so attached to affairs in this life without being delivered?" The possessed girl answered, "Even though my life was short, I still have the relationship from my previous life. I asked King Enma[154] in the Land after Death for a year's respite and I enjoyed spending it with Heiji. Now the time has come for me to return to the Land after Death. Please remember my words." The girl tearfully took Heiji's hands to bid him farewell and honored her parents by joining her palms in prayer. She continued [as if to her younger sister]: "Even after you become Heiji's wife, you will uphold the Way as a woman and faithfully serve your parents. Farewell, and farewell." As soon as these last words were spoken, the younger sister's body shook and she fell down unconscious.

After water had been splashed on her face, the girl came to her senses, but she remembered nothing of what had happened. She was now fully recovered from her illness. In time, the couple made their younger daughter Heiji's wife and offered memorial services for the repose of their older daughter's soul. Everyone who heard this tale thought it most strange.[155]

2-3   A Hobgoblin and a Fox

Koyata Waritake lived in a post town in Musa in Gō Province.[156] He was from Kōka[157] and liked *sumō*[158] because he was naturally strong

---

154. Enma (Yama), the king of Yominokuni (Meido, Myōdo) 冥土, the Land after Death, judges sinners in this world and sends them to the approriate hell according to their sins.

155. The crimson *uchiobi* sash in this story was originally a hair ornament decorated with a gold phoenix in the Chinese text (*SS*, 1-4, 金鳳叙奇記). In the Chinese story, the male protagonist moves away because of his father's work, and the deaths of his parents and his subsequent mourning explain his long absence. The present version incorporated contemporary events, which made the story more plausible to a Japanese audience.

156. Present-day Musa-sho, Ōmihachiman-shi, Shiga-ken.

157. Present-day Kōga-gun, Shiga-ken.

158. Sumō was a favorite sport among warriors, including Nobunaga, who collected strong sumō wrestlers and enjoyed watching sumō matches.

and bold. He moved to Musa in his middle age, rented rooms to travelers, and finally made a living as an innkeeper.

One day when he was on an errand, walking along the Shinohara[159] bank, he noticed the sun was setting and hardly anyone was about. As he hurried home, he saw a fox run out of a thicket and onto the roadside. It had a human skull on its head. It stood up [on its hind legs], faced north, then lowered its head as if in prayer. The skull fell to the ground, and the fox picked it up. Every time it lowered its head to pray, the skull fell off, and the fox replaced it. After several times, the fox managed to keep the skull on its head and appeared more at ease. It prayed, facing north, about a hundred times.[160] Thinking this most strange, Koyata stopped to watch. Then suddenly the fox changed into a woman of sixteen or seventeen years of age. Her beauty was incomparable. The sun had set and it was now dark.

The woman, standing before Koyata, began to cry bitterly. Being a bold fellow, Koyata approached her and asked, "Who are you? And why are you crying so in the dark? Where are you going?" The woman tearfully replied, "I am from Yogo,[161] north of here. A general, Kinoshita Tōkichirō[162] attacked the castle in Yamamotoyama.[163] While they retreated, his soldiers burnt places like Yogo and Kinomoto. My father and brothers died at the castle and my mother took ill out of the fear. Soldiers came to our home and took away all our valuables. When my mother raised her voice in grief, they killed her. I was so frightened I hid myself in a thicket and barely survived. Now I am an orphan, with no one to depend on. I thought of killing myself but sorrow overwhelmed me. I was crying here just now because I thought I was alone."

Koyata said to himself: "So a fox changed itself into a girl and is trying to fool me. Well, I will fool her and profit[164] by it." So he said to the girl, "What a sad thing to hear. You have no one after your par-

---

159. In present-day Yasu-cho, Yasu-gun, Shiga-ken.

160. The fox's facing north suggests her ancestors are buried in the Yogo area.

161. Present-day Yogo-cho, Ika-gun.

162. Toyotomi Hideyoshi was known as Kinoshita Tokichiro when he was young. In 1573, when he obtained the Asai domain, he changed his name to Hashiba.

163. A branch of Otani Castle in present-day Yamamoto, Kohoku-cho, Higshiasai-gun. The castle did not fall in the battle.

164. *Toku* 徳: virtue; translated here as *toku* 得 (to benefit or profit).

ents and brothers were killed. But fortunately I can support another person, although I am poor. If you will look after my household, I would appreciate it and feel I could trust you." With these words, the girl looked greatly pleased, "If you show me mercy and help me," she vowed, "I will serve you as though you were my parents reborn." So the two of them went to Musa, and the girl explained everything to Koyata's wife. Appreciating the girl's beauty, she was very sympathetic and treated her well. Koyata did not say a word about the fox to his wife.

Gō Province finally quieted down at the beginning of the Tenshō era,[165] after the northern county[166] became part of Kinoshita Tokichiro's domain. Ishida Ichinosuke,[167] traveling from the capital [to his home in Gifu], stayed at Koyata's inn in Musa. As soon as he saw the girl, he became infatuated with her and ordered Koyata to give her to him, whatever the cost. The innkeeper replied, "Although many *daimyō* lords have asked me for her, I have not allowed her to leave. But if you offer me something on which I can depend, I may grant your wish." So Ishida gave him one hundred *ryō* of gold and took the girl home to Gifu.

In addition to being intelligent and talented, the girl was able to anticipate people's thoughts and wishes and pleased Ishida in everything. Ignoring his wife, he now loved only her. But the girl, far from being arrogant, considered the wife's feelings and served her day and night, saying, "I am only a mistress. I would never presume to take your place." The wife gave into her kindness and did not harbor any feelings of hatred toward her.

When people came to the mansion, the girl was always ready with suitable gifts, which seemed to appear from out of nowhere: silk kimonos, small silk cloths, needles, face powder. She herself dressed in humble hemp clothes. She knew sewing and painting and *hanamusubi*.[168] Everyone exclaimed, "The Ishida family has acquired a clever woman, indeed!"

Six months later, Ishida was called to the capital. The girl sent him off, saying, "Please do your duty; do not give me a second thought. Do

---

165. In 1573 Nobunaga granted the Asai-Asakura domain to Hideyoshi (*Honchō shōgunki*, 14).

166. The area was north of Lake Biwa, the old Asai domain.

167. Unidentified.

168. 花結び tying or binding flowers with thread; it was considered one of the feminine social graces.

not worry yourself—you, who are worth a thousand pieces of gold—
over trifling matters. Leave your affairs here to me." In the capital,
Ishida met a high-ranking priest, Sōzu Yūgaku[169] of Mount Takao. The
priest carefully examined his face and warned him: "Lord Ishida, you
have been bewitched by a hobgoblin who is draining all of your energy.
Unless you do something to rid yourself of it, you will soon lose your
life. I am unmistaken in such matters."

But Ishida did not believe what he heard and laughed at the priest,
thinking, "I am tired of hearing the false words of wicked priests;
they are said to upset me." But soon Ishida became ill; his face turned
yellow and thin, his muscles withered away. He lost his senses and
could not concentrate. His retainers were surprised and tried all kinds
of medicinal cures in vain. Finally, remembering what the priest of
Takao had told their master, they invited Yūgaku to examine Ishida.
After doing so, he said to Ishida, "There is no mistake in what I have
seen in you. Because you would not believe me at first, you have become ill. Showing mercy is the primary concern of the Way. A prayer
will save you. Quickly go home and wait. I will come and pray for you."
Ishida and his retinue hurried back to Gifu, traveling night and day.

As soon as they arrived home, an altar was set up and decorated
with twenty-four kinds of offerings, twenty-four candles, twelve
standing sticks for sacred *hei* papers,[170] and four kinds of incense. To
ward off the evil spirit, the priest read these holy words:

"Today, in the second year of Tenshō [1574], a man of the Ishida
clan has been bewitched by a wicked fox. Since ancient times, when the
two elements of *yin* and *yang* were separated, and heaven, earth, and
humans[171] were distinguished from one another, beings received their
respective natures and forms. Everyone, everything, is not the same in
nature and status.

"Here a wicked fox has used its tricks at will—changing leaves
into clothes, wearing a human skull on its head as a wig, changing its
form—and has thus bewitched people. Foxes always look suspicious—

....

169. The priest could be Mongaku 文覚 of Jingoji Temple in Takao. Mongaku belonged to the Shingon sect; he lived during the Kamakura period, but his dates are unknown. He was a celebrated
high-ranking priest whose prayers were known to be particularly effective (*Genpeiseisuiki*, 19).

170. *Hei* 幣: pieces of white paper offered to Shinto gods for purification.

171. *Tenchijin* 天地人.

as if they were listening to the ice before crossing it.[172] They stir up curses, producing fire by beating their tails. Because of them, Priest Daian[173] [of China] escaped to the land of *rakan* holy men, and Priest Hyakujō rebuked the karmic rules. The mysteries of a thousand years are revealed in the two legs [of a fox],[174] and the stomach of a man is ruined when he receives a gift from the two hands [of a fox].[175]

"This man of the Ishida clan is a celebrated warrior. Why have you stolen his energy with your wicked tricks? From a lodging house in Musa, you brought lewdness into the bedroom of a good family. You wander around, seeking a partner; your name is Purple.[176] You show your ugliness and shame. Although you would not forget to place your head on a hill when you die, you expose your low trickery when you leech on to a tiger's esteem to fool people. You, quickly leave and leave now. Don't you know the fox with nine tails[177] was punished in ancient times and remained unforgiven for a thousand years? Who does not hate your deceiving lewdness? Unless you leave quickly, all the deities of the small and large shrines of various places will awaken and kill you with the four killing swords and drown you in the six harmful waters."[178]

When the priest finished reading, suddenly black clouds appeared, followed by heavy rain and terrible rolling thunder. The girl was so frightened she fell down and died. The people were shocked to see her turn into a huge old fox lying with a human skull on its head. The girl's gifts to others—the silk kimonos, face power, and needles—turned into banana leaves, rice bran, and pine needles. Ishida instantly recovered; refreshed and energetic, he was curious to see these changed things.

....

172. This and the following expressions are unclear, but essentially they all assert that foxes are wicked and enjoy fooling people with their tricks. This belief was longlived and widespread in both China and Japan.

173. 大安; a monk of Tang China who exposed a woman serving Empress Sokutenbukō (則天武后) as a fox by traveling in his thoughts to the land of *rakan* 羅漢, or Arhats (*Taiheikōki*, 44).

174. A two-legged (standing) fox is wicked and is getting ready to play a trick.

175. The meaning of this sentence is unclear.

176. *Shishi* 紫紫; refers to an old tale of a lewd woman named Purple who changed herself into a fox (*Jibungoshū* 事文後集, 37).

177. *Kyūbi-kitsune* 九尾狐; the fox with nine tails was especially deceitful.

178. *Rikugai no mizu* 六害の水; refers to great rivers like the Kōga 江河 in China.

He buried the fox deep in the mountains and sealed the grave with a *gofu* talisman for purification and protection. He took various medicines such as *tansha* and *kaiō*[179] to regain his energy.

When Ishida visited Musa, he learned that Koyata had moved soon after selling the girl, but no one knew where. Truly, the fox's tricks had deceived many—except Sōzu Yūgaku, whose powers proved the efficacy of his prayers and impressed the people.[180]

3-1   A Man Sees His Wife's Dream

Hamada Yōhei served Ōuchi Yoshitaka,[181] who was the lord of the castle in Yamaguchi in Suō.[182] Hamada's wife had been a courtesan in Port Muro.[183] He fell in love with her, pledged his deep affection,

---

179. *Tansha* 丹砂: a compound of mercury and sulfur. *Kaiō* 蟹黄: crab intestines. Both were used to increase energy and longevity.

180. This story is based on a tale in *SS*, 3-5 (胡媚娘伝). Asai changed it into a Buddhist farce by having a powerful priest upstage a clever fox. Having the bold Koyata fool both the fox and Ishida adds a humorous twist.

181. 大内義隆 (1507–1551); he committed suicide when his subject, Sue (d. 1555), rebelled.

182. Yamaguchi shi, Yamaguchi-ken.

183. 室; in present-day Hyogo-ken, Muro was an important port along the Inland Sea 瀬戸内海.

and finally took her as his wife. Beautiful and discerning, she had a sympathetic heart and knew poetry and calligraphy. It was perhaps due to a karmic link in a previous life that she became Hamada's wife. They were devoted to each other. Everything appeared to her as if in a dream.

Lord Yoshitaka was summoned by the shogun in the capital and was promoted to deputy of the Dazai office [in Kyushu]; he also served [the shogun] as a close attendant of the third rank. He stayed in the capital for a long time. Hamada, too, was forced to remain in the capital. His wife missed him and thought of him constantly. On the fifteenth day of the eighth month, on a cloudy night with no moon, she recited a poem:

omoiyaru
miyako no sora no
tsukikage o
ikue no kumo ka
tachi hedatsu ramu

Thinking
Of the shadow
Of the moon in the capital,
Layers of clouds
Must hide its appearance.

Unable to sleep, the wife, tilting her pillow, gazed up at the [cloudy] sky and lamented missing [her husband].

Earlier that day, Lord Yoshitaka returned to his province. Hamada stayed at the castle and then headed to his home outside the castle gate. It was a cloudy, moonless night. After walking about a half *chō*, he saw a curtain hanging in the thicket by the dark roadside. Behind the curtain were bright lights, and a score of men and women had gathered for a drinking party, hoping to see the moon. "Since the lord has returned, every family must be happy. These people are here to celebrate," thought Hamada. He hid behind a nearby willow tree and watched the revelers. Then he saw his wife talking and laughing among them. "What is this? She should not be there," he wondered in disbelief.

One of the men in the party said, "I wonder how long tonight's moon will remain behind those heartless clouds. And why is there no poem for it?" Everyone urged Hamada's wife to recite a poem. She declined at first but then relented:

kirigirisu
koe mo kareno[184] no
kusamura ni
tsuki sae kurashi
koto sara ni nake

A grasshopper
In the thicket
Of a withered field,
Especially sings his heart out
At the dark moon night.

Hearing her poem, Hamada was filled with compassion for his

---

184. 枯野: withered field. The first two syllables (*kare* 嗄れ) also refer to being hoarse. The grasshopper's voice may have gone hoarse from so much singing.

wife. The party grew more animated as sake cups were passed around. A cup was placed before a young boy of seventeen or eighteen, but he would not take it up. When others tried to force him, he said, "I will accept a cup in exchange for a poem by the lady [Hamada's wife]." She declined: "I have already shared my feelings in a poem. Please excuse me this time." But no one would accept her refusal, so she recited:

yuku mizu no
kaeranu kyo o
oshime tada
wakaki mo toshi wa
tomaranu mono o

The flowing water
Never returns,
Cherish this day
While young
As time never stops.

As the cups went around again, someone cried out, "Now sing a song." So the wife sang a stanza from an *imayō*:[185]

"When I sleep alone in my bedroom, the wind pierces me. When the sound of pampas grass in the wind ceases, I will not lament missing you, but hope the flying geese will carry my letter [to you]."

Someone in the party who was familiar with Confucian works tearfully recited a verse in the Chinese style:

"The light of a firefly penetrates the willows. A sad wind blows the wild grasses. I wonder if this is some kind of game in a dream as I pour and drink a cup of sake in grief."

In response Hamada's wife tearfully asked, "Why is only tonight a dream? Everything in this life is a dream." Hearing this the revelers protested: "You are shedding tears at a party. That is unlucky!" Someone threw a sake cup that hit her forehead. Hamada's wife angrily threw a stone at the culprit; it struck his head and blood began to flow from

185. 今様: popular songs consisting of seven words of five syllables in four stanzas. The wife sings an *imayo* from the *Muromachi kouta* 室町小歌 (Small Songs of the Muromachi).

the wound like a waterfall. As soon as everyone stood up in surprise, the light vanished and then the people, leaving only the insects singing in the thicket. Hamada felt most strange: "Perhaps my wife has died and that was her ghost." Tearfully, he hurried home.

There he found his wife soundly sleeping. When he woke her, she was very pleased to see him and said, "I fell asleep while waiting for you. I dreamed of a score of people carousing in a thicket. At their urging, I recited a few poems and sang a song that expressed my feelings for you. Someone did not like my tears and threw a cup at my forehead, so I threw a stone at him in return. When the people in the party became excited, I woke up from my dream. My head still hurts where the cup hit my forehead." She told him about the poems and the song, which were exactly what Hamada had heard while he was in hiding. In the end he was convinced: "What I saw from behind the willow was my wife's dream."[186]

3-2   Becoming a Demon as He Fell
in the Demon Valley

Hachiya Magotaro lived in Kumakawa in the Onyū District of Jaku Province.[187] His family was wealthy and lacked for nothing. Hachiya concerned himself with neither business nor farming: He engaged solely in studying the works of Confucius. After studying a little, he would say to himself, "There is nothing better than this." When he encountered someone without education, he despised him. When he met someone who was learned, he thought, "I am better than he is."

Moreover, Hachiya slandered Buddhist teachings, scornfully criticizing the concepts of the cause and effect, good and bad deeds, and the transmigration of birth and death for three generations. He laughed at the thought of hell, heaven, *shaba*, and the Pure Land.[188]

---

186. The author recast this tale (based on the Chinese *Gochō shōsetsu* 五朝小説, Muyūroku 夢遊録 [張生]) as a dream story by changing the female protagonist from a housewife to a courtesan.

187. In present-day Kumakawa, Kaminaka-chō, Onyū-gun, Fukui-ken.

188. This life, or the human world, is *shaba* 娑婆, as opposed to the Amida Buddha's Pure Land (*jōdo* 浄土).

He did not believe in demons[189] or ghosts. He stated, "When people die, their souls return to the *yin-yang*.[190] Their forms and bodies turn to dust and nothing is left. In this life, those who are bored with rich food, wear beautiful *kosode* kimonos,[191] enjoy rich lives with wives and children—they are in the Buddha state. Those who suffer from hardship, eat poor food, wear ragged hemp clothes, and sell their wives and children—they are in the hungry ghost state.[192] Those who loudly beg for food at gates do not feel unclean when they eat food left by others, sleep on the grass with stones for pillows, and are naked in the snow— they are in the animal state. Those who commit sins and crimes and are imprisoned, bound by ropes, decapitated, slain by swords when their bones are broken, crucified by water and fire—these people are in the hell state. And those who handle such sinners and criminals are *gokusotsu* prison guards. There is no one else [in this world]. Those who believe in what they cannot see, life after death, illusory ghosts, and the words of monks, *kan'nagi* Shinto priests, and *miko* maiden servants of gods—they are all fools."

If someone cautioned him, Hachiya rebuked the person by quoting from [the Chinese classics], the Four Books and the Six Sutras.[193] Thus he silenced his opponents with his eloquence and false words. His egotistical and arrogant attitude was beyond description. People called him Demon Magotarō and completely ignored him.

One day Hachiya started for Tsuruga on an errand. He left home when the sun was high, so it was dark by the time he arrived at Imazu-Kahara.[194] Because of the fighting in Gō Province and Kitanoshō,[195] he saw neither travelers nor a place that could shelter him for the night. He walked to the riverside and came across many

....

189. *Kijin* 鬼神: someone possessing supernatural powers. *Yūrei* 幽霊: spirits or ghosts; refers to *shiryō* 死霊 (the spirit of the dead).

190. I.e., the Yin-Yang Way 隱陽道.

191. 小袖: a small, sleeved kimono, usually made of silk with lining.

192. 餓鬼道: one of the six realms in Buddhist teachings, which include hell, heaven, and the realms of hungry ghosts, animals, *ashura*, and human beings

193. *Shisho* 四書; *rikukei* 六経.

194. Present-day Imazu-chō, Takashima-gun, Shiga-ken.

195. Gōshū (Ōmi) Province is in present-day Shiga-ken. Hideyoshi 秀吉 attacked Shibata Katsuie 柴田勝家, who committed suicide in 1583 at Kitanoshō Castle in present-day Fukui-ken.

white human bones scattered here and there. The water flowed quietly. After sunset, the mountains in every direction were dark, covered in clouds. He saw no inns.

Wondering what to do, Hachiya looked north and spied a pine grove. He entered it and rested at the base of one of the trees. Owls hooted bleakly and frightening *kitsunebi*[196] appeared. A stormy wind blowing through the pines pierced his body, and he felt helpless and lonesome. He looked around and saw seven or eight bodies lying with their heads to the west and to the south.[197] Then it began to rain; the wind continued to blow and thunder rolled with flashes of lightning. Suddenly the bodies on the ground got up and came staggering toward Hachiya. Terribly frightened, he climbed up a pine tree. The bodies gathered at the base of the tree and shouted, "Let's take him tonight!" At last the sky cleared and an autumn moon began to shine brightly.

A *yasha*[198] came running. He had a blue body, a pair of horns, and a wide mouth. His hair was disheveled. He grabbed one of the bodies, tore off its head and limbs, and devoured it. Then he fell asleep at the base of Hachiya's tree. His snoring shook the ground. "This *yasha* will definitely eat me when he wakes up. It's better to run away now," Hachiya thought, so he quietly climbed down and ran. The *yasha* woke and chased after him. Hachiya noticed an old Buddhist temple at the foot of a mountain, its eaves broken, altar collapsed, and not a priest in sight. All that remained was a large statue.

Hachiya ran into the temple and prayed to it, "Please help me." Moving around the statue, he saw a large hole in its back. He quickly squeezed into the hole and held his breath. Soon the *yasha* entered the temple, but seeing only the statue and not thinking to look inside it, he left. Hachiya was greatly relieved. Then he heard the statue [happily] stamp its feet and slap its stomach, saying, "The *yasha* came in but missed it. I have gotten it with no effort. I have a *tenshin*[199] for tonight!" The statue walked out of the temple, but it stumbled on a stone and broke its limbs, which scattered away. Hachiya crawled out of the hole

....

196. 狐火: fox fire; a phosphorus fire often seen in graveyards.

197. This expression means the bodies were scattered here and there.

198. Or *yakṣa* 夜叉. demons sometimes regarded as protectors of the Buddhist law.

199. 点心: a snack between meals.

and rebuked the statue bitterly: "You tried to eat me, but you were un-lucky and destroyed yourself instead. A Buddhist statue is supposed to help people."

Hachiya continued east and saw a bonfire in a distant field. Encouraged, he hurried toward the field and discovered a group of naked creatures sitting around the fire; some had no heads, others no hands or feet. The shocked Hachiya quickly ran off. Seeing him, the creatures shouted to each other, "That man disturbed us while we were enjoying our sake. Catch him and make him into food that we can enjoy with our sake!"

The creatures stood up and began to chase Hachiya. He ran along the base of the mountain until he came to a river. He barely managed to cross it, but his pursuers gave up and left. Hachiya was still so fright-ened he felt as if all his hair were standing on end, especially when he recalled what the creatures had said, their voices echoing in his ears. He walked about half a *ri*[200] before he came to a bushy and grassy area between two mountains. The moon was tilting toward the west, offer-ing only dim light. Hachiya stumbled on a stone and fell into a pit that

....

200. One *ri* equals 3.9 kilometers.

measured one hundred *jō* deep.[201]

At the bottom of the pit, the frightened Hachiya became aware of a bad odor. Fear penetrated into his bones. After his eyes had grown accustomed to the dark, he found himself in a nest of demons. Some had hair as red as fire and horns, others had blue hair and wings and crossed fangs. Still others had heads like cows and faces like animals with bird beaks. There were demons with bodies the color of crimson or indigo. Their eyes were like lightning and their mouths spewed flames.

When they saw Hachiya, they said to each other, "He will make trouble in our country. Don't let him leave. Catch him and bind him!" They put Hachiya in an iron pillory and copper shackles and dragged him before the demon king. The king addressed Hachiya angrily: "In the human world, this man was very wicked; he rashly criticized, ignored, and despised demon deities and ghosts. The *Chūyō*[202] speaks highly of our virtue. The *Rongo*[203] says humans avoid us out of respect. The Kinoka section of the *Eki*[204] notes our awesome deeds with the expression "loading demons on a cart." The *shōga* section of the *Shikyō*[205] describes our practices. Moreover, the *Sadon*[206] mentions Shin Keikō's dream and Lord Tei Hakuyū in relation to demons. Why do you belittle us and chose only to believe in the words of the *Rongo* and deny the existence of supernatural powers and demons?"[207] And with this, the king commanded his servants to beat Hachiya.

Then he ordered, "Make him tall." The demons gathered [around Hachiya] and pulled his head and feet until he was three *jo* tall, the height of a bamboo pole. All the demons laughed. When they raised him up, Hachiya staggered and fell to the ground. "Make him short,"

....

201. One *jō* equals 3 meters.

202. 中庸: one of the four Chinese classics; the other three are the *Shisho* 四書, the *Daigaku* 大学, the *Rongo* 論語, and the *Mōshi* 孟子.

203. The *Analects of Confucius*. Written by Confucius (551–479 B.C.), the work came to Japan during the reign of Emperor Ojin (r. 270–310).

204. Refers to the *Ekikyō* 易経 (Book of Changes), one of the five Chinese classics (五経); the others are the *Shokyō* 書経, the *Shikyō* 詩経, the *Reiki* 礼記, and the *Shunjū* 春秋.

205. 詩経: the oldest anthology of poems in China (10–6 B.C.).

206. 左伝 (春秋左氏伝): a historical work by Sakyūmei (左丘明), a contemporary of Confucius.

207. *Kairyoku-ranshin* 怪力乱神: the powers of deranged deities. The expression refers to something unreasonable and illogical.

cried the king. The demons began to knead Hachiya like a dumpling until he was flat and wide and crawled like a crab. Again the demons laughed and clapped their hands.

An old demon said to Hachiya, "You have always denied our existence and despised us. Now you have been stretched and pummeled, teased and belittled by us. I pity you and forgive you." He took Hachiya by the hands and threw him, causing Hachiya to regain his original appearance. "Let us return him to the human world," announced [the old demon]. But the others disagreed: "It is no fun to send him back as he is. Let us give him a farewell gift." One of the demons proclaimed, "I give him two horns so he can part the mists when traveling on cloudy paths." The demon planted two horns into Hachiya's forehead. Another put an iron beak in his mouth, saying, "I give him a beak so he can make sounds in the air."[208]

"I give him a mop of red hair," said a third demon, dying Hachiya's hair with red water. The last one said, "I present him with a pair of shiny green eyes" and pushed two round blue jewels[209] into Hachiya's eyes.

Finally, Hachiya was ordered out of the pit. On his way home, he passed Imazu-kawara. By then he was truly a frightful demon with shiny green eyes, flaming hair, a pointed beak, and two horns on his forehead. When he reached his home in Kumakawa, his wife and servants were shocked to see him. He tearfully explained everything and reassured them that his heart was the same in spite of his changed appearance. But his wife said to him, "It is too sad to see you like this" and put a *katabira*[210] kimono over his head. She continued to sob and grieve. His children were so frightened they ran away from him. Curious neighbors came; they were appalled at the sight of him and clapped their hands [in dismay]. Hachiya was so distraught he shut himself in and refused food. Confined to his room, he grew desperate and deranged. Then he became ill and finally died.

Some time later, people saw Hachiya, as his old self, wandering about his home, but after a Buddhist service was held [for the repose

---

208. *Usobuku* うそぶく: to boast or tell lies; underscores the protagonist's arrogant attitude in the human world.

209. *Aokitama* 青き珠; this may refer to a blue iridescent stone that appears green when light shines through it.

210. 帷子: a kimono without lining used for corpses.

of his soul], they no longer did.[211]

3-3   The Peony Lantern

Every family in the capital observed the Festival of Souls,[212] which was held from the fifteenth to the twenty-fourth day of the seventh month. During the festival, familes followed the custom of preparing an altar to worship the departed souls of family members. People decorated altars, eaves, and ancestors' gravestones with lanterns. Pedestrians enjoyed nighttime strolls through streets lit by lanterns with elegant plant, flower, and bird designs. Many *bon* dancers gathered for the occasion and performed as they sang *shōga*[213] in beautiful voices. Thus rich and poor, high and low in the capital enjoyed evenings during the festival.

On the fifteenth day of the seventh month in 1548, Ogiwara Shin'nojō lived in Gojō-Kyōgoku in the capital. His beloved wife had just passed away, and he missed her so much that his sleeves were wet with tears. While at the window, he sadly recalled their past life together. Praying for his wife, he recited a sutra and thought "She has already joined the departed at this Festival of Souls." [Later,] after he had declined invitations from friends, he stood in a daze at his gate, unable to venture out. Shedding tears, he recited a poem:

> *ikanare ba*
> *tachi mo hanarezu*
> *omokage no*
> *mi ni soinagara*
> *kanashi karuran*[214]

> When her visage
> Never leaves me

---

211. This story was adopted from *SS*, 4-2 (大虚司法伝). In the original Chinese story, after his death, the protagonist appeals to the Heavenly Emperor, who destroys all the demons; later the protagonist becomes a criminal law official. The Japanese author skipped this ending and changed the story into a Buddhist tale, following the trend of assimilating Buddhist and Confucian sources.

212. This is *bon* season, when departed souls return to this world.

213. 頌歌: songs praising Buddhist virtues; can also refer to *shōga* 唱歌 (songs in general).

214. A similar poem appears in *Shinshūishū*, Koi, 4.

But always stays with me,
Then, I wonder
Why I am so sad.

The night of the fifteenth was drawing to a close and the streets grew quieter with fewer passers-by.

Just then, Ogiwara saw a beautiful woman of about twenty slowly strolling along the street. She was holding a lantern elegantly decorated with a peony and accompanied by a young girl of fourteen or fifteen. He was fascinated by the woman's beauty: Her eyes were as wide as lotus leaves, and her body as supple as a willow branch. He admired her eyebrows, shapely as a crescent moon, and her glossy black hair. Seeing such a rare creature under the moonlight, Ogiwara wondered, "Is she a heavenly being who has descended from the sky to entertain herself in this world, or perhaps she is Princess Oto[215] of the Dragon Palace at the bottom of the sea, here for amusement? Anyway, she does not look like a woman of this world at all." Unable to control his desire and infatuation, he began to follow her.

Whether walking ahead of the young woman or following behind, Ogiwara tried to get her attention as she traveled about one *chō* block to the west. Suddenly she turned around and spoke to him, smiling slightly, "I am not waiting for anyone in particular. Allured by the beautiful moon, I have been casually strolling like this until it has become late. I am now afraid to return home alone. Will you help me and take me back?"

Ogiwara slowly replied, "It is getting late and your home must be far away. My home is as humble as a dusty hut, but if you don't mind, you can spend the night there." Again smiling, the woman said, "I am glad that you asked me since I usually spend lonesome nights at my window, gazing at the moon. People are easily touched by a kind heart."

Pleased, Ogiwara took her hand and held it until they arrived at his home. Sake was brought in and the young girl served them. They exchanged a few cups until the moon began to tilt. While listening to the woman sweetly express her deep feelings for him, he recalled the

---

215. The legendary Otohime 乙姫 resided in the Dragon Palace. In an *otogizōshi* 御伽草子 (tale), Urashima Tarō 浦島太郎 visited the palace.

old poem "This life is limited only to today . . ."[216] and he thought of their future life together. He recited:

> mata nochi no
> chigiri mada yana
> niimakura,
> tada koyoi koso
> kagiri naru rame[217]

> Should I wait for
> The pledges of new pillows[218]
> Until the next time?
> No, this is the very night
> To exchange them.

The woman answered:

> yuuna yuuna
> matsutoshi iwaba
> kizarame ya
> kakochi gao naru
> kane goto wa nazo

> If you say to come
> Night after night,
> I will come.
> So why do you still
> Look so sad?

Listening to her poem, Ogiwara grew happier and more relaxed. Finally, the couple untied the lower sashes of their undergarments and exchanged their new pillows. Before they had finished their sweet talk, daybreak arrived.

Ogiwara asked the woman, "Where do you live? Tell me your

....

216. See *Shinkokinshū*, Koi, 3.

217. See *Dairingushō* 題林愚抄, Koi, 2.

218. *Niimakura* 新枕: to sleep with someone for the first time.

name as in the legend of the Log Palace."[219] She began: "I am related to Nikaidō Masayuki,[220] a descendant of the Fujiwara clan. Our family was once prosperous, but now that time is over, and we live very humbly. My father, Masanobu, and my brothers all perished during the conflict[221] in the capital. [Since then] my family has been in complete decline, and only I am left, living with a young maidservant near Manjuji Temple.[222] I am too sad and ashamed to tell you my name." Her manner of speaking was very gentle and charming. The clouds in the dawning sky were gathering in the east as the moon sank behind a mountain. The candlelight grew faintly white. Finally, the woman got up and regretfully left him.

She came to him at twilight and left him at dawn as promised. By now Ogiwara was completely enchanted and so enticed by her that he lost his reason. He was only happy when she visited him, saying, "Our pledges will continue for a thousand years." He would see no one during the day. More than twenty days passed like this.

A wise old man lived next to Ogiwara. "A young woman is visiting Ogiwara every night. I hear her singing and laughing. It is strange," he said to himself. One night, he looked through a crack in the wall and saw Ogiwara sitting by a lighted candle, facing a skeleton! Whenever Ogiwara spoke, the skeleton moved its hands and feet; whenever the skeleton spoke, it nodded its skull from time to time. The old man was greatly shocked. As soon as morning arrived, he called on Ogiwara: "I hear you have a guest every night. Who is it?" Ogiwara kept silent, not wanting to reveal anything. The old man continued: "You will definitely be visited by misfortune, so why should I hide anything from you? Last night, I looked into your house through a crack in the wall and I saw what was going on. When you are alive, you have a strong positive *yang* spirit, clean and pure. But when you die, you have a neg-

---

219. Konomarudono, or Kinomarudono, 木の丸殿, was the log palace of Empress Saimei (r. 655–661) located in present-day Asakura, Fukuoka-ken. Those who wanted to enter the palace had to identify themselves.

220. The Nikaidō 二階堂 clan had important administrative roles in the Kamakura and Muromachi governments. In 1487 Masayuki (Masatsura) 政行 joined the shogun Ashikaga Yoshihisa's army (see *Rokuon nichiroku* 鹿苑日録, 1). The Fujiwara clan was in power during the Heian period.

221. This may refer to the private war between the Hosokawa and the Miyoshi in the capital.

222. 万寿寺; in present-day Honchō, Higashiyama-ku, Kyoto-shi, Manjuji is one of the five Zen temples in Kyoto.

ative *yin* spirit and are defiled.[223] This is why people have a deep hatred of death and avoid it.

"In your ignorance, you have chosen to associate with a ghost, to sleep with a defiled demon. Your *yang* spirit will quickly be lost and you will be overcome by illness. Once you are sick, neither medicine nor *mogusa*[224] treatments will work. Consumption will fill your decaying lungs. Although young like fresh grass, you will quickly turn into an old man and wither. Given your sudden invitation to the Land after Death, you will soon be buried beneath the moss. What a pity!"

Ogiwara was shocked to hear this and told the old man everything that had happened. The man suggested: "If the woman says she lives near Manjuji Temple, why don't you go and see her?" So Ogiwara went west of Gojō and searched the Madenokōji area. He walked on the dyke, looked through the willow groves, and asked the people there about the woman to no avail. Toward sunset, he entered Manjuji Temple. While resting there, he toured the grounds and saw an old *tamaya*[225] to the north, behind the bathhouse. There he found a coffin bearing the inscription: "Zen Nun, Ginshōin-Reigetsu; Iyako, a daughter of Nikaidō Masanobu[226] Saemon'nojō." Next to it was a *togibōko*[227] with the name Asaji written on its back. An old lantern with a peony design hung in front of the coffin. Realizing that this was the coffin of his lover, Ogiwara became so frightened every hair on his body stood up, and he ran out of the temple without looking back. All his love and infatuation were completely gone. He forgot his yearning for evening to arrive and the resentment he felt at daybreak when the woman left him. He was even afraid to return home, thinking, "What shall I do if she comes tonight?" He asked the old man to stay at his home that night.

When Ogiwara asked the man for help, he was told, "Lord Kyō of

....

223. This idea is based on the Yin-Yang Way.

224. According to the *kyū* 灸 treatment, fluid made from heated *mogusa* grass cures ailments.

225. 魂屋: a place where coffins were kept.

226. Masanobu is unidentified. Both the daughter and father are fictional.

227. *Otogibōko* 伽婢子: dolls buried with a deceased person. *Bōko*, or *hishi* (婢子) originally referred to maidservants who were buried with their deceased mistresses. Later, dolls were substituted. *Togi* 伽: to entertain. Thus the doll was buried to entertain the departed soul as a companion.

Tōji Temple[228] is known for his learning and dealings with the occult. Go and see him." As soon as Lord Kyō saw Ogiwara, he said to him, "A demon is consuming your blood and energy. You will die in ten days." After Ogiwara told Lord Kyō his story, the priest wrote out and gave him a protective *gofu* talisman[229] and told Ogiwara to put it on the gate of his house. After he did so, the woman no longer came to him.

About fifty days later, Ogiwara visited Tōji Temple to express his gratitude to Lord Kyō. The lord invited him in for a drink. When Ogiwara left, he was slightly drunk, and perhaps because of this, he began to miss the woman. He went to Manjuji Temple and looked in at the gate. Then suddenly the woman appeared. She said resentfully, "Your early promises have weakened. In the beginning, I gave you everything because I believed in your deep feelings for me. I visited you every evening and left you at dawn with the promise that our relationship would last forever like an *itsumade-gusa* eternal vine. But someone named Lord Kyō interfered and changed your heart. Tonight I feel most fortunate that you have come back like this. I am so glad to see you again. Please come in." Saying this, she took his hand and led him into the inner part of the temple. Ogiwara's servant, who was with him, ran home and reported what had happened. But alas, when his family arrived at the temple, Ogiwara was already dead; he was found embracing a white skeleton in a woman's grave. The temple priests thought this disturbing and moved the grave to Toribeyama.[230]

Later, on rainy and cloudy nights, anyone who saw Ogiwara strolling hand-in-hand with a woman accompanied by a young maid carrying a peony lantern became seriously ill. People in the area were distraught. Ogiwara's family was obliged to perform a dedicatory service wherein the *Lotus Sutra* was recited one thousand times and one thousand copies of the sutra, made in a single day,[231] were buried in

....

228. *Kyō no kimi*; Lord Kyō is unidentified. Tōji Temple 東寺, in present-day Minami-ku, Kyoto-shi, is the headquarters of the Tōji school of Shingon sect.

229. A sentence or passage from a Buddhist sutra was written on these to dispel evil spirits.

230. 鳥部山. a burial ground in present-day Higashiyamaka-ku, Kyoto-shi.

231. *Ichinichi tonsha* 一日頓写.

the woman's grave. Since then, the apparitions have ceased to appear.[232]

3-4   The Plum Blossom Screen

At the end of the Tenmon era [1531–1554], the Miyoshi and Hosokawa families continued to wage a feud in the capital of Kyoto.[233] Shogun Kōgen'in Minamoto Yoshiteru[234] tried to quell the turmoil, but no one would join him: Imperial power was too weak [to influence the situation].

Ōuchi Yoshitaka,[235] assistant director of police in Kyushu and the lord of Suō Province,[236] received junior second rank as an imperial attendant.[237] Concurrently serving as director of the military,[238] his prestige and power increased, and many noblemen of Kyoto joined him in Yamaguchi to avoid the disturbances in the capital. In Yamaguchi Castle, elegant parties and feasts hosting poetry and music recitals were held day and night. Over time, Ōuchi Yoshitaka neglected the warrior's way. While he surrounded himself with entertainers, politics fell into the hands of certain sycophants. Taking advantage of

....

232. In the original Chinese text, SS, 4-2 (牡丹灯記), the male protagonist, the woman, and the maidservant visit a Taoist priest to appease their souls and are finally sent to hell. The Japanese author ignored this portion of the story and introduced more romantic and mysterious elements. In the original, the fifteenth night of the first month is celebrated with lighting lanterns; here the time period is changed to coincide with the *bon* festival, when a ghost sighting would have been more likely for Japanese readers. Also, Asai skillfully combines the descendants of the Nikaidō clan, including the woman, and the *bon* festival to create a Buddhist tale. This ghost story, translated into Japanese (*Kiizōdanshū* 奇異雑談集), was so popular that Hayashi Razan 林羅山, a contemporary Confucian scholar, composed a poem for it. It later became known as a typical *kaidan* 怪談, a strange (ghost) tale, and was narrated by Sanyūtei Enchō 三遊亭円朝 (1839–1900), a celebrated Edo storyteller. The Chinese story includes no poems, but three *waka* poems, all related to the *Shūiwakashū* 拾遺和歌集 (1005–1007) , appear in the Japanese version.

233. The fighting began in 1548 and lasted until 1551. Hosokawa Harumoto was defeated by Miyoshi Chōkei.

234. 光源院源義輝: the thirteenth shogun of the Muromachi shogunate from 1546 to 1565.

235. 大内義隆 (1507–1551); Yoshitaka's decline was blamed on his "soft" lifestyle as described in the *Kōyōgunkan* 甲陽軍艦.

236. In the eastern part of present-day Yamaguchi-ken.

237. *Jijū* 侍従.

238. Hyōbukyō 兵部卿.

this situation, Elder Sue, a governor of Owari, rebelled.[239] Yoshitaka retreated to Daineiji Temple[240] in Nagato, where he committed suicide. Eventually, Elder Sue, now established at Yamaguchi Castle, appointed as his lord Ōtomo Yoshinaga, governor of Bungo[241] and a younger brother of Ōtomo Sōrin.[242] Elder Sue controlled political affairs himself.

Among the noblemen from the capital were Former Regent Fujiwara Tadafusa[243] and Former Minister of the Left Fujiwara Kinyori,[244] who left Yamaguchi Castle during the revolt and died after being struck down by arrows. Fujiwara Chikayo of the junior second rank[245] took the tonsure. Middle Councilor Fujiwara Motoyori[246] excelled in tactics as well as poetry, calligraphy, and painting. He was familiar with the military arts, including riding and swimming. He swam as fast as a fish and could remain underwater for half a day. While Yoshitaka was in Kyoto, Lord Motoyori helped him in various ways. He was granted an official rank[247] and familiarized himself with the manners and customs of the imperial court. Yoshitaka especially welcomed Lord Motoyori to Yamaguchi, building him a new mansion near the castle and treating him well. Lord Motoyori brought his entire household to Yamaguchi, where he enjoyed a peaceful life.

Meanwhile, a rebellion by the elders took place. One night, Lord

....

239. After the rebellion, Fujiwara Tadafusa and Kinyori committed suicide and Fujiwara Chikayo took the tonsure according to an article in the *Kugyōbunin* 公卿補任 on the twenty-ninth day of the eighth month in 1551.

240. 大寧寺: a temple of the Sōtō sect in present-day Nagato-shi, Yamguchi-ken. Yoshitaka committed suicide there.

241. Present-day Ōita prefecture.

242. 大友宗麟 (1530–1587); Sōrin was a Christian *daimyō* 大名. His younger brother Ōtomo Yoshinaga 大友義長 was invited by Elder Sue to serve as the lord of Yamaguchi (*Honchō shogunki*, 9).

243. 藤原伊房; Tadafusa was killed at the age of fifty-six, after Yoshitaka's death (*Kugyōbunin*, *Tenmon*, 20).

244. 藤原公頼; Kinyori, who received junior first rank, was killed at the age of fifty-four (*Kugyōbunin*, *Tenmon*, 20).

245. Fujiwara Chikayo 藤原親世 actually received third rank and took the tonsure at the age of fifty-eight.

246. 藤原基頼: unidentified. He could have been Fujiwara Motoki 藤原基規, who took the tonsure at the time of the rebellion (*Kugyōbunin*, *Tenmon*, 20).

247. With the exception of shoguns, receiving imperial rank was unusual for a man from a military family (*buke* 武家).

Motoyori left Yamaguchi for the capital with his wife, close attendants, and valuables. When their boat reached Takasago-Tadanoumi in Agei Province,[248] they stopped and waited for the tide to change. As they waited, the lord's wife tearfully composed a poem:

tada no umi
ika ni ukitaru
fune no ue
sanomi ni araki
nami makura kana

Aboard the boat
Floating[249] on the Tadano Sea,[250]
Why is my slumber
Disturbed so much
On the rough waves?

As the night deepened and the moon tilted further, Lord Motoyori had his servants prepare sake, and her ladyship took a sip of it. He also shared food from a *warigo*[251] with the boatmen.

The boatmen came from Nōchi,[252] one and a half *ri* east of Tadanoumi. Seeing the lord's costly furniture, items decorated in gold and silver, and silk kimonos in the cargo, they devised a wicked plan: "Let's kill them tonight and take their valuables. No one will blame us for robbing them in these desperate times." They waited until it was late and the moon had disappeared.

They began by throwing a few servants into the sea. At the noise, the lord awoke, and they immediately pushed him into the sea. "What happened?" cried his surprised wife. The chief boatman caught her and said, "Remain calm. I will not kill you. I have two sons. The older

---

248. Present-day Tadanoumi in Takehara-shi, Hiroshima-ken. The author could have mistaken Takasago for Takasaki in the same city.

249. *Ukitaru*; the word also means weary or detesting.

250. The place name, Tadanoumi, suggests *tadano* (mere or ordinary); thus "Aboard a boat floating on an ordinary sea, why is my slumber (suggested by *makura* [pillow]) disturbed so much?" The poem expresses the wife's anxiety.

251. 破子: a wooden food container with a lid.

252. Present-day Nōchi, Yukisaki-cho, Mihara-shi, Hiroshima-ken.

one is already married, but the younger one is still single. I will let him have you as his bride." The chief and his men took the boat to Nōchi, where they sold all the valuables for cash. Motoyori's wife thought up an excuse: "Right now I am very upset. Please wait for a while. I will marry your younger son after I am settled." The chief agreed.

In the meantime, he invited his family, including his wife, children, and in-laws, to a moon-viewing party on the boat on the thirteenth night of the ninth month. That night, as it grew late, everyone got drunk and fell asleep. Motoyori's wife thought, "If I miss this chance, I will never be able to escape." She silently slipped out of the boat, swam to the beach, and ran. At dawn, she arrived at Mount Karei in Kitsunezaki.[253] Her feet, cut on stony beaches and thorny mountain paths as she ran for her life, were covered in blood.

In the morning mist, she saw a [small] temple in a forest. As she ran into it, she heard someone reciting sutras and chanting Amida Buddha's names. A nun appeared and confronted her cautiously, "You are a stranger. Why are you here so early in the morning and barefoot?" Motoyori's wife answered, "I come from Tomari in Mekari.[254] Since my husband left for the capital and was killed in battle, I have been serving my mother-in-law. But she is very mean and she and my in-laws treat me badly. I have been suffering day and night on account of their false charges and slander. Last night at a moon-viewing party on a boat, I was made to serve sake and dropped a [precious] sake cup by accident into the sea. I ran all night to avoid punishment and ended up here." Thus the wife tearfully told her story to the nun.[255]

"In that case, I suggest you return home now. I will come with you and apologize for you. But if you would rather stay here, I will help arrange for your remarriage. I am offering to do this because you seem very miserable," said the nun sympathetically. But the wife, while showing her gratitude, did not accept her offer and said, "Please make me a nun."

The nun explained, "Long ago, when the consort of Emperor Junwa [r. 823–833] took the tonsure, she was called Nun Nyoi[256] and confined

253. Present-day Ushiroji of Tomo-cho, Fukuyama-shi, Hiroshima-ken.

254. Unidentified.

255. The wife is changing her story so the nun will accept her.

256. The story of Nun Nyoi, Urashima's treasure box, and Kūkai appears in the *Genkōshakusho* 元亨釈書.

herself to the mountains in Muko.[257] While practicing the Way, she came to this temple, deposited the treasure box of Urashimako[258] and invited Priest Kūkai[259] to hold a dedicatory service for it. Since then, the temple has been reduced to ruins. The treasure box was eventually deposited in the bosom of the Noirin Kannon[260] statue, which was carved from a cherry tree. The statue became a miraculous Buddhist image. The governor of this province stole it, and eventually he was destroyed in a fire along with his house.

"This temple, located close to the beach, is surrounded by the sound of rough waves and has hardly any visitors, only wild *yomogi* thickets. Our only friends are the cries of monkeys in the mountains behind us and of plovers over the waves facing the temple. There is no one to talk to except the wind blowing through the pines and the waves crashing on the beach.

"There are three nuns here who are in their fifties and a young one acting as a servant who is discreet. Changing your beautiful flowery robe into a black one and shaving your head like a widow to become a nun will garner you sympathy. Unless you enter the Way and leave behind your worldly attachments, your life will be illusory and as transient as dew. Once you enter the Way, the clouds of disillusion will be dispersed in meditation, the darkness of ignorance will be illuminated by candlelight, and the heart and mind will be cleansed by the fragrance of incense. Picking flowers [in the garden] will cool your agitation. You will spend your time eating rice gruel in the morning, taking *toki*[261] at noon, and accepting the karmic relation from [your] past life.[262] Have neither grudges nor envy and your life will be calm and peaceful. Instead of involving yourself in secular matters and seeking

---

257. In present-day Muko-gun, Osaka-fu.

258. 浦島子. According to a legend, Urashimako received a treasure box from Princess Oto of the Dragon Palace.

259. 空海, or Kōbōdaishi 弘法大師 (774–835): founder of Kongōbuji Temple on Mount Kōya. Kūkai introduced the Shingon teachings to Japan. His writings include *Sangyōshiki* 三教指帰.

260. 如意輪観音: one of the three Nyoirin Kannon of Japan. The statue is presently kept in Manisanjinjuji Temple in Nishinomiya-shi, Hyogo-ken.

261. 斎: a Buddhist meal taken between twelve and two o'clock in the afternoon.

262. *En ni shitagai* 縁にしたがい. The expression means to accept the karmic (cause and effect) relation from one's past existence. One who committed sinful deeds in a previous life should accept the results or effects of these acts in his or her present life.

suffering and anxiety in your future life, know that nothing is superior to leaving worldly affairs behind."

After hearing the nun's speech, the wife advanced to the altar and had the young servant cut off her hair. She took Rishun as her Buddhist name. Since her early days, she had been familiar with poetry and calligraphy and had read the classics and Buddhist writings. After taking the tonsure, she read and understood the profound meanings of sutras and taught the head nun theories of the Law and interpretations from the sutra commentaries. She recited a poem to express her feelings:

> nakanaka ni
> uki ni shizumanu
> mi nari seba
> minorino umi no
> soko o shrameya

> Since I have sunk myself,
> In the sea of suffering,
> I wonder
> If I have come to know
> The bottom of the sea.[263]

Indeed, it is said: "A Buddhist seed rises from a relation."[264] Rishun stayed in the temple and rarely saw anyone from the outside world.

One day a man visited the temple and asked the head nun to perform a service. After the recitation of the sutra, the man placed his offerings, including a painting of a plum blossom, on the altar and left. The head nun pasted the painting on a screen. As soon as Rishun saw the painting, she recognized it as one she had put in a box when she left Yamaguchi.

"What sort of a man was it who left the painting?" asked Rishun. The nun answered, "He is a boatman from Nōchi and a parishioner of this temple. But people say he kills and steals. That is his means of

---

263. *Minori no umi no soko*: the depth or profound meaning of the Law.

264. I.e., knowledge or enlightenment stemming from relationships between parents and children, men and women, humans and animals, etc.

living. I am not sure if it is true." Rishun was convinced the man was one of the pirates but she did not say anything to the nun. Instead she quietly took a brush and added a poem to the painting:

waga yado no
ume no tachie o
mirukarani
omoi no hokani
kimi ya kimasamu

Having seen
The upward branch
Of the plum in my garden,
My dear one
Might return by chance.

The nun, not knowing the true meaning of the poem, only admired her beautiful calligraphy. The poem differed slightly from an earlier one but conveyed Rishun's fervent wish.[265] Later the painting was acquired by Honji Kyūbei[266] of Tomo in Bingo Province.[267] During a visit to the temple on an errand, he was attracted to the mysterious style and mood of the painting and the calligraphy, and he asked the head nun for the screen.

After having been thrown into the sea, Middle Councilor Lord Motoyori, the expert swimmer, swam about ten *chō*[268] before arriving at a beach. At Tomonotsu he hid his identity and went to the mansion of Yamana Genban-no-kami.[269] A servant noticed the unusual refinement of the visitor and reported this to his master. Yamana met the lord, invited him into a private chamber, and asked to hear his story. After Motoyori explained everything, Yamana said, "Your story is very sad. The conflict in the capital is not yet settled. Even if you return

265. The original poem, *Haru*, by Taira Kanemori, appears in the *Shūishū* 拾遺集. A *tachie* 立枝 is a branch that grows upward, suggesting Rishun's hope.

266. Unidentified.

267. Present-day Ushiroji, Tomo-cho, Fukuyama-shi, Hiroshima-ken.

268. One *chō* 町 equals 99.17 acres.

269. Unidentified. The Yamana were appointed governors of Bingo Province in 1379.

there, you will find no place to stay. Why don't you remain here for a while and see what happens?" Yamana treated Motoyori most cordially.

Now Honji Kyūbei happened to serve Yamana, and he told him about the plum painting when he visited him. Motoyori also heard Kyūbei's story and became very curious about the painting. He asked to see it and, upon doing so, he began to weep. When Yamana asked him to explain, Motoyori said, "This is the painting I made and the calligraphy is undoubtedly by my wife. At Tadanoumi, all my people, including my wife and servants, were thrown into the sea. The pirates took our valuables. How did my wife survive? And how was the poem added to the painting?" Yamana immediately summoned Kyūbei, who explained how he had obtained the painting at the temple. The head nun verified his story. Rishun had told her about the pirates, hiding nothing. Now it became clear that Rishun was undoubtedly Motoyori's wife.

Immediately Rishun was called to Tomonotsu to be reunited with her husband. She felt as if she were dreaming. Both appeared older and more weary than before. They stayed in Tomonotsu until the situation in the capital improved. Miyoshi and Matsunaga were dead and Shogun Yoshiaki's fortunes improved.[270] While preparing to return to

....

270. Miyoshi Yoshitsugu died in 1573 and Matsunaga Hidehisa in 1578. Shogun Ashikaga Yoshiaki 足利義昭 (1537–1597) was the fifteenth Muromachi shogun. To his advantage, Honganji Temple and the Mōri, Uesugi, and Takeda clans united to attack Oda Nobunaga.

the capital, Motoyori suddenly fell ill and died. His wife became a nun [again] and, twenty days later, following her husband, she also passed away.

Yamana buried them both in the same place. On the last day of the *chūin*,[271] after the funeral, people saw white smoke rising from their graves, heading west. A pleasant fragrance permeated the air and eventually filled the mountain and valley. No one failed to be impressed by this incident.[272]

4-1 Asahara is Resurrected upon Visiting the Hell

Asahara Shinnojō[273] came from Miura Dōsun's[274] clan in Kamakura, Sō Province.

Talented and eloquent, Asahara was interested solely in studying the works of Confucius and did not believe in the Buddhist Law. Whenever someone mentioned the transmigration of lives and karmic cause and effect, he would express derision and disdain the Law. He showed Buddhist priests little respect, slandering them and arguing with them most unreasonably. Next to Asahara lived a rich man, Magohei, who had been greedy since his youth. He loved to fish and never sought a future life in the Law.[275] One day, Magohei fell ill and passed away. His wife and children prayed [for his recovery]. Because his chest was still warm, they did not bury him but asked a Buddhist priest to recite the sutras and decorated the altar.

On the third day, Magohei revived and reported what had hap-

....

271. 中陰: forty-nine days after death.

272. This story is based on *SS*, 4-4 (芙蓉屏記). In the Chinese version, the pirates are caught and endure harsh punishment; the patron (Yamana) dies, and the couple (Motoyori and his wife) bury him. In the Japanese text, Motoyori and his wife die to emphasize the futility of life during the warring period. Asai used historical events taken from the *Kōyogunkan* and *Kugyōbunin* to enhance the story.

273. Unidentified.

274. 三浦道寸or Yoshiatsu 義同 (d. 1516): a son of Uesugi Takahira of Ōgigatani, Kamakura. Dōsun was his Buddhist name.

275. Fishing and hunting usually result in killing. A good Buddhist never fishes or hunts and always wishes for rebirth in a future life.

pened: "After I died, I went to the Land after Death,[276] traveling on a dark and difficult path. I saw no one from whom I could ask the way. Finally, after walking about one *ri*,[277] I came to a gate. Passing through it, I saw an official standing at the bottom of a staircase. He beckoned to me and said, 'You have come here after your death. Your grieving wife and children spent much money holding Buddhist services and prayers, so I will let you return to the world.' Greatly pleased, I remembered to step through the gate and am now revived." Everyone agreed, "The prayers and Buddhist services were not in vain."

Hearing Magohei's story, Asahara sneered and laughed, saying, "The greedy, cunning *jitō* [278] and their wicked assistant *daikan*[279] extort commissions. When they do not get enough profit for themselves, they force the innocent to be the sinful. So the rich win dishonest lawsuits[280] while the poor lose [even though] they are in the right. I thought such injustice was found only in this world, but officials in the Land after Death are no different from officials here.[281] If one spends a great amount of money to hold a Buddhist service, a dead person may revive, and those who have sunk into hell may float. The poor are powerless. As for the results of good and bad deeds, only those who spend much gold and silver can expect an easier future life. Once Igen, who lived in Han China,[282] said, 'Instead of leaving thousands in gold to your son, it would be better to teach him a [Buddhist] sutra.' But he is wrong because even King Enma [in hell] forgives a sinner with money." Asahara, clapping his hands with glee, composed a poem:

....

276. Meido 冥土 or Myōkai 冥界. King Yama 耶麻天 (Enma 閻魔王) judges the dead and sends sinners to the various hells. *Myōkan* 冥官: officials who serve Enma.

277. One *ri* equals 3.9 kilometers.

278. A *jitō* 地頭 received a fief from his lord and administered his domain.

279. *Daikan* 代官: local officials in charge of various administrative duties (e.g., collecting taxes and looking after lawsuits) for the lord of a manor. They were notorious for showing little mercy when collecting taxes.

280. *Hikuji* 非公事.

281. *Watakushi ari* 私あり: to profit privately. In other words, officials in hell expect profit for themselves.

282. Igen 葦賢, a man of Su of the Former Han (202 B.C–8 A.D.). The saying appears in *Mōkyū* 蒙求 (II) and *Myōshinhōkan* 明心宝鑑, 10 (kunshi-hen).

osoroshiki
jigoku no sata mo
zeni zo kashi
nenbutsu no shiro ni
yoku o fukagare

The frightful hells
Depend on coins
Think of your desires
When chanting the Buddha's
Names and the price.

Sometime later, when Asahara was sitting alone at home in the candlelight, two demons suddenly appeared. They were so frightful Asahara felt his hair stand on end. They announced, "We are King Enma's messengers.[283] Quickly, come with us!" Pulling him by his hands, neither flying nor walking,[284] they soon arrived at what looked like a palace of justice.[285] Once inside Asahara saw someone who appeared to be a great king with a crown on his head. He sat on a carpet and was flanked by officials who sat according to their rank. The two demon messengers took Asahara before the king, who said in an angry voice, "You have engaged in Confucian studies and slandered the Buddhist Law, sneering and abusing it in your ignorance. You also deny the existence of the Land after Death. You have done all of this with your mouth. You will quickly be sent to the hell where tongues are pulled out and plowed by cows!"[286]

Touching his forehead to the ground, Asahara excused himself, explaining, "I am neither sinful nor against the human way." I have upheld the five Confucian ways[287]—of the lord and the subject, the father and the son, the husband and the wife, the older brother and the younger, and friends. I have done nothing against the Way. I have

....

283. *Myōkan;* they often have the heads of cows and horses (*gozumezu* 牛頭馬頭).

284. *Ayumu tomo naku tobu tomonaku* あゆむともなく飛ぶともなく: soon, shortly.

285. *Hyōjoba* 評定場.

286. *Batsuzetsu-nairi* 抜舌奈梨: the hell where a sinner's tongue is beaten and stretched, then plowed.

287. *Gorin no michi* 五倫の道.

preached the pure and genuine way of heaven and reason,[288] and up-held the virtues. Although I have not practiced the Buddhist way, there is no reason to send me to hell."

"Then who was it who recited the poem that said 'Private desires[289] compel the *myōkan?*'" the king asked angrily. "The hell depends on whether you are rich or poor. So think of the price when reciting the Buddha's names."

Asahara replied, "In the ancient times of the three emperors and the five [sacred] emperors,[290] there was no talk of demons and heavens. During the three dynasties,[291] the mountain and river gods were first enshrined. Since the Buddhist Law was transmitted in the Later Han,[292] it has taught us the theory of cause and effect in relation to heaven and hell. People believed in the spirits and gods of the mountains, rivers, and shrines. Many wooden and painted images revealed something miraculous. But now people have lost their reason and commit sins without regret. The strong take advantage of the weak while the rich disdain the poor. A child feels no filial duty toward a parent. There is no loyalty between a lord and his subjects, and no cordiality among family members. People devour and covet for money and treasure. Without knowing righteousness, they are indiscreet and scatter to col-lect profits while forgetting obligations. By spending gold and silver for Buddhist services, the sinful avoid hell and are reborn in heaven. If this continues, only the rich and the wicked will be reborn in heaven and only the good and the poor will fall into hell. Even in the court of King Enma, I hear that the rich and the wicked are judged worthy of rebirth in the Pure Land because their families paid for costly Buddhist ser-vices. This is not honest judgment, but bribery. After coming to these conclusions, I composed a *kyōka*[293] criticizing these times. Great king, please consider well my situation."

....

288. *Tenriseibun*天理性分: natural reason.

289. *Watakushi* 私; translated here as private desires or private profits, i.e., taking bribes to satisfy one's private desire.

290. Sankō-gotei三皇 五帝: ancient China's three legendary emperors and the five eminent emperors.

291. Ka 夏, In 殷 , and Jō 周.

292. Buddhism came to China at the time of Emperor Mei 明帝, (r. 57–75).

293. *Kyoka* 狂歌: poems or songs of thirty-one syllables; these were popular for their comical and critical themes from the Kamakura to Muromachi periods.

The king, who had been listening carefully, responded, "What you say is reasonable and truthful. I should not punish you. All of this started when Magohei was returned to the secular world because his family spent gold and silver to perform a Buddhist service. Quickly, bring Magohei here!" When Magohei was brought in, the king ordered, "Take him immediately to hell in fetters, and return Asahara to the world!" Two officials escorted Asahira away. He asked them, "In the human world, I engaged in Confucian studies and never believed in the hells described in the Buddhist Law. Now I am here. Please let me see them and make me believe in them."

"We should ask Shirokujin,[294] deity of records," said the officials. They led Asahara through the western hall to another building where the records of people's good and bad deeds while alive were piled high like a mountain. The officials explained the situation to Shirokujin, who then gave them a tally. The officials and Asahara walked for a half *ri* to the north, where there was a forbidding iron castle surrounded by high copper walls. Black smoke blanketed the sky above it, and crying voices echoed all around them. Many demons with cow and horse heads stood guard on both sides of the castle gate. The officials handed them the tally then ushered Asahara into the castle, which was full of sinners.

The demons caught a few sinners and made them lie flat on the ground, where they skinned them, squeezed out their blood, cut their stomachs open, hollowed out their eyes, and sliced off their ears, noses, limbs, and other flesh. Their echoing cries from the excruciating pain filled the air. Hunters and fishermen, these men had committed the sin of killing while in the human world.

Next Asahara saw a man and woman staked on two copper poles. The demons cut open their bellies with swords, filled sake bottles with boiling water, and poured the hot water into their stomachs, which festered and melted. Both the man and the woman cried out, only their heads remaining. When Asahara asked the reason for their punishment, the demons replied, "The man was a doctor who treated the woman's husband. They had an affair. The doctor gave the sick man the wrong medicine; the wife treated her husband harshly. After the husband was dead, they remained together. Eventually they died and are now tortured like this in hell."

....

294. 司録神: one of the eight deities of hell; Shirokujin records the deeds of sinners committed in this world.

Asahara also saw many naked monks and nuns crouching on the burning iron floor. The demons covered them with the hides of cows and horses, and they immediately became cows and horses. They were forced to pull heavy rocks. When lashed by iron whips, their skin and flesh broke, and blood gushed from their wounds like a waterfall. Again Asahara asked the reason for the punishment and was told, "When they were monks and nuns in the human world, they ate as much as they wanted without cultivating any rice fields and dressed themselves warmly without weaving any cloth. Even though they took the tonsure, they neglected the precepts, showed no mercy, did not study, and ate offerings. They have become animals to atone for their misuse of offerings and other sinful deeds."

At another place Asahara saw more sinners suffering as cows and horses. "These were *daikan* who overtaxed peasants and sold their wives and children. Taking what peasants worked hard for is the same as misusing offerings, isn't it?" reasoned the demons. Lastly, Asahara came to a hell where the flames were highest, and several hundred fettered sinners were sitting on the hot iron ground. Their bodies were on fire in the high flames. Poisonous serpents appeared; they coiled around their bodies and sucked the blood out of them. Meanwhile, hawks with iron beaks perched on their shoulders, hollowed out their eyes, and pecked at their flesh. When the sinners tried to cry, their throats were filled with smoke. Their sufferings were indescribable. When their flesh was exhausted, their bones became visible. After they died, a cool wind blew, and soon they were revived.

A demon explained, "Here we have Mekada Shinsuke,[295] his younger brothers Chōsaburō and Saburōsuke, and his relatives. Shinsuke was the son of a nurse of Lord Ryūwaka, who was a son of Lord Uesugi Norimasa[296] in Kamakura. After Norimasa's fall, Shinsuke delivered his lord, Ryūwaka, to their enemy, Hōjō Ujiyasu.[297] Eventually, Ujiyasu killed Shinsuke and his relatives because they had betrayed their lord. After they died, they all landed here, where they will suffer for a long period of time.[298] Other sinners here have also been disloyal, deceiving their lords and ruining the country."

As soon as Asahara was led outside the gate, he was revived. When he asked [his family], "How is Magohei, our neighbor?" he learned that the man had died again. Asahara left his Confucian studies, went to Kenchōji Temple, [299] learned the Law, and became an expert on enlightenment.[300]

4-2   Pledging Love in a Dream

During the Daiei era [1521–1528], there lived a man called Funada Sakon. He left the warrior class, became a commoner,[301] and lived in Yodo[302] in Yamashiro. Gentle at heart, well liked, and incomparably handsome, he came from a wealthy family and owned some rice fields

....

295. 妻鹿田新介; a subject of the Uesugi clan who took his lord Ryūwaka to Hōjō Ujiyaasu (*Korōgun monogatari*, 5; *Kōyōgunkan*, 10, I.).

296. Norimasa was attacked by Hōjō Ujiyasu in 1551. His heir, Ryūwaka 竜若, was beheaded in Odawara.

297. 北条氏康 (1515–1571); Ujiyasu destroyed the Uesugi clan. See *OT*, 2-1.

298. *Okumangō* 億万劫: a Buddhist term meaning a long period of time.

299. 建長寺: one of the five Zen temples in Kamakura, founded by Hōjō Tokiyori (1227–1263).

300. *Dōnin* 道人: a master who has attained perfect enlightenment by meditating on Zen teachings. The Japanese version of this tale, based on *SS*, 2-1 (令狐生冥夢録), introduces the various hells in the latter part of the story with critical comments on contemporary officials, including *daikan*.

301. *Bonge* 凡下: the common class; i.e., those without official rank and learning.

302. 淀; in the southern part of present-day Fushimi-ku, Kyōto-shi. It was a place of some importance because it was where the Yodo, Kizu, and Katsura rivers met.

in Hashimoto.[303] At the age of twenty-two, Funada had no wife and was known to be amorous man.[304]

One autumn day, he decided to work in his rice fields, so he took a boat to Hashimoto. On the way, north of Hashimoto, he saw a house that sold sake. It looked very popular and appeared clean and neat. After mooring his boat on the bank behind the house, Funada attempted to buy some sake. The master of the house came out. "This way, please," he said and ushered Funada into a sitting room on the slope. To the west, Funada saw a willow tree, its hanging branches interspersed with red maple leaves. The lower leaves of several *hagi* appeared heavy with dew while their blossoms lay strewn about, felled by a past storm. Lamenting the passing of autumn, insects sang faintly beneath pampas grass. Chrysanthemum hedges bloomed, releasing an enchanting fragrance.

To the north, Funada saw the Yodo river and heard seagulls here and there; he imagined them playfully flying over the river waves. Yōji Island[305] as well as the Nagisa Detached Palace[306] appeared close by. From where he sat, Funada had a commanding view of Mizuno,[307] Yamazaki,[308] Udono,[309] and Mishimae.[310]

The master of the house offered him a sake cup [and a number of dishes], saying, "This is not sea bass from Zungō [in China][311] but the marinated Yodo carp that is praised by Priest Gen'e in his book *Teikinōrai*."[312] And "This is not *junsai* water-grass from Gochū [in

---

303. 橋本; in present-day Hashimoto, Yawata-shi, Kyoto-fu. It was a *shukuba* 宿場 (station or inn) town that connected Kyoto and Osaka. Hashimoto was also popular because it was located near the Iwashimizu Yawata Shrine.

304. *Irogonomi* 色ごのみ: a man who loves women. *Iro* (color, love, sex); *gonomi* (to like).

305. 楊枝; a small island where the Yodo and Uji rivers meet. It was famous for plovers.

306. Nagisa-no-in 渚の院: a detached palace on a beach in present-day Hirakata-shi, Osaka-fu.

307. In present-day Mizu-cho, Fushimi-ku, Kyoto-shi.

308. In present-day Shimamoto-cho, Mishima-gun, Osaka-fu.

309. In present-day Udono, Takatsuki-shi, Osaka-fu.

310. In present-day Mishimae, Takatsuki-shi.

311. Zungō 松江; located in Wu-song-jiang, Jiang-su-xing, China.

312. Priest Gen'e 玄恵 (?–1350) was a Tendai sect monk believed to be the author of the *Teikinōrai* 庭訓往来.

China],[313] but the Mizuno pond dropwort that Ki no Tsurayuki[314] used to pick [in his poems]." Thus Funada was treated cordially and he had several cups of sake to acknowledge the master's hospitality.

The master had an eighteen-year-old daughter who was not yet married and staying in the room adjoining the sitting room. Because her parents were wealthy, she had many books on poetry, and her writing style was as smooth as a flowing stream, although her calligraphy was not perfect. She had a gentle and sensitive heart. As soon as the girl glimpsed Funada in the sitting room, she was in love. Peeping through an opening in the screen, she showed her face first and later passed in and out of the room. Dazed yet unable to hide her shyness, she was completely taken by him.

Similarly, Funada was impressed by the girl's radiant and matchless beauty and felt as if his heart were lost in her sleeves. Both tried to communicate their feelings not with words but by exchanging glances. Soon the sun was tilting to the west; Funada stood up and returned home.

Funada thought only of the girl as he felt the cold autumn wind pierce his body. Unknowingly, he shed tears in his lonely bed. That night he had a dream: He went to Hashimoto, entered the gate behind the house, and found himself in the girl's room. It faced a small garden with many layers of rocks that reminded him of a valley [at the bottom of] a summit, with a path meandering from its base. [All the rocks] were tastefully arranged, layer upon layer. A clear pond set in the middle of the garden had many small fish swimming in it. *Shinobugusa*[315] grew by the water. It was the end of autumn: The light of fireflies was fading, and the singing of *suzumushi* insects was growing faint. A birdcage hung under an eave, and the intoxicating fragrance of incense disturbed and aroused him.

Inside the room, Funada saw a few chrysanthemums in a beautiful vase and an inkstone on a desk. Various interesting books such as *The Tale of Genji* and *The Tales of Ise* were piled on the floor. Gazing

....

313. *Junsai* is a kind of water-grass belonging to the lotus family.

314. 記の貫之 (868–945): a famous poet who compiled the *Kokinshū*. Mizuno pond dropwort is unidentified in Tsurayuki's writings.

315. 忍草: a fern; *shinobu* (to yearn for, worry about, bear).

at a koto[316] placed against a wall, he thought of the girl playing the instrument to console herself and express her feelings. As soon as the daughter saw him, she came closer with a happy smile, took his hands, and led him to her bedroom. There they talked about everything that was in their hearts[317] and pledged their love to one another. They wondered if they would be like a current split in two by an island[318] that eventually comes together again or if they would be like *shinobugusa* ferns and worry about their love attracting the unwanted attention of others.[319] They pondered if such obstacles would cause them pain. Soon their talk was interrupted by the noisy crowing of cocks ignorant [of their part in signaling] the lovers' sad separation. Dawn broke, the torchlight faded, and Funada woke from his dream.

From that night forward, Funada dreamed of visiting the girl and each night they pledged their love. One night she played *Sōfuren*[320] on the koto. She played it so beautifully and with such deep feeling that the music echoed in clouds. On another night, she was sewing a white kimono when he visited her. While he was fixing a candle, the tip of the wick accidentally fell on the kimono, leaving a dark mark. In another night's dream, the girl gave him a silver incense box and, in exchange, he offered her a crystal ball. When he awoke, he found the incense box by his pillow but not the crystal ball. He felt this most strange and composed a poem:

> *kimi ni ima*
> *auyo amata no*
> *katarai o*
> *yume to shiritsutsu*
> *samezu aranamu*

---

316. 和琴: a Japanese lute with six strings.

317. *Koto o ha momo yo mo tsukiji*: their words would not be exhausted even for a hundred nights; i.e., the two lovers had a lot to talk about.

318. *Chigiri wo kawasu*: exchanging a pledge. Here *kawasu* is a pun on Kawanakajima 川中島, an island in the middle of a river that splits the current.

319. *Hitome o shinobu-gusa*: to worry, to be concerned about attracting attention; implies that their love should be kept secret.

320. 想夫恋: to think of a husband and yearn for him; the original Chinese tune (想夫憐) appears in the *Hakushi bunshū* 白氏文集, 68.

Seeing you night after night
We talk of many things
I know all is
In my dreams,
And I wish I would not wake

Unable to resist his feelings, Funada rowed to Hashimoto, stopped at the house, and asked for a cup of sake. The master was very pleased to see him and invited him in with special courtesy. The master began, "I have one daughter who is not yet twenty years of age. When you came here last autumn, she saw you, and since then she has been sick with love. She has been depressed and constantly sleeps, talks to herself, and acts as if she is drunk on sake. A doctor's cure had no effect at all. A *yin-yang* master offered prayers, but she became worse and her condition continues. Sometimes she mentions your name. Yesterday, she said, 'Tomorrow he will surely come.' We thought she said this in her usual confused state, but now you have come. This is truly a god's revelation. Please make my daughter your wife. Although I do not have much, I offer you everything I own."

So the master and Funada exchanged names and were formally introduced. Funada agreed [to the master's proposal] and entered the girl's room with him. Everything in the room and the front garden was identical to what he had seen in his dreams. Soon the girl raised her head from her pillow; she was herself again. Funada noticed that her face, her manner of speaking, and her voice were just as same as in his dreams.

The girl confessed, "Since I saw you last autumn, I have been in love with you. You and your image have never left me, and every night I dream of our pledging our love to each other. It is most curious." Funada learned that his dreams were the same as the girl's, even down to the dark wick mark on her kimono, the song she played on the koto, and the gift of the incense box. Everyone who heard their story was amazed and agreed that their two souls[321] must have communicated with each other and that their pledges of love were so deep that they had dreamed the same dream.[322]

....

321. *Tamashii* 神; i.e., *reikon* 霊魂. souls or spirits.

322. This Japanese story is based on *SS*, 2-5 (渭塘奇遇記). The Chinese version includes five poems.

4-3   A Dream of Thirty Years

Hosokawa Takakuni[323] and Hosokawa Haremoto[324] fought at Tennōji Temple[325] in Sesshū during the sixth month of the fourth year of Kōroku.[326] Takakuni was defeated and escaped to Amagasaki. He later committed suicide[327] while pursued by the enemy.

Yusa Shichiro,[328] a subject of Takakuni, became a masterless samurai and hid in a village in Akutagawa.[329] In time he thought of seeking a position in Kyoto, so he started for the capital with a *chūgen*.[330] While resting at Takaradera Temple[331] in Yamasaki, Yusa became very sleepy. He took a nap in the eastern corridor of the temple, and there he had a dream.

Yusa stepped out of the temple and saw a man dressed like a laborer, standing [at the gateway] with a basket of plums.[332] He asked him, "Whom do you work for?" The man replied, "I am a servant of Katano Jizaemon of Yamasaki.[333] Master Katano served the shogun[334] and died in battle. He left a daughter who became the wife of Ishio Gengo of Nishinooka.[335] After Master Gengo was killed during [an attack] by the Miyoshi, the wife became a widow and returned to her home. She is only twenty-one years old. Her mother is over sixty and a very clever woman. She says, 'If there is someone who is a descendant of our family, I will offer him all [I have] as the bridegroom [of my daughter].'" Now Yusa thought and thought: "Katano's wife is my aunt.

323. 細川高国 (1484–1531): a son of Masaharu. He was defeated by Miyoshi Motonaga and Akamatsu Masamura.

324. A son of Sumimoto (1514–1563). He attacked Takakuni with Miyoshi Masanaga and Motonaga.

325. See *Shōgunki*, 10.

326. Or Kyōroku: 1531.

327. Takakuni died at Kōtokuji Temple in present-day Daimotsu-cho, Amagaki-shi.

328. Perhaps from the Yusa 遊左 family, who served the Hatakeyama clan.

329. In present-day Akutagawa-cho, Takatsuku-shi, Oaka-fu.

330. 中間: a person who belongs to the servant class below samurai and above *komono* 小者.

331. Hōshakuji Temple 宝積寺 in present-day, Ōyamasaki, Otokun-gun, Kyoto-fu.

332. *Yamamomo* 楊梅子; translated here as "plums."

333. Unidentified. Katano is in present-day Katano, Hirakata-shi, Osaka-fu.

334. Perhaps Ashikaga Yoshiharu. The battle could have taken place in 1527, when Yoshiharu was driven from Kyoto by Yanagimoto Kenji.

335. Unidentified.

I hadn't heard anything about her in a long time and had no idea of her whereabouts. But now she lives in Yamasaki. I should visit her."

So Yusa accompanied the servant back to his mistress, who was undoubtedly Yusa's aunt. After introductions were made, the woman shed happy tears, invited him in, and asked after her relatives. Yusa told her that everyone had died but him. His aunt said, "I have only a daughter on whom I depend. You are my nephew, a close and kindly relative. Instead of going to the capital, why don't you become my son-in-law? Then you will have no worries in the future." Hearing this, Yusa was very pleased. He gave his aunt his promise, gathered some close friends, and prepared for the wedding. He thought, "Tomorrow will be an auspicious day!" He was also very happy to see that his bride-to-be was an elegant beauty. Preparations for the wedding were truly elaborate. Many friends and guests arrived daily for the banquets. Yusa proudly enjoyed himself and was content.

One day Yusa received two messengers[336] from the capital. He was being summoned by the shogun. Immediately, he went to the capital and found the shogun in a good mood. Yusa was appointed governor of Kawachi with a ten-thousand *kan* fief. He served in this position for two years in Kyoto. While in the capital, he also associated with prestigious *shōbanshu*[337] officials.

After returning home to Yamasaki, Yusa selected a good place to build a castle and made many changes to his household. He now had countless samurai, servants, and visitors. Tethered horses were constantly seen outside his gateway as increasing numbers of messengers and visitors from various provinces visited daily.

Nearly thirty years passed. Yusa had been blessed with seven sons and three daughters. Four of his sons had gone to the capital to serve the shogun, and two of his daughters had married into a celebrated warrior family, the Hosokawa in Kawachi, Tsu Province.[338] He had

---

336. *Ryōshi* 両使: a master messenger (*seishi*) and his assistant (*fukushi*).

337. 相談衆: a group of government officials of the Muromachi shogunate. It included the families of Yamana 山名, Isshiki 一色, Hatakeyama, Hosokawa, Akamatsu 赤松, and Sasaki 佐々木.

338. Tsu (Settsu) Province belonged to the Hosokawa family for generations.

eight grandchildren, both inside and outside his family.[339]

Yusa was at the peak of his prosperity when suddenly, with a terrible war cry, over three thousand cavalry surrounded his castle from all directions and set fire to it. His terrified wife and children cried out, and his servants fled. Yusa had no means to defend his household. Just as he was about to cut open his belly, he was caught by enemy soldiers. He fought desperately. Perspiring, he woke from his dream.

Yusa got up and asked his servant, "What time is it?"

"It is the hour of the sheep"[340] was the reply. Thirty years had passed in a dream. Like the dreamer in the Kantan story,[341] Yusa realized that whether good or bad, this life was nothing but a dream. He immediately dismissed his servant and decided[342] to enter the Way. He confined himself to Mount Kōya[343] and became an ascetic dedicated to the Way.[344]

4-4   The Mystery of the Resurrected After Buried

Stories of the dead returning to life before or after burial or during cremation[345] have been handed down to us. In every case, those revived were not allowed to return home but were killed on the spot.[346]

Some people appear dead temporarily because of serious illness; others stop breathing for some reason. (A few actually die and see the Land after Death.) In any case, their set life span[347] or natural life

---

339. *Uchimago* 内孫: grandchildren born "inside the family," i.e., the children of sons. *Sotomago* 外孫: grandchildren born "outside the family," i.e., children of daughters who have married into other families.

340. About two o'clock in the afternoon.

341. The story of Kantan 邯鄲 (邯鄲一炊夢) was popular in Japanese literature and Noh drama. A young man of Tang China visits an ascetic in Kantan. He enjoys great success but then wakes after a short nap to find that he has been dreaming.

342. Hosshin 発心: decision.

343. Kōyasan 高野山: the headquarters of the Shingon sect.

344. This story is based on the Chinese tale *Muyūroku* 夢遊録 (桜桃青衣).

345. *Kasō* 火葬: a Buddhist funerary custom.

346. This practice was observed during the Warring States period.

347. *Jōgō* 定業; this was already fixed in one's previous lives.

span[348] is not yet exhausted or their life register[349] not yet eliminated [in the Land after Death]. In Japan these people were regarded as dead and were quickly buried in coffins. Anyone who revived was killed. This is most regrettable.

In foreign lands, people do not bury the dead so quickly: They observe the *karimogari*.[350] Many stories tell of those who revived within three, seven, or ten days of dying; after [ten days] there are no accounts. One should be careful and not die without warning or suddenly from fear.

Those who revived during their funerals were killed for the this reason: The *Ekiden* by Keibō[351] states: "When the dead come alive, *yin* elements turn to *yang*, and the low becomes the high." Resurrection was regarded as an omen of *gekokujō*, a time when those occupying lower positions overtook their superiors. Thus those resurrected were killed.

When a female attendant died at the mansion of Lord Ōuchi Yoshitaka,[352] she was taken to the burial ground, where she revived. Out of pity she was brought back to the mansion. She became a nun, lived about half a year, then died again. In that very year, Sue, the elder of Lord Ōuchi, rebelled, and Yoshitaka was forced to leave his province [Yamaguchi].

A servant died in the household of Lord Kōgen'in.[353] His body was sent to the Senbon burial ground, where it revived after two days. The servant begged for his life, crying and asking for mercy. Feeling pity, the attendants took him back to the mansion, where he fully recovered in four to five days. Later that year Shogun Yoshiteru was killed during a rebellion led by Miyoshi Yoshitsugu and Matsunaga Hisahide.

A corpse is *yin* but it becomes *yang* when revived, and this was

---

348. *Tennen* 天年.

349. *Myōjaku* 命籍: the life span recorded in registers kept in Myōdo (Meido), the Land after Death.

350. During this period, bodies were taken away to await burial.

351. The *Gekokujō* 下克上 in the *Ekiden* 易伝 by Keibō 京房 (a fortune-telling scholar of Han China) was used to explain the great upheavals from the Kamakura through the Muromachi periods.

352. Shogun Yoshiteru. See *OT*, 3-4, n.3.

353. See *OT*, 3-4, n.2.

taken as a sign that people of higher status would be overtaken by those below them. Thus the resurrected were killed at gravesites. Was this reasonable or not? Whatever the answer, it must have been very difficult for people to kill their relations if they happened to revive.[354]

4-5 A Ghost Speaks
with Her Husband

Chūta of Noji[355] was from Gō Province. His wife was the daughter of a commoner[356] from Yasu District.[357] The couple had a daughter, who died at six months, and they had remained childless since then. In a year near the end of the Eiroku period [1558–1570], Chūta went to Kamakura on business, but he was unable to return home for about three years because disturbances in his and other provinces had caused the roads to be blocked.

One night Chūta dreamed he saw his wife first standing behind a cherry tree and tearfully lamenting the scattering blossoms, then looking into a well and laughing. Upon waking, he went to a fortune-teller and told her about his strange dream. She replied, "The blossoms must have been scattered by the wind and the well reflects the way to the Land after Death. This dream is not good." Three days later, Chūta heard that his wife had died of cold. His grief was boundless.

After he returned home, Chūta shed many tears because everything around him reminded him of his wife. He wondered how she must have felt during her last moments, and his grief deepened every time he thought of her. Whether awake or asleep, he missed her. He composed a poem:

354. This story is based on the Chinese tale of Ganki 顔幾 in the *Shūishi* 集異志, who revived while in his coffin. It is used to explain inexplicable historical events: How Ōuchi could be overthrown by his subject, Sue, and how Shogun Yoshiteru could be betrayed and killed by his own vassals.

355. 野路; in present-day Nojicho, Kusatsu-shi, Shiga-ken

356. *Jigenin* 地下人: a person without official rank or title

357. 野州; in present-day Moriyama-shi, Shiga-ken.

omoi ne no
yume no ukihashi[358]
todae shi te
samuru makura ni
kiyuru omokage

Missing you in my sleep
You appear in my dreams
But when I wake,
Your image disappears
On my pillow.

For days Chūta said to his wife, "If you feel how much I miss you, at least come and show yourself to me in my dreams."

One night in the middle of autumn, the moon was bright and the wind pleasant. Hearing the singing grasshoppers on the wall and the incessant sounds of other insects in the thickets, Chūta shed tears as the dew set in; he was restless and could not sleep. As the night advanced, he heard a woman weeping, faintly at first. Straining his ears, he thought the sobbing voice resembled his wife's. He said in his heart, "If that is my wife's ghost, why doesn't she come to see me now? Certainly she hasn't forgotten our love even after her death, no matter how far this life is from the Land after Death." From the window, a woman's voice announced, "I am your wife. Because I could not bear hearing your grief and sadness in the Land after Death, I have come here tonight." Chūta tearfully replied, "What I have in my heart cannot be described in writing or in poetry; words are inadequate. I wish you would show yourself to me just once and I will stop grieving." Thus he tried to persuade his wife to appear before him, but she tearfully responded, "The human world and the Land after Death are different, so seeing each other will be difficult. And even if I show myself to you, you may doubt what you see."

As his sadness grew, Chūta saw his wife just beginning to appear; she was accompanied by her young maid servant, Yoshiko. "I heard that Yoshiko died three years ago after she returned home. Why is she here?" he asked. The maid replied, "While concerned with my mistress'

---

358. 夢の浮き橋: dream's floating bridge; i.e., a dream that is as fragile and futile as a floating bridge. This poem appears in the *Dairingushō*, Koi, 4, and the *Shinshūishū* 新拾遺集, Koi, 1.

well-being, I unexpectedly took ill and became worse after I returned home. I died, and soon afterward my mistress came to the Land after Death looking for me. Since then, I have been serving her." Taking up a candle, Chūta invited them in. Then he saw an old woman [behind them]. "Who is she?" His wife answered, "This is my wet-nurse. After my death, I had no one to protect me, so she drowned herself. She followed me here tonight.

"The living are *yang*, the deceased are *yin*. In spite of our being in separate worlds far apart, our love is unchanged. The officials in the Land after Death were moved by your sincere grief and gave us a short reprieve. I am so glad to see you [even if it is only] once in a thousand years, but I will be sad when I must be separated from you again." She shed tears like rain.

Chūta asked, "I have been wondering what you eat after death?" His wife replied, "We don't like anything fishy[359] in the Land after Death. The only thing we have is rice gruel." So he prepared some gruel and offered it to them. (The three spirits appeared to take it, but later Chūta noticed the gruel was untouched.)

His wife asked, "Don't you want to see our child, who died as a baby?[360] She is now grown up."

"She was only two years old when she died.[361] Does one add years to one's age in the next world?" asked Chūta. "Yes, we add months and years to our age as in the human world. We count our ages just as you do as people hold the *chūin* memorial services, forty-nine days after one's death and the fiftieth service starting from the first year after one's death." The dead child appeared and knelt by her father. She was about seven years old with a sweet and bright disposition and beautiful features. Chūta spoke as he tearfully stroked her hair, "If you were here, I would regard you as a remembrance of my wife. After you left us, we were childless. If you stay, you would be sweet to me and I would be so happy. But, alas, I will not see you again after tonight. How sad it is!" Saying this he tried to hold her, but she disappeared like a puff of smoke, leaving nothing in his arms.

Chūta asked [his wife], "Where do you live in the Land after Death?"

....

359. *Kusaku-namagusa*: something smelly; generally refers to fish and meat.

360. *Mutsuki* 襁褓: a diaper; i.e., a baby.

361. There is a discrepancy in the text.

"The patriarch of the Noji family, your ancestor, occupies the first position; he looks like a demon king.[362] Everyone else is dispersed, filling heaven and earth. Your grandparents, parents, sisters, and brothers are all in the same place. My position is to the right of your parents," replied his wife. Chūta asked, "If one has a set place in the Land after Death and has become a spiritual being,[363] how can one assume one's previous form?"

"When you die, your positive soul returns to *yang,* your negative soul to *yin.*[364] The Shimei[365] and Shiroku officials in [the Land after Death] keep all the records [of your deeds in this life], and your [physical] form turns to earth. So once you are registered in the demon book,[366] you cannot return [to this life] whenever you wish. For example, you can't remember your place in a dream; only your soul sees various things. After your death, you don't know where you died or where you were buried or where your past form was."

While they were reminiscing, the night deepened further. Chūta continued to question his wife. "Do the men and women in the Land after Death marry?"

"Sometimes, yes. But a man who knows the Way will not take another wife. After his wife dies, he will join her in the Land after Death. A faithful wife will not take another husband. After her husband in this life dies, she will join him [and they will be] a couple in the next life. But if they had wicked minds and had committed evil deeds, both the husband and wife will fall into hell and will not be able to marry again. Similarly, when a man in this life commits a crime and is imprisoned, he cannot be with his wife. I, myself, was sought as the wife of a high-ranking man of the west, but being faithful to my husband, I thwarted his plan and now live alone."

Chūta was so unhappy [at the thought of his wife's departure] he wished this one night would last as long as a thousand. The sounds of birds and bells could now be heard, clouds on the mountain parted, and the sleeves of those near and distant became visible. His wife

....

362. *Kiō* 鬼王; suggests Enma, the king of hell.

363. *Shinrei* 神霊.

364. This idea is based on the *yin-yang* (*onyōdō* 隠陽道) concept.

365. 司命: an official serving King Enma who examines the good and bad deeds of the deceased. For *shiroku,* see *OT,* 4-1, n.22.

366. *Kiroku* 鬼録: the book in the Land after Death in which the names of the deceased are recorded.

tearfully untied the collar of her kimono and recited a poem:

> *wakarete no*
> *katami nari keri*
> *fujigoromo*[367]
> *eri ni tsutsumishi*
> *tama*[368] *no namida wa*

> My tears of pearls
> Wrapped in the collar
> Of a wisteria robe,
> A remembrance
> Of our parting.

Chūta tearfully received her token and said, "If you don't forget me in the Land after Death, please console yourself by looking at this." He handed her a silver incense burner as he recited a poem:

> *naki tama yo*
> *koto naru michi*[369] *ni*
> *kaeru tomo*
> *omoi wasuru na*
> *sode no utsuriga*[370]

> Your departing soul
> Returning to
> A different place,
> Do not forget
> The fragrance on your sleeves.

Chūta asked his wife, "When can I see you again?" She replied, "From now on, we must wait forty years to renew our love." She wept

....

367. 藤衣: a wisteria robe created by weaving wisteria vines used for mourning. It also refers to the coarse hemp robe worn while in mourning.

368. A piece of jade, a pearl, or a jewel; translated here as "pearls."

369. 異なる道: a different road or way; i.e., the way to the Land after Death.

370. 移り香: a transferred fragrance; refers to the fragrance of incense on the sleeves.

loudly before disappearing in the morning mist.

Afterward, Chūta felt everything in this life was futile. He shaved his head, dressed in a black robe,[371] and traveled to various places, unable to settle down. Finally, he went to Mount Kōya, recited the sutras and Buddha's names, and prayed for the repose of his wife, hoping for deliverance on the same seat[372] [as her] in a future life.[373]

5-1   Wadō Coins

Emperor Junna [r. 823–833] had a palace to the west of Omiya[374] and to the north of Shijō in Kyoto. This area was called Sain,[375] and it was home to the Grand Consort of Tachibana.[376] Many generations later, peasants would live where the palace once stood.

During the Bunmei era [1469–1487], a learned *sōzu*[377] named Shōkai lived in Nagara.[378] Avoiding secular matters, he retired to the village in Sain, built a grass hut, and quietly practiced the Way. One day he had a strange visitor who appeared to be around fifty years old. His hat was round on the top and square on the bottom. His light green *naoshi*[379] robe appeared to have been woven from thread as thin and light as cicada wings. He introduced himself as Chichibu Kazumichi, saying, "I am from the Chichibu District of Mushashi Province.[380] Since middle age, I have been traveling. I have been everywhere and seen everything in Japan."

....

371. *Koromo wo sumi ni some* 衣を墨に染め: to dye a robe black (with soot); i.e., to renounce the secular life or enter the priesthood.

372. Ichizakedai 一座花台: to sit on one seat (*ichiza*) together with one's wife; the seat is a flower stand (*kedai*), implying the white lotus flower seat in the Pure Land of Amida Buddha.

373. This story is based on the Chinese *Reikishi* 霊鬼志 (唐胆) of the Gochō shōsetsu (Five Dynasty Fictions). The description of the customs in Land after Death is mostly adopted from the Chinese version.

374. Perhaps present-day Nishiōjidōri 西大路通.

375. 西院; in present-day Saiin, Ukyo-ku, Kyoto-shi.

376. Tachibana no Ooikisai 橘の太后 (橘嘉智子) was in fact the mother of Empress Junna, who lived in Sain after Emperor Junna passed away.

377. 僧都: a priest who ranks below a *sōjō* 僧正 (abbot).

378. In present-day Yodogawa-ku, Osaka-shi.

379. 直衣 ; everyday attire for a nobleman.

380. Present-day Chichibu-gun, Saitama-ken

Sōzu thought, "This creature is no mere human." After conversing with Kazumichi for a while, he found him quite knowledgeable about the three esoteric Shingon sutras,[381] the mandalas of the two worlds,[382] the *inmyō-darani*,[383] and the *kanjō*.[384] Kazumichi talked about many things of which Sōzu was ignorant. He also went on about events in the past and present as if they were happening right before his eyes.

Sōzu remarked, "Your hat does not look like anything made in Japan. Why is it round on the top and square on the bottom?" Kazumichi replied, "Although everything in this life comes in various forms and shapes, there are basically only two: round and square. In my case, my outside is round, and my inside—my mind—is square. The form of heaven is round while that of earth is square. A round character is one without prejudice. If one is square, one's mind is straight. So my way [view] is unprejudiced; it is right and correct in everything. To show this, I put this hat on my head."

Sōzu questioned Kazumichi further. "Your robe looks very light and thin. Where was it made?" The visitor replied, "This is called five *shu*[385] silk. Heavenly people wear robes made from the silk of three *shu* while those under heaven wear five or six *shu* silk robes." Still convinced that Kazumichi was not human, Sozu inquired, "Who are you really? Tell me your name." Laughing, Kazumichi answered, "Since you are a pious man, I have come here and told you all kinds of stories. I don't need to tell you my real name; it will eventually become known to you. The sun is setting now and I must be leaving." Kazumichi stood up and walked off. Sōzu followed and watched him vanish before a bamboo grove twenty *ken*[386] to the east of his hut.

The next morning Sōzu asked some villagers to dig a hole [where Kazumichi had disappeared the previous day]. They found a box

381. The *Dainichikyō* 大日経, the *Kongōchōkyō* 金剛頂経, and the *Soshitsujikyō* 蘇悉地経.

382. *Ryōkai mandala* 両界曼荼羅; the two worlds, Kongōkai 金剛界 (Diamond World) and Taizōkai 胎蔵界 (Womb World) are universal truths in the Mikkyō (密教) esoteric Buddhist teachings.

383. 印明陀羅尼: hand signs and incantations recited for protection.

384. 灌頂: an esoteric Buddhist ceremony in which sacred water symbolizing the future Buddha's wisdom is sprinkled on a person's head after he has transmitted the Law.

385. Twenty four *shu* (銖) equal one *ryō*, or 10 grams.

386. One *ken* equals 1.82 meters.

about three *shaku*[387] down containing one hundred coins and nothing else. Sōzu examined them and learned they were the old coins of Wadōtsūhō.[388] Carefully reflecting on everything that had happened the day before, Sōzu was now convinced that the visitor, Chichibu no Kazumichi,[389] was the spirit of the Wadōtsūhō coins.

Sōzu told the villagers: "I was curious about our strange visitor. During the reign of Empress Genmyō [r. 707–715],[390] the forty-third ruler of this country, some copper arrived in the capital during the seventh month [of the fifth year of Keiun][391] from the Chichibu District of Musashi Province. At that time, the capital was in Naniwa in Tsu Province,[392] and the fifth year of Keiun was changed to the first year of Wadō.[393] In that year, the copper was made into coins. I'm guessing that these must be the old coins of Wadōtsūhō.[394]

"[Our visitor's] hat was round on the top and square on the bottom just like the Wadōtsūhō coin. The light green color of his robe resembles the patina of copper coins and five *shu* refers to the weight of a coin. His name, Kazumichi, is an abbreviation of Wadōtsūhō. His native place, Chichibu, was the place where the copper was first produced. His traveling to the capital as well as many other provinces can be interpreted as the circulation of coins. The round shape of a coin denotes heaven and the square hole in the middle indicates earth. *Yin* and *yang* correspond to the front and back of the coin. The four characters on the coin are the four directions, as the coins were regarded as a popular treasure under heaven. The characters also indicate the year of casting.

"Coins run far without feet and fly high without wings. Difficult people smile at the sight of coins, and those who do not talk much

387. One *shaku* equals 30.3 centimeters.

388. 和銅通宝.

389. The two characters of *kazumichi* 和通 are the first and third characters in *wadōtsūhō* 和銅通宝. *Wadō* 和銅 is Japanese copper.

390. 元明天皇: the fourth daughter of Emperor Tenji.

391. The year 708.

392. The government was in Fujiwara-kyo in present-day Kashiwara-shi, Nara-ken.

393. *Shoku nihongi*, 4.

394. On the first day of the fifth month of the first year of Wadō (708), silver coins called *wadōkaichin* 和銅開珎 were cast; copper coins were cast on the fifteenth month of the eighth month of that year (*Shoku nihongi*, 4). This round coin had a square hole in the middle. *Wadōtsuhō* may derive from *kaneitsūhō*, a coin widely used in the early Edo period.

open their mouths. Just as Toyo[395] was inclined[396] toward the *Saden,* Rakuten[397] toward poetry, and Hankō[398] toward currency, everyone has a special feeling for coins. There is nothing more powerful than coins to subjugate demons and soldiers. At the sight of them, the avaricious act like starving people thinking about food. When the greedy obtain coins, they resemble a sick man seeing a physician. A coin is a true treasure." Sōzu laughed, distributed the one hundred coins to the villagers, and chanted the Shingon *darani* to finish his practice.

It is said that the villagers became wealthy and prosperous and respectfully served Sōzu. But later, following a disturbance by the Yamana clan, the villagers scattered, knowledge of Sōzu's whereabouts was lost, and all the coins were dispersed.[399]

5-2   Ghosts Criticize Many Generals

Tsuruse Anzaemon[400] lived in Kō Province.[401] Previously he was called Anzōsu and worked as an *anja*[402] at Keirinji Temple.[403] He was favored by Takeda Shingen[404] for his talent and personality and received a small fief. Eventually he was secularized and named Tsuruse Anzaemon.

....

395. 杜預: a man of Jin who was devoted to the study of Chinese classics (*Saden,* or *Shunjūsashiden* 春秋佐氏伝).

396. *Kuse* 癖: a habit; translated here as an inclination toward something.

397. Hakurakuten 白楽天, or Hakukyoi 白居易 (772–846): a Tang poet whose work greatly influenced Heian literature.

398. 樊光: a government official of the Sung dynasty.

399. This story, based on the Chinese tale *Hakuishi* 博異志 (岑文本), explains how the first Japanese coins, *wadōkaichin,* were circulated.

400. 鶴瀬安左衛門; for Tsuruse and his career with Oyamada and Takeda Shingen, see *Kōyōgunkan,* 8 and 19.

401. In present-day Tsuru District, Yamanashi-ken; the temple belonged to the Oyamada clan, which was under Takeda control during the Muromachi period.

402. 行者: a servant in a Zen temple who did not take the tonsure.

403. 恵林寺; in Oyashiki, Shioyama-shi, Yamanashi-ken. Keirinji is a Zen temple of the Rinzai sect and was founded by Musō Kokushi 夢想国師 (1275–1351). It was Takeda Shingen's family temple (*bodaiji* 菩提寺).

404. 武田信玄 (1521–1573); a son of Nobutora, Shingen expelled his father in 1541 and controlled Kai Province. He fought against Uesugi Kenshin several times at Kawanakajima. He died of illness while attacking Noda Castle in Nobunaga's domain. Shingen was his Buddhist name.

On the fifteenth of the seventh month of the year of the Tiger of Eiroku [Eiroku 9, or 1566], Tsuruse observed an *urabon* ceremony. He went to Kōfu to attend the memorial service for his family. Toward evening, he headed to Nishigoori[405] to see Priest Kaisen[406] of Keirinji Temple. Because he missed his *chūgen* and *komono*[407] servants on the way, he walked alone. When he finally arrived at the temple, he saw Tada, a governor of Awaji,[408] outside the gate. Tsuruse thought, "Tada was a valued commander[409] of Shingen's footmen. His strength and talents were well known among his colleagues and samurai generals of other provinces. He slayed a demon on Mount Togakushi in Shinshū.[410] But I know he died of illness on the twenty-second of the cold month[411] last year. I must be dreaming to see him here like this." Tsuruse approached Tada cautiously and said, "Some people are gathering in the temple garden for an *urabon*. Let's go in and enjoy ourselves." Tada accompanied him to the temple compound.

Inside the gate, a straw mat was spread on the ground and some servants were kneeling, waiting for guests. Naoe, a governor of Yamashiro[412] who was a subject of Lord Nagao [Uesugi] Kenshin[413] of Echigo,[414] arrived. He was closely followed by Hōjō Saklemonnosuke,[415]

---

405. 西群; in Yamanashi District, Nishigoori was on the way to Keirinji Temple.

406. 快川 (d. 1582): a Zen monk of Keirinji Temple

407. For *chūgen* 中間 see *OT* 4-3, n.8. *Komono* 小者 are the lowest servants in a samurai's house.

408. Tada Awajinokami 多田淡路守 was a subject of Shingen who died of illness in 1563 (*Kōyōgunkan*, 9, I).

409. *Ashigaru-daishō* 足軽大将.

410. Mount Togakushi is located near the boundary of Shin'etsu in present-day Jōsuinai-gun, Nagano-ken. Tada's slaying of the demon appears in the *Kōyōgunkan*, 9, I.

411. *Gokugetsu* 極月: December.

412. Unidentified; perhaps Kagetsuna, a governor of Yamato, who died in 1577 or 1578.

413. 上杉謙信 (1530–1578); a son of Nagao Tamekage, Kenshin controlled Echigo, Kaga, and Noto. Later he received the name Uesugi and often fought against the Hōjo and Takeda Shingen.

414. 越後; in present-day Niigata-ken.

415. Hōjō Saemonnosuke 北条左衛門介 could refer to Hōjō Tsunanari, who died at the age of 73 in 1587.

a subject of Hōjō Ujiyasu,[416] and Yamamoto Kansuke Dōki,[417] Takeda Shingen's military advisor. Kansuke took the senior seat, followed by Naoe and Hōjō. Tada joined them. Soon they began to talk about the military tactics of various lords.

Hōjō began: "Lord Takeda Shingen is a splendid and prudent warlord, blessed with courage and talent. His fighting style has always been firm and his soldiers' spirits high and strong. They fight like flowing water, with no distraction, and their victorious merits are as radiant as the stars shining in a clear sky. Shingen's character can be compared to a crystal ring. However, because he is fiercely proud of his valor, he does not ask his generals to seek peace and is now surrounded by enemies. He upholds the idea of *kyojitsu,* the true and the false,[418] in his fighting style. But he lacks the technique of *kisei,*[419] sudden and measured attacks. So he gains small profits, but not large ones. Until now, he has not lost much and has suffered little, but he has accomplished no greater feats even with his prestige. His own province has never been violated, but he will end his life without accomplishing the great task."[420]

Following Hōjō, Kansuke spoke: "No lord is without merit and virtue, but many lack a free and intuitive technique,[421] so they will never carry out the great task. Lord Nagao Kenshin is a strong general from Hokuestu.[422] No one is more steadfast or formidable. He remains in Echigo, so his fame is known in the northeast. He has never lost a fight. His fighting style is quick and sharp; he uses free and variable techniques at will, moving his armies as if they were his own hands and feet. Facing great enemies, he ignores them as if they were crawling bugs and he swiftly moves his soldiers to scatter them like sand. Who

....

416. Ujiyasu was the third head of the Hōjō clan. He destroyed the Uesugi and controlled Kantō's eight provinces: Musashi, Sagami, Kōzuke, Shimotsuke, Kazusa, Shimōsa, Awa, and Hitachi.

417. 山本勘助道鬼 (d. 1561); Dōki served Shingen as a military advisor and died at the Battle of Kawanakajima. Dōki was his Buddhist name (*Kōyōgunkan,* 9).

418. *Kyojitsu* 虚實; here the true refers to exercising caution and examining the situation at hand, the false to acting recklessly and being caught off guard by the enemy.

419. 奇正.

420. *Taigyō* 大業: a great task; i.e., the unification of Japan.

421. *Henka-muhō* 変化無方.

422. See *Koyogunkan, Hyōban,* 10. Hokuetsu 北越 generally referred to Echigo Province in present-day Niigta-ken.

dares oppose the tip of his spear? However, because he depends on his valor, he deploys too many soldiers in small battles. Thanks to his faithful soldiers he has enjoyed great success, but without reflecting on the past and strengthening his armies, he will not accomplish the great task."

After listening to these two speeches, Naoe began: "The virtues of these lords soar to the blue sky, while their faults sink to the bottom of a deep pool. Their merits and faults are not fixed but vary depending on the situation. However, they will never carry out the great task unless their intentions accord with the will of heaven.[423]

"Among these lords, Lord Hōjō Ujiyasu has governed his people with a most gentle heart. He is steady and well disciplined in the Way. His fighting style is quite relaxed but firm at the foundation. He does not depend on swords alone to subjugate his enemies; he analyzes situations well to avoid wasting his soldiers. Patiently waiting for heavenly luck, he evades dangerous fights. It may take him a long time to win, but once he wins he will not lose what he has gained. He is modest and faces others with restraint. But only a bold general can extricate his troops in an emergency. Because Ujiyasu values peace and begrudges his soldiers, he can't compete with Shingen and Kenshin as far as valor and courage are concerned. Because he governs with laws and letters,[424] he will not take on the great task when his prestige lessens."

Finally, Tada advanced and spoke: "All your comments are reasonable. However, how can we know a superior general's secret tactics? Every lord must have his own private thoughts and reservations. There is a saying: 'A small hole made by ants can cause a great dyke to crumble.'[425] It is true that Shingen, Kenshin, and Ujiyasu have been the greatest generals during this warring period. But we must know that there are many local lords who are gathering soldiers and waiting for the chance to attack their superiors. Shingen, Kenshin, and Ujiyasu are like the three legs of an iron pot.[426] Their powers are obvious to each other, but they should not overlook the rise of lesser local lords.

....

423. Tenmei 天命: the Chinese philosophical concept of the legitimacy of rulers.

424. *Shubun* 守文.

425. I.e., a slight mistake can cause a great work to fail.

426. Tada is likening the three lords, equal in strength and necessary to maintain balance, to the three legs of an iron or copper *kanae* 鼎 pot.

"Oda Nobunaga[427] of Bi Province, whose great intention [to unite Japan] has subjugated his neighbors, now leads powerful armies. In the second year of Kōji [1556],[428] he defeated the army of the celebrated Lord Imagawa Yoshimoto[429] of Suruga in a single morning. With discernment and foresight, Nobunaga has sought a close relationship with the strong and tactful Shingen.

"He had his aunt marry Akiyama, a governor of Hōki.[430] He also had his niece marry Takeda Katsuyori,[431] while constantly sending messengers and tribute to Kōfu to pay his respects to Shingen as if he were his subject. Currying Shingen's favor and appearing servile were all part of Nobunaga's plan to appease Shingen and other powerful lords behind him[432] while he crushed his enemies before him. First, he gathered a large army with the pretext of supporting Lord Yoshiaki,[433] who was the younger brother of Lord Kōgen'in Yoshiteru,[434] and defeated [Yoshiaki's] enemies. Second, Nobunaga followed the tenets of *honmatsu-zengo*.[435] He first routed the weak clans and families of the five areas[436] to increase his own power, then made peace with powerful enemies in the north and Tōkai in the east so he could attack them later. Finally, Nobunaga

....

427. Nobunaga came from Owari (Bi) Province in present-day Aichi-ken. He tried to unify Japan but committed suicide after he was attacked by Akechi Mitsuhide.

428. The Battle of Okehazama took place in 1560; Yoshimoto's 45,000 soldiers were defeated by Nobunaga's 3,000 (*Shinchōki*, I).

429. 今川義元 (1519–1560); a son of Ujichika, Yoshitomo spread his influence as far as the provinces of Suruga, Tōtomi, and Mikawa, but was defeated by Nobunaga at Okehazama.

430. Akiyama, Shingen's subject, married Nobunaga's aunt, a widow of the Iwamura family.

431. 武田勝頼 (1546–1582); Shingen's fourth son and the last lord of the Takeda clan, Katsuyori married Nobunaga's adopted daughter and niece, a daughter of Tōyama Kantarō.

432. *Ushiro wo kokoro yasuku shite* 後ろは心安くして; Nobunaga was confident as he prepared to engage the powerful lords in the northeastern provinces, which were located behind his home province of Owari.

433. 義昭 (r. 1568–1573); Yoshiaki became the fifteenth Ashikaga shogun of the Muromachi government with Nobunaga's assistance.

434. 光源院義輝 (r. 1546–1565): the thirteenth shogun of the Muromachi government.

435. *Honmatsu* 本末: beginning and ending. Governing one's country is *hon*, attacking one's enemy is *matsu*. *Zengo* 前後: front and behind. Controlling one's army is *zen*, destroying one's enemy is *go* (*Kōyōgunkun, Hyōban*, 3).

436. Gokinai 五幾内 included Yamashiro, Yamato, Kawachi, Izumi, and Settsu provinces.

threatened weak enemies in Chūgoku and Seikai[437] to the west while condescending to those lords in the north. He enlarged his domain with many soldiers and quelled the disturbance in the capital before anyone else. Nobunaga can carry out the great task of unifying Japan. Shingen, Kenshin, and Ujiyasu will end their lives exhausted from trying to maintain their provinces and neighboring areas."

While everyone was agreeing with Tada, Nagano,[438] a governor of Shinano who was once the lord of Minowa Castle in Jō Province,[439] joined the group. He was a strong and exceptionally talented subject of Uesugi Norimasa[440] of Kantō. He had fought against Takeda Shingen for seven years before dying of illness. His son, Ukyōnoshin,[441] had inherited the castle but had lost it to Shingen.

Nagano surveyed the party and spied Yamamoto Kansuke proudly occupying the senior seat. Without greeting him, Nagano advanced to a seat higher than Kansuke's and said to him with his hand on the hilt of his sword, "I do not understand your insolence. What great achievements have you earned to justify such arrogance?" He pressed Kansuke further: "You committed three great sins. People do not yet know that you are going to steal the name of a military expert many years in the future. I am going to expose your sins." Kansuke replied nonchalantly, "Speak quickly. I am listening."

Nagano began: "When Shingen was young and too much involved with women to bother with affairs of state, Itagaki Nobukata[442] remonstrated him. Shingen rectified his conduct and plotted tirelessly to defeat his neighboring enemies and expand his territory. At this time, Hafuri Yorishige[443] of Suwa in Shinshū surrendered to Shingen and went to

....

437. 中国西海; refers to the midwestern provinces of Japan, including present-day Okayama, Hiroshima, Yamaguchi, Shimane, and Tottori.

438. Nagano Narimasa 長野業正 (1499–1561) led a military group called Minowashū; he opposed Nobunaga.

439. The castle was in present-day Minowa, Gunma-gun, Gunma-ken.

440. See OT, 4-1, n.24.

441. 右京進, or Nagano Narimori (1548–1566). Narimori inherited the castle after his father, but committed suicide when it was taken by Shingen.

442. 板垣信形 (d. 1548); Nobukata reprimanded the nineteen-year-old Shingen for his wicked deeds involving women (Kōyōgunkan, Hyōban, 1).

443. Suwa Yorishige 諏訪頼重 (1516–1542) married Nobutora's daughter; he committed suicide after he was attacked by Shingen.

Kōfu to serve as his subject. You advised Shingen, saying, 'Unless you attack Yorishige now and take his castle, you will never obtain his lands to increase your own. Plot to kill him and perhaps you may gain his province.' At your urging, Shingen killed Yorishige. Even a hunter does not kill a bird that has flown into his bosom. Wasn't it a most cruel and merciless action, contrary to all human feeling, to destroy Yorishige, who had surrendered to Shingen? Would you call it a military tactic or a dirty plot? It was truly a merciless deed, contrary to the true martial code, something born of the savage minds of tigers and wolves. Moreover, because Yorishige's daughter was beautiful, Shingen wanted her for his mistress. When he secretly consulted you, you, Kansuke, told him, 'Nothing stands between you and your desires.'"[444] So Shingen made Yorishige's daughter his mistress. Your fawning counsel was most despicable. Why didn't you reason with him, warn him? Beheading the father, then taking the daughter to satisfy his desire, ignoring her feelings: These actions were utterly inhuman. The mistress, a shrewish woman, gave a birth to a son, Katsuyori, and ill-treated her stepson, Yoshinobu,[445] Shingen's official heir. She hated her stepson so much she abused him with various slanders. Shingen was a discreet man but, overcome by lust and desire, he killed his heir and some eighty faithful subjects, including Iitomi Hyōbu, for no reason.[446] All this was due to your flattery. You failed to give your master proper advice and closed your mouth to righteousness. That was your first sin.

"Nobutora,[447] the father of Shingen, was an obstinate but brave and strong-minded general. When Shingen was still young and called Harunobu, his father favored his second son, Nobushige, and expelled Shingen, his heir. Later, with the help of his father-in-law,[448] Imagawa Yoshimoto, Shingen expelled his father and regained his position.

444. Kansuke tried to strengthen his ties with the Suwa family by recommending that Shingen take Yorishige's daughter as his mistress (*Kōyōgunkan*, 9, 1).

445. Takeda Yoshinobu 武田義信; Shingen's first son. He committed suicide after being suspected as a traitor in 1567.

446. See *Kōyōgunkan*, 10, 11.

447. 信虎 (1494–1574); Nobutora unified Kai Province in Shinano by 1532. After being expelled by his son, Shingen, he lived in Suruga Province in 1541. Upon Imagawa Yoshimoto's death in Suruga, Nobutora went to the capital, where he was temporarily employed by Shogun Yoshiteru. He died in Shinano.

448. Shingen's elder sister was Yoshimoto's wife.

Relying on Imagawa Ujizane,[449] his frustrated father wandered in Suruga. After a while, Shingen realized his mistake and wanted to return his father to Kōfu. At the time, you, Kansuke, advised him wrongly, saying, 'If you bring your father here, he, given his wicked mind, will again cause the family trouble. Leave him be.' Thus you encouraged Shingen to act shamefully, to be a bad son. That was your second sin.

"At the Battle of Kawanakajima,[450] [Shingen] put you in charge. Believing that the headquarters of your enemy, Uesugi Kenshin, was at Mount Saijō,[451] you failed to place capable soldiers along the river and did not notice Kenshin crossing the river at night. Only after the morning mist had lifted were you aware of the enemy's movements. Kenshin's men on the left bank were pitted against your ally's army on the right, led by weak generals such as Yoshinobu and Mochizuki,[452] who were eventually defeated. Kenshin's army advanced directly to Shingen's headquarters. Thanks to the timely return of an ally force from Mount Saijō, Shingen was barely saved,[453] but many good men were not, including Tenkyū Nobushige, Morosumi Bungo, and Hajika Gengorō.[454] Although Shingen won the battle, he lost countless soldiers and you, Kansuke, were yourself ignobly killed in the battle. All this was due to your weak battle tactics. How could you call yourself a military expert? That was your third sin.

"You, Kansuke, came from Ushikubo in San Province[455] and traveled widely when you trained as a warrior. You met Ogata in Shikoku, taught him military strategy, and in return you learned how to build— and breach—castles.[456] But where is there a castle you have constructed?

....

449. 今川氏真 (1538–1614); a son of Yoshimoto, Ujizane inherited his father's domain, including Suruga, Mikawa, and Tōtomi, in 1560. He lost Mikawa to Ieyasu and died at Shinagawa in Edo.

450. Kawanakajima 川中島 in Nagano-shi, Nagano-ken, was an old battleground for Kenshin and Shingen. The Chikuma river joins the Saikawa river near Kawanakajima. The battle mentioned in the text in 1561 was their fourth (*Kōyōgunkan*, 10, 2).

451. 西条山; this is Mount Saijo 妻女山 in Matsushiro-cho, Nagano-shi.

452. For Shingen's inferior formation during in the battle, see *Kōyōgunkan*, 10, 2.

453. *Manshi o dete* 万死を出て: coming out of ten thousand deaths; i.e., to be barely saved (*Jōganseiyō* 貞観政要, 1).

454. For their deaths in the Battle of Kawanakajima, see *Kōyōgunkan*, 10, II.

455. Sanshū 三州 was in Mikawa 三河 Province. Ushikubo 牛窪 is present-day Ushikubo-cho, Toyokawa-shi, Aichi ken.

456. *Shirodori no nawabari* 城取りの縄ばり: plans and designs used to construct castles.

"Spurned by the Imagawas, you wandered about Kōfu, where Shingen finally kept you occupied with a fief. Later you returned to Suruga and boasted of accomplishments—a foolish throwback to your younger days. Although you were fortunate enough to spend many years as Shingen's military advisor, your master failed to attain reknown on the battlefield. What does that say about your abilities?

"You belong to an enemy clan. Because the great king in the Land after Death does not allow us to forgive our enemies, I have no choice but to say these things." Nagano ended his speech and Kansuke, without a word, stood and relinquished his place to Nagano, announcing to all, "Among you celebrated lords and generals, I am the only one who was lord of a castle. But excuse my insolence in taking the first seat."

Tada addressed the group: "Now we should not hold any grudges. Everything is over and done with; it all sounds like a dream after so much time has passed. So drink up and enjoy yourselves." He procured food and drink, and everyone exchanged sake cups several times. Soon Nagano sang, "Righteousness is heavy while life is as light as a bird's feathers. Our bodies disappear and some are hidden in grass thickets. As mountains are razed and deep pools are filled, we vow that our souls remain here and our principles lofty."[457]

Hōjō continued: "The way to the Land after Death stretches to eternity and separates life and death. Why do you seek glory in battle? Everything in the past, present, and future is a dream. We clearly listen to the sounds of the wind in the Land after Death."[458]

Naoe sang: "Everything changes as numerous autumns pass. Birds cry, blossoms fall, and water flows for no reason. Why do humans grieve so? The rich as well as the poor return to a handful of earth."[459]

Kansuke said, "Unfamiliar with the world of words, I have known only the battlefield. Taking a seat here [among you], how can I keep silent?" He began to sing: "Tactics fill my mind. My sword is sharp, my spirits high. Why should I vainly discuss the rise and fall [of these warlords] after my death? I pity the grudging souls that grieve in deep thickets."[460]

....

457. See *Sentōyowa*, 3-3.

458. See *Sentōyowa*, 2-2.

459. See *Sentōyowa*, 7-1.

460. See *Sentōyowa*, 3-1.

Tada sang last: "Our souls return to the Land after Death, our spirits to the Yellow Spring.[461] We resent only the fame and reputation bestowed in the human world. The three-foot-high solitary mound is blanketed with moss. We meet guests from the Land after Death for a while in Keirinji Temple."[462]

Seeing and hearing all of this, Tsuruse felt most strange. "Is this a dream or not? This is the compound of Keirinji Temple. All the people I am seeing are from the past. I wonder if I am dead and in the Land after Death. I have to question someone closely." Then he heard the sounds of drums and conch shells. He heard the others say "Understood!" to one another. Taking their swords, they hurried off and eventually disappeared, leaving Tsuruse sitting alone in the temple compound. Day gradually broke.

Overwhelmed by the strange experience, Tsuruse quickly returned to Kōfu, saw Shingen, and told him what had happened. Shingen laughed at him and said, "Taken in by a fox's tricks, you must have seen some foolish things," before losing interest. Badly shaken, Tsuruse returned to his district. It is said that he wrote everything down and placed what he had written in a box.[463]

5-3   Destined Destruction by Fire

A kind and compassionate man, Tonda Hisanai lived in Nishinokyō.[464] One day he left home to visit the Tenjin shrine[465] in Kitano. On his return home, he rested at a teahouse. While sitting on [a bench], he met a twelve- or thirteen-year-old monk.[466] The boy looked pale and thin. "Where are you from?" Hisanai asked. The young monk

---

461. *Kōsen* 黄泉: the Land after Death.

462. See *Sentōyowa*, 7-1.

463. This story, based on *SS*, 4-1 (竜堂霊怪録), is a commentary on various Japanese warlords during the warring period. Asai used the *Kōyōgunkan* and the *Kōyōgunkan hyōban* (1653) as sources. The *kanji* verses in the text are adopted mainly from the Chinese verses in the *Sentōyowa*.

464. 西の京; located west of Kyoto, in the western part of present-day Nakagyo-ku, Kyoto-shi.

465. Kitanotenmangū 北野天満宮 in Bakurō-chō, Kamigyō-ku, Kyoto-shi.

466. *Kobōshi* 子法師: a young novice.

answered, "I am from Higashiyama.[467] I have been running errands since this morning but have had nothing to eat. It is mentally and physically exhausting to follow my master's orders." Hisanai felt sorry for the boy, so he gave him some rice cakes. Eventually both Hisanai and the monk left the teahouse and came to Uchino Field and the Ukon riding ground.[468]

Turning to Hisanai, the boy said, "I am not human. I am a messenger of the fire deity and have been carrying out my master's instructions. Because you are a kind and merciful man, I will tell you this. Tomorrow Kitano, Uchino, and Nishinokyō will be completely destroyed by fire. I don't want to burn your house down, but it is in the designated area. Quickly return home and move to another place with your valuables and property. I will come after you [have moved]." And with that the boy disappeared.

Although he thought it strange, Hisanai hurried home, removed his valuables and property, and took them away. Curious neighbors asked Hisanai why he was moving, but he did not reply. Finally, when he was pressed to answer, he relayed what the boy had told him, but people just laughed and said, "Here is a man who has been tricked by a fox. He listens to its foolish talk and hastily removes[469] his furniture and property. He probably wastes his money on reconstructing his house," his neighbors sneered.

Around the third month of that year [1444], both Nishinokyō and Higashinokyō merchants established a za[470] to control the sale of sake kōji.[471] Soon there was a breach in the union,[472] and the Nishinokyō

....

467. 東山: refers to the mountain range east of Kyoto and the area near the Yasaka shrine. Higashinokyō 東の京, east of Kyoto, included the area near Nijō Castle.

468. Uchino 内野: the field southeast of Kitano Shrine. Ukon no baba 右近馬場, the riding ground of the imperial guard of the right, was located to the east of the shrine.

469. *Uchihazushi* 打ちはずし: to strike and move; i.e., Hisanai removed doors and shelves.

470. 座: a merchants union or association in medieval Japan.

471. 麹; made from steamed rice, wheat, beans, and bran mixed with bacteria, *kōji* is used to make sake, soy sauce, and miso.

472. Ignoring the special rights of the Nishinokyō merchants, the Higashinokyō continued to produce sake *kōji*. For the lawsuit and its results, see *Nihon'ōdaiichiran* 日本王代一覧, 7, and the entry for the thirteenth day of the fourth month of the first year of Bun'an in the *Kōfuki* 康富記.

faction appealed to the government. Hatakeyama Tokuhon,[473] the *kanrei* of the Muromachi shogunate, judged that the Higashinokyō acted reasonably. The Nishinokyō lost the lawsuit because they had breached the contract. Frustrated, they gathered together other malcontents and confined themselves to Kitano Shrine. In spite of the good offices of the *kanrei*, they insisted they would attack the Higashinokyō sake *kōji* dealers. Finally, the controller ordered Kyōgoku of the office of the samurai [474] to catch and imprison all those who were holed up in the shrine. The Nishinokyō merchants set fire to a shrine building on the twelfth day of the fourth month of the first year of Bun'an [1444][475] and then committed suicide. A strange, strong wind[476] rose up, and the main hall, priests' living quarters, pagoda, and corridors of the shrine were burnt to ashes in a moment. The fire also consumed the commoners' houses, including those of the Nishinokyō. A field now stands in their place.[477]

5-4 Hara Hayatonosuke was Born of a Ghost[478]

Hara Hayatonosuke Masakatsu,[479] was a subject of Takeda Shingen[480] of Kō Province. He was a son of Kaganokami Masatoshi,[481] who came

---

473. Hatakeyama Nyūdo Tokuhon 畠山入道徳本, or Hatakeyama Mochikuni 畠山持国 (1398–1455), was *kanrei* 官領 (controller) of Kyoto at the time of the incident. Tokuhon was his Buddhist name. *Nyūdo* received the tonsure but remained in the secular world.

474. *Samurai-dokoro* 侍所: the office responsible for law and order in the capital. Its director (*shoshi* 所司) was selected in turn from one of four families: the Yamana, Akamatsu, Isshiki, and Kyōgoku 京極. Kyōgoku Mochikiyo is the *shoshi* mentioned in the text.

475. The fire actually happened on the thirteenth day of the fourth month (*Ken'naiki* 建内記); it started in the priests' western living quarters (*Kōfuki*).

476. *Mafū* 魔風: a demonic wind.

477. In this story, adapted from the *Shūishi* 集異志 (漢末魔竺云々), the fire deity is a boy; in the original Chinese version, the deity is a woman. The struggle among Kyoto's sake *kōji* dealers is based on a historical fact mentioned in the *Kōfuki* and *Honchōshōgunki*. Asai should be credited for skillfully incorporating historical facts into a strange tale.

478. *Kitai* 鬼胎: inside the body of a ghost (鬼); i.e., someone born of a demon or ghost.

479. 原隼人左昌勝 (d. 1575); Hayatonosuke was Shingen's *samurai-daishō*, or chief of samurai.

480. See *OT*, 5-2, n.5.

481. 昌俊 (d. 1549); the father of Hayatonosuke, Masatoshi served both Nobutora and his son, Shingen. He taught Hayatonosuke the topography of the provinces (*Kaikokushi* 甲斐国志, 96).

from Takahatake[482] of Kō Province. While employed by Shingen, Masatoshi accomplished many military feats. Before he died, he said to his son, Hayato, "Birds, animals, and even crawling bugs have their own virtues and none are without talent.[483] You are a man, the son of a samurai. You should be grateful and honor your lord by developing your skill as a warrior. If you are without a sense of duty—wastefully receiving a fief, eating your fill, dressing warmly, harboring evil desires—you are no better than a thief and lower than an animal. You must improve yourself to serve your lord. The sun, moon, clouds, fog, trees, and grasses—all have their merits. Without talents and abilities, one cannot benefit others, only harm them. Think well on everything I have said and be prudent."

Following his father, Hayato served Shingen with utmost loyalty and became a great warrior. He was always one step ahead of the ally's armies, attacked deep in the enemy's territory, and fought bravely.[484] He knew where to camp and where to fight. He traveled unfamiliar mountains, rivers, valleys, and summits without a guide. He walked every route, including small paths. He advanced ahead of the ally's soldiers without making mistakes. Few of his colleagues ever doubted him. He selected the best places to camp and fight even in provinces unfamiliar to him, and he never failed to find back routes and water. People wondered if he was blessed with divine powers.[485]

[Hayato's mother] was the daughter of a man of the Henmi.[486] Her husband was very busy and hardly at home; he spent many days and months traveling and staying in military camps. The family lived near the Jizō hall of Kamijō.[487] After she died in childbirth, Masatoshi was overcome with grief. He could do nothing but bury her in a grave

....

482. In present-day Takahata, Kōfu-shi.

483. *Ete* 得手.

484. For Hayato's remarkable fighting skill, see *Kōyōgunkan*, 8.

485. *Jintsū* 神通: someone with mysterious or divine powers and talents.

486. 辺見; the family was related to the ancestors of Takeda Shingen.

487. Bodhisattva Jizō, dressed in a priest's robe, saves sentient beings in hell by interceding on their behalf with King Enma; see Yoshiko Dykstra, "Jizō, the Most Merciful: Tales from *Jizōbosatsu reigenki*," *Monumenta Nipponica* 33 (1978): 179–200. Kamijō 上条 is in present-day Hacchōme, Kokubo, Kōfu-shi.

mound behind Hōjōji Temple.[488] Before his wife died, she had prayed to Jizō, facing his hall with her palms joined: "I have worshiped you for many years. Please fulfill my true vow." She took her last breath reciting Jizō's name. Masatoshi, too, put his faith in Jizō and asked that the bodhisattva lead his wife to the next life.

One night, a hundred days after the woman's death, an eighty-year-old man— with drooping eyebrows[489] as white as frost and crystal beads in his hands—knocked at the Hara [gate]. Masatoshi opened the gate and saw that the old man, leaning on a pigeon stick,[490] was accompanied by his wife, recently revived.

Greatly surprised, Masatoshi invited them in and asked the man, "Now, old priest, how is it that you come to be here with my wife?"

The priest replied, "I live in Hōjōji Temple. This evening when I came out of the hall, a grave mound suddenly collapsed and a woman appeared. 'Who are you?' I asked, and the woman answered, 'I am the wife of Hara, a governor of Kaga.' So I have brought her to you. Take good care of her." As soon as he finished his story, he vanished. Feeling this most strange, Masatoshi sent his man to Hōjōji and learned that a grave mound had indeed collapsed. "So it is true," he thought as he gave his wife some gruel. She was dazed for a while but recovered in seven days. She did not like bright places. The following year she gave birth to a baby boy.

One evening, after the boy had turned three years old, Masatoshi's wife tearfully announced, "I am not human. Because of my deep feelings for you, Jizō of Kamijō ordered one of the officials in the Land after Death to release my soul. I returned here and have been with you for the past three years. But now the time has come for me to bid you farewell and return [to the Land after Death]. Please do not neglect my grave." The wife left the child with Masatoshi and disappeared. When he went to her grave, it was intact and covered with grass. This must surely have been one of the skillful means[491] used by Bodhisattva Jizō. When Shingen heard this story, he restored the Jizō hall in Hōjōji

....

488. The temple had Bodhisattva Jizō as its principal image and is in present-day Tōkōji-chō, Kōfu-shi.

489. *Mayu ni hachiji* まゆに八字: eyebrows in the shape of the character for *hachi* 八 (eight).

490. A walking stick with a pigeon carved at the top.

491. *Hōben* 方便: a Buddhist term referring to the means to teach and lead sentient beings.

Temple and renewed his worship of Jizō.

Masatoshi never took another wife. The child mentioned in the story was Hayatonosuke, which would explain why he seemed to enjoy divine protection since his first battle at the age of eighteen.[492]

6-1 Ise Hyōgo Travels to a Hermitage[493]

Hōjō Ujiyasu[494] of Izu Province controlled the eight provinces[495] in Kantō and was famous for his prowess as a warrior. One day, while on a beach, he looked to the south and said, "Long ago Chinzei Hachirō Tametomo[496] was exiled to the Izu islands. When he saw some birds flying in the offing, he thought, 'An island must be out there. Those birds are flying to it this evening.' So he followed the birds and arrived at Onigashima,[497] where demons are said to live. The island is now called Hachijō. I have never heard of anyone visiting it. I wonder if someone would go to the island and tell us what it is like." Two men, Sakamioka Kōsetsu[498] and Ise Hyōgo no Kashira,[499] came forward and said, "We will investigate the island and give you a detailed report." Two large ships were constructed. The samurai generals[500] Kōsetsu and Ise each took twenty dōshin[501] horsemen aboard. On a fine day they sailed south in high spirits.

....

492. This story is based on the *Chūchōkoji* 中朝故事 (代説鄭略云々). The Japanese version follows only the outline of the Chinese original.

493. *Senkyō* 仙境: a place where *sen'nin* 仙人 (Taoist recluses or hermits) reside. The word refers to an otherworldly, ideal place like Shangri-la.

494. See *OT*, 2-1, n.53.

495. Musashi, Sagami, Kōzuke, Shimotsuke, Kamiusa, Shimousa, Awa, and Hitachi.

496. 鎮西八郎為朝 (d. 1170) : the eighth son of Tameyoshi. Tametomo was a warrior lord celebrated in many legends. He was exiled to one of the Izu islands after he was defeated in the Battle of Hōgen (1156).

497. 鬼島: demon or goblin island; the island is well known because of the popular folktale *Momo Tarō* (Peach Boy).

498. 坂見岡江雪; a subject of Hōjō Ujinao (1562–1591). Kōsetsu also served Hideyoshi and Ieyasu. Kōsetsu was his Buddhist name (*Hōjō Godaiki* 北条五代記, 5).

499. 伊勢兵庫頭; difficult to identify because men of the Ise clan traditionally occupied the *kashira* 頭, or chief position, at the *hyōgo* 兵庫 (weapon storehouse).

500. *Samurai-daishō* (or *taishō*) 侍大将: a head or chief of a group of samurai.

501. 同心: a group of soldiers under a *samurai-daishō*.

There are seven islands[502] off the coast of Izu. When they approached [one of them], the wind suddenly changed. The waves became as high as snowy mountains. Kōsetsu barely reached the island of Hachijō. He observed conditions there and the island's people, then returned home.

Meanwhile, Ise, who had been blown south, wandered for about ten days, not knowing if it was day or night. As the wind subsided, he drifted to a strange island. When he landed, he saw tall rocks: Some were as blue as blue jewels, some as white as snow, some as yellow as steamed millet, some as red as crimson flowers. He saw many kinds of rocks and stones unknown in Japan. The plants, flowers, and fruits were also unfamiliar to him. On the beach he saw a strange person wearing a hat made of a thin material, a *hitatare* robe[503] woven from various plant fibers, and shoes decorated with flowers. He was about twenty-years-old with a very fair complexion, intelligent brows, and teeth dyed black. He appeared to be Chinese yet he understood Japanese. Seeing Ise, he asked, "Who are you?" After Ise explained his situation, the man said, "This place is called Sōrō.[504] It is three thousand *ri* south of Japan and is near the Fudaraku Pure Land of Bodhisattva Kannon.[505] At the time of Emperor Junwa,[506] Priest Egaku visited the Fudaraku world by order of Empress Tachibana.[507] I heard that the priest came to this island on his way there and shared his story.

"You must be very tired after being at sea for such a long distance. Please come this way and rest yourself." The man led Ise to his home, where he offered him drinks made from the *shōbu* iris with nine joints[508] and the *hekitō*[509] blue peach, served in a jeweled cup. After several cups,

....

502. Ōshima, Ritō, Shintō, Kamitsushima, Miyakejima, Mikurajima, and Hachijōjima.

503. The *hitatare* was the official clothing for a nobleman and a samurai.

504. 滄浪: the color of water, or light blue.

505. 補陀落世界; this place was presumably located in the southern sea. For Kannon, see Yoshiko Dykstra, "Tales of the Compassionate Kannon: The *Hasedera Kannon genki*," *Monumenta Nipponica* 31 (1976): 113–143.

506. 淳和天皇 (r. 823–833).

507. 橘皇后 (786–850): the wife of Emperor Saga. The time of Priest Egaku, who went to China during the Showa era (834–848), does not correspond with the reign of Emperor Junwa.

508. A drink made from an iris with nine joints on the stem.

509. 碧桃: a food for *sen'nin*. Here the drink is made from the pistil of the peach blossom.

Ise felt refreshed. The tales of Hōgen and Heiji[510] told by his host made him feel as if the battles were taking place right before his eyes.

The house, decorated with gold and gems, the furniture, and other items appeared otherworldly. There was a rock measuring two-foot-square called Shōfūseki (Pine-Wind-Stone)[511] in the alcove. It resembled a transparent blue and yellow jewel. Sand of the seven jewels surrounded the base of the rock, which was placed on a tray decorated with the seven jewels. On the rock were paths leading to a valley and a summit. A waterfall, its spray made of white jewels, looked as if it were flowing. No water was heard, but there were wave crest patterns on the rock. It was a superb *bonsan*.[512] A foot-high pine tree grew beside the rock. The aged pine had passed a thousand springs and autumns; one almost felt like asking it about the old days. A cool wind blew through its branches and filled the room. The fresh appearance of the slanting branches and trembling pine needles would have caused us to forget the heat of mid-summer.[513]

There was a three-foot-long Chinese agate chest in the bedchamber. The carvings of animals, birds, and plants on the chest were beyond the abilities of any human. A purple vase large enough to hold a *koku* of rice stood near the chest. It was translucent and as radiant as crystal, but when lifted, it was as light as a feather. The vase was filled with sake and labeled "the most refined and rarest sake." A shiny white jar, two *tō*[514] in size, contained incense; according to the label it was the celebrated "Descending Dragon's True Fragrance." Ise also saw a high tower with silver railings, gold pillars, and curtains. Its walls were decorated with paint made from the crushed pieces of every kind of gem. "Descending Divine Hermits"[515] was framed and hung [on one of the walls].

In the garden, strange plants and flowers were blossoming as if it were early spring. Peacocks, parrots, and other birds that Ise could not identify were singing in curious voices among the trees and flower-

....

510. The Battle of Hōgen (保元の乱) in 1156 and the Battle of Heiji (平治の乱) in 1159 involved the samurai class who, for the first time, participated in government affairs.

511. 松風石: a rock or stone presented to Emperor Wu of the Tang (618–907).

512. 盆山: a miniature mountain landscape created with small stones and trees grown in a tray.

513. *Kyūkasanpuku* 九夏三伏: ninety days in mid-summer; i.e., the hottest time of the year.

514. One *tō* equals 10 *shō*; one *shō* equals 1.8 liters.

515. *Kōshin* 降真.

ing plants. The horses in the fifteen-*ken*-long stable were magnificent dragon horses[516] measuring eight-feet-four-inches tall. Their colors varied from green and blue to white, black, and spotted grey. Their fodder looked like the *chigaya* plant with its small white flowers; it was unmixed with other grasses. Jujubu fruits as blue as lapis lazuli and chestnuts as shiny as coral and the size of pears hung from branches.

Beyond a hedge, Ise saw all kinds of beautiful buildings made of gold, silver, jade, and purple jewels soaring above the clouds with roof tiles as colorful as rainbows. Music echoed in the sky and the smell of incense wafted through the air.

Ise went to the base of a mountain and saw a waterfall. The water in the basin was green and flowed into a river. There was a two-*chō*-square pool containing water so hard that gold and silver would not sink in it. Truly, if someone had thrown a stone into the pool, it would have floated on the surface. Thus the people of the island amused themselves on iron boats. The sand at the bottom of the pool was golden, which reminded Ise of how the roses in Ide [in Kyoto], reflected in water, resembled golden flowers in bloom. Four-footed fish shone as bright as gold in the pool.

....

516. *Ryūme* 竜馬.

Nearby Ise saw a wide field where grasses with gold-colored stems and blue leaves grew wild. Peony-like blossoms with leaves resembling those of chrysanthemums bloomed there. The flower was yellow on the outside and red within with white pistils resembling bunches of thread. The flowers moved like flitting butterflies in the slight breeze. The women decorated their hair with these flowers, which remained fresh for ten days. The men and women all appeared to be in their twenties and were very good looking, unlike their counterparts in Japan. He saw no elderly people.

"I wonder if I could live here," Ise said to himself, but then he recalled, "I went to sea on my master's orders and was brought by the wind to this place, where I have seen the most miraculous sights. If I stayed here, I would be branded unfaithful and disloyal after my death. I must return home at all costs." Ise shared his feelings with his host, who was greatly impressed and said, "In that case, I will raise a good wind to take you home. A horse and a parrot will be on the ship as tokens of your visit." Ise bid the man farewell and boarded a ship that was laden with cargo, including chestnuts and jujubu fruits in porcelain containers. As soon as the mooring line was cut, a favorable wind began to blow. With the sails raised, the ship arrived at Izu in about a day.

Shortly after coming ashore, Ise went to the castle and found that his master, Ujiyasu, had fallen sick and died,[517] and that Ujimasa[518] had taken his place. Grieving, Ise tearfully described the island he had visited, saying, "In olden times, Emperor Suinin[519] ordered Mamori of Tamichito to go to Tokoyo Ever Land. Mamori brought back the fragrant fruit known as the *tachibana*[520] tangerine. When he returned, the emperor had already passed away. Mamori died of grief, saying, 'I failed.' Returning after my master's death, I too have failed." And with that, Ise committed suicide by cutting open his stomach. His story was recorded and later circulated.[521]

....

517. Ujiyasu died in 1571.

518. 氏政; Ujimasa inherited control of the Hōjō clan in 1559.

519. The *Nihongi* (日本紀) mentions Emperor Suinin 垂仁 (r. 29 B.C.–70 A.D.) sending Mamori of Tamichi 田道間守 to Tokoyo 常世 Ever Land.

520. 橘.

521. This story is based on *Toyōzōhen* 杜陽雑編, 2 (処士元蔵幾云々). In the Chinese version, the protagonist returns home after spending two hundred years on a south seas island. He wanders about for several decades with the appearance of a foreigner.

6-2   A Long-lived Taoist[522]

Satomi Yoshihiro[523] of Awa, a celebrated warrior, governed his province well. One day he brought an old man to his mansion from the Asaina District.[524] When Yoshihiro asked the man his age, he answered he could not remember exactly but he was several hundred years old at least. Judging from his complexion, he appeared to be in his fifties. His white hair and beard changed color and at times resembled golden threads. He had blue eyes, long ears, and hair that reached to the floor when he sat down. His name was Toji Iwata,[525] and he told [Yoshihiro] that he had accompanied Miura Ōsuke[526] on a hunting trip to Nasuno in Shinshu[527] during the time of Ex-Emperor Gotobain.[528] On that occasion, he had caught a nine-tailed fox[529] and crushed a *sesshōseki* stone.[530] Many people were badly affected by the poison: Some became deranged and died of a high fever. He related the story as if it were unfolding before his eyes.

The man continued: "I was eighteen years old when I became despondent about this sad life. My parents and brothers had died after the hunting incident. I confined myself to a mountain to practice the Way. A hermit[531] appeared and gave me medicine.[532] As soon as I took a blue pill, I felt my body become light and my mind refreshed. The

522. *Dōji* 道士: a master of the Taoist way; the equivalent of a *sen'nin*, a Taoist hermit or recluse.

523. 里見義広 (1525–1578); Yoshihiro was the sixth head of the Satomi family; he fought against the Hōjō clan.

524. Near present-day Chikura-chō, Awa-gun, Chiba-ken.

525. Unidentified.

526. Miura Ōsuke Yoshiaki 三浦大介吉義明 (1092–1180) was a warrior from present-day Yokosuka-shi. The legend of his defeating a monster appears in the Noh drama *Sesshōseki*.

527. In present-day Nasu-chō, Nasu-gun, Ibaragi-ken.

528. Emperor Toba (r. 1107–1125).

529. *Kyūbi no kitsune* 九尾の狐, or *kyūbi-kitsune* 九尾狐: a legendary mysterious fox that appears in the *Sankaikyō* 山海経 and the *Nanzankyō* 南山経 and is often compared to a powerful, beautiful woman. Here the fox is Tamamonomae, a favorite concubine of Ex-Emperor Toba.

530. 殺生石: a killing stone. The monk Genō crushed the stone to dispel the evil spirit of a mysterious fox, but the poisonous effects of the scattered pieces of the stone are unknown.

531. *Sen'nin;* these Taoist recluses are often associated with *senyaku* 仙薬 (herbal medicines for longevity).

532. Varieties of *senyaku* medicines appear in the next few sentences of the text.

hermit and I flew in the sky until we landed on the summit of a strange mountain. I was taken to a [building and] was made to sit on the floor. Some red chestnuts[533] and a drink of condensed mist[534] were given to me. After a while, I became intoxicated and lost consciousness. I was made to drink another half cup of "Sweet Dew of Heaven,"[535] which roused and refreshed me.

"The hermit asked me, 'Have you ever seen cranes and turtles?[536] They breathe calmly[537] so they don't waste their energy and have long lives free of sickness. Ninety years from now, your eyes will turn a shiny blue and you will be able to see in the dark. In a thousand years, your bones will be changed[538] and in two thousand years your skin and hair will likewise be changed. After that, your shape and figure will never age, your years will remain fixed, and your life span will be limitless. In general, people in the world are badly affected internally by the seven feelings[539] and externally by wind, cold, heat, and moisture. They act according to their desires and eat voraciously. Their emotions rise like flames while their heart beat grows irregular and their internal organs are disturbed. Their 900 muscles atrophy. Outwardly, their 49 folds of skin and 80,000 pores deteriorate. Their 14 veins and 15 arteries[540] become tangled and loosen. Their joints come apart. Many kinds of illness are born from these phenomena and their life span is shortened. Hardly anyone lives for a hundred years.

"'Grief and sadness alternately disturb and bind their hearts and minds like summer insects flitting around a flame. Their desire for fame and profit never cease like fish that feed on anything—even poisonous food—in streams. Their souls and energy are exhausted in vain. Their small minds are full of high waves of delusions. Their envy and jealousy toward each other are more violent than those of any

....

533. *Tanrichi* 丹栗.

534. *Kashō* 霞漿.

535. *Genten no kanro* 玄天の甘露.

536. Both cranes and turtles are symbols of longevity.

537. Breathing is an important factor in longevity.

538. According to Taoist teachings, bones can change into wings after years of practicing the Way.

539. Joy, anger, sadness, fear, love, evil, and desire.

540. *Keimyaku* 徑脈, *rakumyaku* 絡脈: the vessels that carry and circulate blood, nutrition, and air inside the body.

beast. This is why a Buddhist sutra calls the human world the House of Fire[541] and the Taoists regard the body as a great source of anxiety. If you are able to escape from all this and look at the human world, it looks like boiling water. Would you throw yourself into boiling water?

"'When a person controls his three-foot-tall body[542] and polishes his one-inch-long heart, he can ascend to the sky, enter the ground, ride on clouds, and run across water. He goes through thousands of changes at will, going and flying whenever he wishes. He feels superior even to an emperor. Who in this world is better than him?' Saying this, the hemit taught me how to make medicines.[543]

"Since then, I have confined myself deep in the mountains and learned the Way. I eat pine needles[544] and *bukuryō*.[545] I seek *toshishi*[546] and *bōkon*[547] and use a salve made from stones.[548] I also eat sweets made from frost and the condensed dew of hundreds of flowers. After taking these medicines without any grains for so long, I no longer have an appetite. My mind appreciates the wind in the pines and the bright moon. I console my heart with a waterfall and am free of desires and anger."

Yoshihiro asked, "If I decide to follow the hermit way,[549] is it something I can learn?" The old man replied, "If you calm your mind and control it, relinquish sexual and other desires, avoid tasty foods, ignore pleasure and sadness, and practice virtuous and unprejudiced deeds, then you will live according to nature, the way of heaven and earth, with the blessing of longevity. You will not see, hear, speak, or behave in vain. You will not go, come, rise, or retire needlessly. You will always maintain the disciplines."

Hearing this, Yoshihiro said, "Then the way of this [secular] world is contrary to everything you've mentioned. If we try to attain the Way

....

541. *The Lotus Sutra* compares this world with *Kataku* 火宅, the House of Fire.

542. The three-foot-tall body is one's insignificant body or self.

543. *Senyaku.*

544. *Matsunoha* 松葉: pine needle resin.

545. 伏苓; *bukuryō* grows at the roots of pine trees. Its meat is soft and red like a yam but becomes white and hard when dried. It is often used in herbal medicine.

546. 兎糸子: the seed of the *nenashi-kazura,* or convolvulus.

547. 茅根: an orchid root or root of the *chigaya* plant.

548. Another *senyaku,* this is a salve for longevity made of eight kinds of stones or red sand.

549. *Senjustsu* 仙術.

by avoiding all wordly things, we would be like monkeys and deer and there would be no point in living a long life." Saying this, he urged the old man to eat all the foods he had shunned. The old man refused to do so, but he drank a great deal without becoming intoxicated. Because of his strange appearance, the young women attending the feast laughed at him. The old man said to them, smiling, "You'll be sorry." As soon as he pointed at the fifteen or sixteen of them, from seventeen to twenty-four years of age, they turned into old women with the skin of chickens that was as rough as shark scales. Their complexions darkened and their hair turned white. Appalled, they grieved [for their youth] and begged the old man's forgiveness, shedding tears like rain. They apologized, putting their palms together. The old man said, "Now you have learned your lesson." Again he pointed his finger at them, and the women returned to their former selves.

Seeing this, Yoshihiro became very angry and thought of killing the old man. Immediately the old man sensed his intention and wrote him a note: "If you do as you intend, your province will not last long. Five hundred months later, you will surely suffer misfortune." As soon as he finished writing, he rose from his seat and disappeared. No one knew where he went. Yoshihiro's men searched for the old man throughout the province, including the mountains, in vain. Yoshihiro said to them, "The old man's note mentioned five hundred months. That is forty some years from now. I may not live that long." But when his men examined the note, they found that Yoshihiro had mistaken 箇 [*ka*, a numerical unit] for 百 [*hyaku*, a hundred].[550]

Five months later, Yoshihiro was defeated at the Battle of Kōnodai[551] by Hōjō Ujiyasu[552]—just as his people had feared. It was said that nothing more was known about the old man, Toji Iwata—where he was from, who his parents were, or where he died.[553]

6-3   The Courtesan Miyagino[554]

Miyagino was a courtesan at an inn[555] in Suruga Province.[556] She was good-looking and good natured. Because she had a tender and sympathetic heart, she excelled in calligraphy and poetry. Many men in the vicinity admired her. Men of taste, as well as men who were amorous of her, were filled with regret when they had no contact with her. An incomparable courtesan for many years, Miyagino entertained men of high and low standing without discrimination, modeling herself after Toragozen[557] and Rikiju.[558]

A group of young men had gathered for a moon-viewing party at the inn on the night of the fifteenth of the eighth month, in the middle of autumn. Miyagino joined the party and recited two poems:

....

550. I.e., five months, not five hundred months.

551. In 1564 the Satomi family was defeated by the Hōjō at present-day Ichikawa-shi, Chiba-ken

552. Hōjō Ujiyasu, the third head of the Hōjō clan of Odawara, defeated the Uesugi clan of Kamakura and took control of the eight provinces of the Kanto area.

553. This story is based on Zuyōzatsuhen 杜陽雑編, 2 (羅浮先生軒輾集云々).

554. Unidentified.

555. *Tabiya* 旅屋: inns for travelers; they customarily kept courtesans and prostitutes.

556. Present-day Shizuoka-shi.

557. Toragozen 虎御前 was a courtesan in Ōiso (present-day Ōiso, Kanagawa-ken) and a mistress of Soga Sukenari 曾我祐成, the eldest of the Soga brothers and one of the protagonists of the *Soga monogatari* 曾我物語. Toragozen appears in the *Azumakagami* 吾妻鑑 and the *Soga monogatari*.

558. Rikiju 力寿 was a courtesan in Awataguchi in Kyoto and a mistress of Satō Tadanobu 佐藤忠信, a retainer of Minamoto Yoshitsune 源義経 (1159–1180).

nagamureba
sore towa nashini
koishiki o
kumoraba kumore
aki no yo no tsuki

Somehow I miss someone
By gazing at the moon,
If you want to hide behind a cloud
Hide yourself,
The autumn night's moon.[559]

iku yo ware
oshi akegata no
tsuki kage ni
sore to sadamenu
hito to wakaruru

How many times
Have I parted from
Strangers
Under the moon's shadow
At the break of dawn?[560]

Some of the men laughed at hearing poems that expressed the courtesan's personal feelings, but others were touched. One of these men was Fujii Seiroku. His ancestor came from the capital and had served a provincial governor. His family had settled in the area and become prosperous farmers and land owners, and his descendants were still known for their wealth in the province. Seiroku showed great sensitivity in matters of the heart. Because his father was dead, he lived with his mother. Still unmarried, he had joined the party to appreciate

---

559. The more the poet gazes at the moon, the more she misses her beloved and the sadder she becomes. Thus she admonishes the moon to hide behind a cloud (*kumore:* to be cloudy). The poem is adapted from *Kinyōshū* 金葉集, Koi, 1.

560. The poem tersely expresses the unhappy life of the courtesan (*Shinshūishū*, Koi, 2). A *sadamenu hito* is a person who is not committed to being one's beloved. It is translated here as "stranger."

the autumn moon. After hearing Miyagino recite her poems, he was so impressed by her beauty and superior talent that he paid a great sum to the owner of the inn to free her and make her his wife.

Hearing the news, his mother said to him, "Because our family is very wealthy, I had hoped someone from a celebrated family would be my daughter-in-law. It was not my wish for you to marry a courtesan, but if she is your choice, I have nothing to say. Quickly bring her here."

When Seiroku's mother finally met Miyagino, she was impressed with her looks and gentle heart. Much pleased, she said to herself, "Even if she had been the daughter of a *daimyō* or from a cerebrated family, she would be of no use unless she were good natured. This woman, although from a humble family, excels in the ways of womanhood. My son has reason to be attracted to her." She appreciated the bride very much, and Miyagino served her mother-in-law faithfully and with the utmost sincerity.

Seiroku had an uncle, his mother's younger brother, in the capital. The uncle became seriously ill and believed he was dying. He sent for a messenger, saying: "Bring Seiroku to the capital. I have something to tell him."

[Upon receiving her brother's message,] Seiroku's mother implored her son, "Hurry and see [your uncle]. I would fly to his side if I could. It is difficult for a woman to travel to the capital, but you, being a man, can do it easily. Go and see how he is." Seiroku lingered, wondering [if he should leave his new bride]. Miyagino said to him, "If you do not heed your mother's wish and go to the capital, first, she will think you have forgotten your uncle on account of me; and second, you will fail in fulfilling your filial duty to her. So please go. However, given her age, your mother may become ill. An old saying tells us, 'The more time you spend working, the less time you have to serve your parents.' Your mother is like the moon sinking behind a mountain in the west.[561] Go quickly and return quickly."

The couple exchanged a cup of sake in farewell. Although they knew they would see each other again, they were both filled with sadness anticipating even a brief separation. Miyagino tearfully recited a poem:

....

561. The setting sun behind a mountain in the west suggests death; the Amida Buddha's paradise is located in the west.

utatenado
shibashi bakari no
tabi no michi,
wakaruto ieba
kanashi karuramu

Lamenting
Only a short trip,
Why do I become
So sad when we
Talk of separation?

Seiroku also recited a poem in tears:

tsune yori wa
hito[562] *mo wakare o*
shitau kana
kore ya kagiri no
chigiri naruramu[563]

More than usual
She is grieving
Our separation,
I wonder if this
Might be our last pledge.

Hearing his poem, his mother said, "How ominous to talk about a [last pledge] when you are going on such a short trip!" and she hurried her son on his way.

When Seiroku arrived at the capital, he found that his uncle had grown worse and he soon passed away. His uncle had a young child. Seiroku gave all of his uncle's valuables and property to his wife's family so they could look after the child. After he finished making the arrangements and was ready to return home to Suruga, war broke out in various provinces. Barriers were set up and people were unable to

....

562. Here *hito* (a person) refers to the reciter's wife.

563. *Dairingushō*, Koi, 2.

travel. Every day there was fighting in nearby villages and provinces, and, under such conditions, news of people away from home and their relatives grew scarce. Because Seiroku could not travel as he wished, he was forced to wander from one place to another for a year.

Meanwhile in Suruga, Seiroku's mother was very distressed when her son failed to return home. "If I had known this was going to happen, I would not have sent him to the capital. I greatly regret that. I don't know whether he is alive or dead," she cried. She became sick with grief and spent days in bed.

Miyagino looked after her mother-in-law day and night. She tested medicines on herself before she administered them and cooked rice gruel for her. She even prayed to the gods and Buddhas, saying, "Please save her by taking my life instead."

But all her efforts were in vain. About six months later, when her mother-in-law felt there was no hope of recovering, she called Miyagino to her bedside and said, "My son has gone to the capital and has been unable to send word because of the disturbances. I have been seriously ill and you, my daughter-in-law, have served me better than even my own daughter could have. Your filial piety is unprecedented. I have nothing more to say. I am going to die without rewarding you for your faithfulness to me. You will have a child of your own in future. But I will die without seeing my grandchild. Your child will certainly be as filial and faithful to you as you have been to me. If heaven shows the truth, there will be no falsity in my words."

Saying this, she died and did not revive. Miyagino's grief was so deep that she shed tears like rain. She performed a proper funeral service and observed the mourning period of forty-nine days.[564] Her tremendous devotion[565] left her exhausted. Her skin and complexion became dull and her hair lost its luster.

Lord Takeda Shingen invaded Suruga Province in 1568.[566] He attacked the castle and set fire to the houses in the town. Lord Imagawa

....

564. The Buddhist mourning period is forty-nine days.

565. *Bungen* 分限: to do something beyond one's ability and economic status.

566. Takeda Shingen invaded Suruga on the thirteenth day of the eleventh month in 1568 (*Kai sengoku shiryōsōsho ōdaiki*, Eiroku, 11).

Ujizane[567] lost the castle and abandoned it.[568] The Takeda soldiers looted and plundered every house, committing atrocities. They found the beautiful Miyagino and tried to rape her. She ran into the inner part of the house, where she committed suicide by hanging herself. Impressed by her chastity, the soldiers buried her at the foot of a persimmon tree behind the house.

Takeda soon took over Suruga; the fighting subsided and calm returned to the province. The local lords along the highways made peace with each other and people could finally travel again. Seiroku returned home. Arriving in his town, he found things greatly changed. He saw no one in his home. The main pillar was slanting and the eaves were collapsed. Grass and plants grew profusely in the yard and garden. He looked for his mother and wife in vain.

When he was about to leave, he saw a servant passing by, one who had served his family for a long time. When Seiroku questioned him, the servant told him everything—how his mother had become ill and passed away in spite of Miyagino's devoted care, how Miyagino had prayed for her recovery and offered her own life. He also relayed the news of Takeda's invasion, Imagawa's defeat, and finally Miyagino's chastity, which had so impressed the enemy soldiers.

Hearing the servant's story, Seiroku was consumed by grief, like one shedding tears of blood. He tearfully exhumed his wife's body and found it unchanged: It was as if she were still alive. He missed her and grieved bitterly in agony; he felt himself close to death but could do nothing but bury her by his mother's side.[569] Offering flowers and incense before the grave, Seiroku spoke aloud to his wife, "You were always intelligent and blessed with deep affection. You conducted yourself well in my stead.[570] Your death was unlike that of other wives. It was not my fault that I could not send word to you. It was all due to the way of this futile world, in which we are helpless. Even though you are at the bottom of the Land after Death, if you hear me, please show yourself to me just once." He went to her grave

567. Imagawa Ujizane, a stepson of Imagawa Yoshimoto, controlled the three provinces of Suruga, Mikawa, and Tōtomi. His mother was an older sister of Takeda Shingen and his daughter was married to Shingen's eldest son.

568. Ujizane escaped to Kakegawa Castle. He later went to Izu and was protected by Hōjō Ujiyasu.

569. This indicates that Miyagino was finally accepted as a member of Seiroku's family.

570. *Hito ni kawarite*: in place of someone; i.e., Miyagino fulfilled Seiroku's filial duties.

in the morning and returned home in the evening. Thus he spent the next twenty days.

One night, with the moon dark and the stars shining, Seiroku sat alone in the candlelight. Miyagino suddenly appeared like a shadow before him and said, "I have come here tonight because you have longed to see me. I asked permission from the Shiroku deity."[571]

She told him all that had happened, standing before him helplessly. Seeing her, Seiroku was overwhelmed with gratitude for her looking after his mother and upholding her chastity at the cost of her life.

Miyagino continued, "I was not the daughter of a nobleman or of anyone of high rank or title. I was drifting in this futile life. I associated with many men but never gave my heart to any of them. I left them in the morning, feeling nothing. Adorning myself in colors and flowers, I enchanted travelers. I was like a willow along the roadside or a flower by the hedge, expecting to be picked by any passerby. With amorous looks and skillful words, I bid farewell to guests one day and welcomed new guests the next. I became the wife of the man who was heading down to the west and the wife of one who was traveling up [to the capital][572] from the east. I exchanged false pledges with these men and like a boat drifting on the waves I spent days and months in meaningless love affairs. But after I met you, I became a real wife, remaining true and abandoning all my old habits and customs. Unfortunately I met with misfortune because of bad karma from my previous life. But thanks to my filial piety and chastity, the kings of heaven and earth will change my feminine nature to a masculine[573] one in my next life. Go and see Takakura, a wealthy man of Kiridōshi in Kamakura. I will be reborn [as his son] tomorrow. When I see you, I will smile at you and that will be the sign." When she finished, she vanished like melted snow.

Seiroku, still grieving, went to Kamakura seven days later, visited Takakura, and asked him, "I wonder if a baby boy has been born to you lately. Please let me see him."

Takakura replied, "The baby was in his mother for twenty months and has never stopped crying since his birth." He brought the baby

....

571. Shirokujin is one of the eight deities of hell; he records the sins and crimes of those in hell.

572. Travelers coming from the east to Kyoto went "up to the capital" and those heading west went "down from the capital."

573. *Henjōnanshi* 変成男子: to change into a man. This is a concept found in the *Lotus Sutra*, which says that women can be delivered only after they are changed into men.

in his arms. As soon as the baby saw Seiroku, he stopped crying and smiled at him. Thereafter, the baby no longer cried but was always happy. Seiroku told Takakura everything and both families exchanged pledges; people said their relations have continued ever since.[574]

6-4 The Spider's Mirror

During the Eishō era [1504–1520], a merchant lived near Mount Tonami[575] in Ecchū Province. He made his living by gathering *shiba* brushwood, cultivating a mountain field, and raising silk worms, which required him to go deep into the mountains to obtain mulberry leaves.[576] In the summer, he went to villages to buy thread and cotton, which he then sold at a profit.

While traveling through the mountains, he often came upon deep ravines that were very difficult to cross. Sometimes a big rope of wisteria vines was stretched from one side of the ravine to the other and both ends were bound around the base of large trees or moss-covered rocks. Travelers would hang onto the rope to cross the ravine. [If one fell,] one would be dashed against the rocks and would perish in the current below, which flowed as swift as an arrow. At another place, a traveler would put himself into a bamboo basket hung from a rope of grapevines that stretched from east to west. Someone on the opposite side of the ravine would draw the rope while the person in the basket helped it along. But if the rope broke, the traveler would fall into the rapids, hit a rock, and die.

One day in the middle of the fifth month, the merchant wanted to buy some thread and cotton, so he traveled through the mountains. He came to a deep ravine. The sides of the ravine were as straight as

....

574. In the original tale, SS, 3 (愛卿伝), the son leaves his mother and bride to advance his career, but here he leaves to look after a sick uncle, which Japanese readers must have found more affecting. Miyagino's chastity is contrasted with the immoral conduct of Takeda's men. The author uses Takeda Shingen's attack on Suruga in other *Otogibōko* stories (5-2, 12-5). The original Chinese has three poems, while the Japanese has four *waka*, which creates a more romantic atmosphere. As with other *Otogibōko* stories, the author includes Buddhist elements: Miyagino's rebirth as a baby boy points to the Buddhist concepts of *rinnetenshō* 輪廻転生 (the cycling from one birth to another) and the idea of *henjōnanshi*.

575. Between present-day Koyabe shi, Toyama-ken, and Kahoku-gun, Ishikawa-ken.

576. Raising silk worms generally starts in the third month of the year.

standing screens, and the water below was as blue as indigo dye. The trees grew so thickly that he could not see a chink of sunlight. The merchant saw a large, round mirror [on his side of] the ravine that shone brightly with the reflection of the water below. The diameter of the mirror was about three feet. The merchant thought, "This mirror is superior to the Bright King Mirror[577] in the [bed chamber] of Yōkihi in China and to the Divine Mysterious Mirror of Chōki[578] in Ben Province. I wonder if the One Hundred Polishes Mirror[579] has appeared here—or the Heavenly Mirror?[580] This surely must be a miraculous mirror. I will take it and turn a profit." The merchant returned home and talked to his wife, who said, "Why in the world would such a mirror be left in a ravine? And even if it is [what you say it is], why risk your life to obtain it? If you miss a step and fall into

....

577. Myōōkyō 明王鏡 was placed by the pillow of Yōkihi 楊貴妃, the favorite concubine of Emperor Gensō 玄宗皇帝 (r. 712–756), to ward off evil spirits while she was ill.

578. Unidentified.

579. Hyakuren no kagami 百練の鏡: a mirror polished one hundred times and offered to an emperor. It appears in a poem by Hakurakuten. See *Kokinbunshū* 古今文集, Hyakurenkyō 百練鏡.

580. *Tenjō no kagami* 天上の鏡; may refer to the moon.

the water, it would be no use regretting it later. Don't do it." But the merchant insisted, "I will not make a mistake. I should get it before someone else does and make a profit." He could hardly wait for day-break, when he set out, carrying a sword. His worried wife followed him with their son and a servant, who carried a hatchet and a rusty spear.

After traveling deep into the mountains, they came to the ravine and saw the big mirror, shining brightly. The merchant began climbing down to the mirror. Suddenly a great shout was heard—and then nothing. The surprised wife, son, and servant quickly climbed down the ravine until they came upon the merchant, wrapped in the cob-web of a huge black spider. They immediately attacked the spider with the hatchet and spear and cut open the cobweb with the merchant's sword. But alas, the merchant was already dead and bleeding from a head wound. The giant spider looked like a huge wheel with its out-stretched legs.

The wife and son tearfully gathered some *shiba* wood, built a fire, and burned the spider, which gave off an odious smell that filled the mountains and valley. They took the merchant's body home and buried it. It is said that the spirit of the merchant possesses the mirror and [uses it to] occasionally deceive people.[581]

6-5   The Ghost of the White Bones

Nagamano Sata was from Jō Province.[582] During the Bunki era [1501–1504], he was summoned by the shogun to Kyoto. After completing his duties in the capital, he did not return home because he had renounced secular concerns. He composed this poem:

wasure temo
mata te ni toraji
azusayumi
moto no ieji o
hiki hanarete wa

---

581. Based on the *Dakukōki* 諾皋記 (元和中蘇湛云々).

582. Sata cannot be identified. Jō Province is present-day Mino Province, the southern part of Gifu-ken.

Even though I forget,
I would not take
An *azusayumi*[583] bow
After I have left
My way home.

After finishing the poem, Sata built a grass hut at Kashiwano,[584] north of the capital. Instead of begging for food, he bought *shiba* wood, sold it for firewood in the capital, and made a small profit.

Sometimes he ate rice cakes, drank sake, and went home tapping his behind while singing songs. Other times he cleaned temple gardens, dusted the altars before Buddhist images, and spent the night under the temple eves when it was too late to return home. At dawn, he went out to buy more *shiba* wood to sell later. He did not mind his one-layer *shibuzome*[585] kimono becoming torn.

Ishizu, a servant of Lord Toki Nariyori,[586] came from the same province as Sata. He gave Sata a lined *kosode* kimono and three hundred copper coins, saying, "Come and have dinner with me now and then." Sata took the gifts home but returned them [to Ishizu] four or five days later, saying, "Keeping things is for someone who has a wife and children; I have neither. I am all by myself, have no particular place to stay, and I eat when I have something to eat. Because I have detached myself from things, my pleasure is limitless. But with this kimono and money, I feel I have to come home early when I am out. When I leave my hut, I have to close the door because of thieves, and my pleasure is completely gone. Worrying about these small things is truly pitiful."

One day Sata went to Kitano. By the time he reached Rendaino[587] on the way home, it was already late. There was an old grave mound by the road. Suddenly it collapsed and opened. The strong-minded

---

583. 梓弓: made of *azusa* wood. A *makura-kotoba*, this word is associated with drawing and shooting. The poet can never return to his old ways just as an arrow can never return once it is released.

584. In present-day Kita-ku, Kyoto-shi.

585. 渋染: a dye made from the juice of persimmons.

586. 土岐成頼 (d. 1497: the ninth head of the Toki family and a *shugo-daimyō* of Mino Province.

587. 蓮台野; located west of Funaoka Hill, this was a burial ground like Adashino in the west and Toribeno in the east.

Sata was not frightened at all but stopped to look inside the mound, which released a light like a torch. He saw a white skeleton, complete from skull to foot bones. It had no flesh or sinew. The skeleton rose up and clung to Sata firmly. Being a strong man, Sata forcefully pushed it away. The skeleton fell on its back; the skull and other bones broke into pieces and remained still. When the [torch] light was extinguished, it was pitch dark. [Sata] did not know whose grave it was. When he returned to the spot in the morning, the grave was disturbed and the skeleton was lying in pieces. Later Sata perished but no one could say how.[588]

6-6   An Omen of Death

One day, during the Kōtoku era [1452–1540], Isonoya Jinsuke,[589] a servant of Hosokawa Ukyōdaifu Katsumoto,[590] was taking a nap. His wife was outside when she saw a strange man run from the house with a sword in his right hand and Isonoya's head in his left.

Shocked, she quickly went in and found Isonoya sleeping soundly. She was so stunned that her hands and feet were paralyzed, and she felt as if she were dreaming. After she woke her husband, he sat up and said, "I just dreamed someone cut off my head and took it away. This is most strange and something I should be concerned about." Soon he hired a *yamabushi* and had him perform the Changing the Dream Ritual.[591]

At the end of the month, when Lord Katsumoto did something that infuriated[592] the shogun, he made his servant, Isonoya, his scapegoat, ordered his head cut off for no reason, and thereby excused himself.[593]

....

588. This story is based on the *Keishashi* 撲車志 (劉先生云々); the first half can be found in the *Kan'ninki* 堪忍記, 4 (*Shōnin no kan'nin*).

589. The name Isoya 磯谷 appears in the *Honchō shōgunki*, 9.

590. Hosokawa Katsumoto 細川勝元 was *kanrei* from 1452 to1464.

591. The *yamabushi* 山伏 (mountain ascetic) performed the ritual to change Isonoya's bad dreams into good omens.

592. Katsumoto was involved in the inheritance affairs of the Hatakeyama family, which developed into a political struggle that upset Shogun Yoshimasa (*Honchō shōgunki*, 9).

593. This story is based on the *Shūishi* (北斎云々). The author of the *Otogibōko*, Asai, used the Chinese story and related it to a historical incident (Isonoya losing his head) recorded in the *Honchō shōgunki*.

7-1   Jealousy in an *Ema*[594]

The popular Gokō Shrine of Fushimi Village[595] was a celebrated shrine of Empress Jingū.[596] If visitors prayed earnestly at the shrine and dedicated *ema* while sprinkling hot water on them,[597] their wishes were fulfilled. The *ema* placed before the altar were illustrated with tethered horses, walking horses,[598] sailboats, birds, flowers, plants, and beautiful women amusing themselves.

During the Bunki era [1501–1504], a merchant of Shichijō[599] in the capital traveled to Nara for business. One day toward the end of the ninth month, he left Nara and headed home to Kyoto. As the autumn day was short, it soon became dark. The man saw hardly anyone when he arrived at Fushimi Village after crossing the Ogura dyke.[600] At the foot of the mountain, he saw fox fires[601] and heard wolves howling in the distance. Frightened, he decided to spend the night at Gokō Shrine.

[In the faintly lit shrine hall,] the merchant lay before the altar with his arm for a pillow. He listened to the cool wind blowing through the pines—it was as if it were his friend. As he began to doze off, someone stood by his head and woke him up.

A man dressed in a blue *naoshi* robe and *eboshi* hat[602] addressed him. "A noble lady is coming here," he said. "Move to the side and remain there." Although he felt this was a strange request, the merchant got up and did as he was told. Soon a beautiful lady came into the worshiping hall with a servant girl. A silk carpet was spread over a straw mat and a standing lamp was brought. The lady, sitting on the carpet, took out *sake* and food. Looking around her, she spied the merchant

....

594. 絵馬: a wooden tablet or votive; originally *ema* were illustrated with horses, but later other subjects were depicted, depending on what devotees wished for.

595. In present-day Gokōgu-monzenchō, Fushimi-ku, Kyoto-shi.

596. 神功皇后: the mother of Emperor Ōjin (r. 270–310).

597. Sprinkling hot water with bamboo leaves is a shrine rite.

598. Horses in noblemen's processions were led by the reins and called *hikikuma* 引馬.

599. Many Kyoto merchants in the Muromachi period lived in the area near Shichijo 七条 ("seventh avenue"). They sold textiles, handcrafts, and agricultural products.

600. The dyke was in present-day Ogura-chō, Uji-shi, Kyoto-fu. The pool was on the way to the Nara highway.

601. *Kitsunebi*, or *onibi* 鬼火: demon fire; phosphorus fires seen burning at night.

602. The everyday outfit of a nobleman.

crouching in the corner of the hall. Smiling, she asked, "Are you a traveler? They say it is lonesome to spend the night in a place like this when the sun has set as it has in your case. Come and relax." Hearing this, the merchant gladly drew closer but remained at a modest distance. The lady invited him to sit on the carpet. "Come closer, relax, and have a drink," she offered.

Facing her, the merchant said to himself, "I have heard that Lady Yōkihi[603] had eyebrows like willow leaves and a face like a *fuyō* peony blooming by the Taieki of Biyō Palace.[604] Lady Ri[605] could bring about the downfall of a entire country if one looked back at her once and a city if one looked back at her twice.[606] But because I have never seen her, I don't know. Now this lady before me, I wonder, what kind of person is she? What karma[607] has brought her here? I don't know if this is a dream or not. I am too fascinated by her to know if this is real."

The maid sevant appeared to be seventeen or eighteen years of age and her appearance was unusual. The shape and color of her eyebrows resembled the delicate lines of distant mountains, fragrant with the scent of mountain trees. Her teeth were as white as snow. Her waist was as supple as bunched threads, and her fingers were like new bamboo shoots. Her voice was clear and her speech elegant. When her mistress took up a sake cup and offered it to the merchant, he received it and, without thinking, drank three cups[608] of sake. Meanwhile, the maid brought out a *kukō* harp and began to play. The lady had a koto harp and tuned it with a *kotoji*.[609] Then she began to sing in a small voice. Completely enchanted, the merchant drank several more cups of sake and sang a popular song, "Namimakura" ["Wave Pillow"]. He had a good voice that suited the melody well when accompanied by the koto and *kukō*. Their music filled the shrine, brushed the dust off the beams, and echoed to the clouds. The drunken merchant fumbled at

....

603. Lady Yōkihi was the most beautiful consort of Emperor Gensō of the Tang.

604. Taieki 大液 was a large pool commissioned by Emperor Wu (r. 141–78 B.C.) of the Han. Biyō Palace 未央 was built during the Han.

605. 李夫人: the wife of Emperor Wu.

606. The verse appears in a poem by Lady Ri's elder brother.

607. *En* 縁.

608. Guests were served sake in large, medium, and small cups (*sankon* 三献) at drinking parties.

609. 琴柱: a device used on a harp for tuning.

his bosom, took out a box with a white flower design, and offered it to the lady. He wrapped a set of *kotozume* picks made of turtleshell and gave them to the maid. He took her hand and held it firmly. Smiling, the maid squeezed his hand in return. Watching this, the lady became jealous and recited a poem:

> *ayaniku ni*
> *sanomina fuki so*
> *matsu no kaze,*
> *waga shime yuishi*
> *kiku no magaki o*

> Wind in the pines,
> Don't blow
> So strongly over
> The chrysanthemum hedge
> That I have made myself.[610]

The lady threw a sake cup stand at the maid's face, which began to bleed. Seeing her sleeves turning crimson, the surprised merchant stood up and woke from his dream.

After dawn broke, he saw an *ema* before the shrine that depicted a beautiful lady sitting on a brocade seat, playing a koto. Her maid played a *kukō* and a man dressed in a blue robe sat beside them. The maid's face was damaged. Everything was exactly as it had been in his dream. Even the violent emotion shown by the lady in his dream was evident on the tablet. The merchant now understood that a woman is a jealous being. No one knew who painted the tablet.[611]

....

610. The maid, like the chrysanthemum hedge, has been personally trained by the lady. Similar poems appear in *Dairingushō, Koi,* 3, and *Shinsenzaishū* 新千載集, *Koi,* Tameuji. The term *shime yuishi* (to squeeze, tie, or bind) refers to the merchant and maid squeezing hands.

611. This story is based on the *Reikishi* (勝児). A *Konjaku* tale (*Konjaku monogatarishū* 今昔物語集, 13:34) also tells of an *ema* picture that came to life.

7-2   The Honest Servant Who
Became an Official after Death

Ashinuma Jirōemon Shigetoki[612] died of illness while he served as a
daikan[613] in Fujisawa for Lord Uesugi Norimasa, who was *kanrei* of
the Kantō region. His nephew, Mihono Shōhachi, succeeded him.
Ashinuma had taken neither wife nor mistress and had led a life free
of avarice. He had set store by neither studies nor future deliverance.
Straightforward and honest by nature, he had been merciful to peasants and cultivated no desires or indulgences. His nephew, however,
was greedy and abused the peasants, who all hated him and hoped he
would not last in his position.

One night Shōhachi dreamed of a strange man who looked very
angry. The man [a general] had a score of attendants carrying bows,
spears, and long swords. They turned to their commander and said,
"Shōhachi has accumulated bad deeds. Tie his arms and legs and cut
his head off." At that moment, his deceased uncle, Ashinuma, appeared
and [begged the general], "All Shōhachi has done is against human
nature. But please forgive him and just shave his head." Smiling, the
general reasoned, "It is to be expected that you feel sorry for him because you were his uncle. But will he rectify his conduct and do good?"
The frightened Shōhachi apologized for his evil deeds. The general
ordered, "Shave your head before me." Someone gave Shōhachi a razor
and made him shave his head.

When Shōhachi woke from his dream, he touched his head and
found that all of his hair had been shaved off and was on his pillow.
He had become a monk. His wife and children grieved for him in vain:
Shōhachi left them and became an ascetic of the Way—but he had
no faith at all. Finally, he confined himself to Kōmyōji Temple[614] and
recited Amida Buddha's name.

Ashinuma again visited Shōhachi in a dream and asked him, "Why
are you here?" Then he continued, "Since you entered the Way you have
not visited my grave. Be sure to go there tomorrow and erect a stupa."

612. Unidentified.

613. A local administrator who represented land holders or feudal lords in the capital. He dealt
directly with peasants when he collected taxes.

614. 光明寺; in present-day Zaimokuza, Kamakura-shi. Kōmyōji was an academic temple of
the Pure Land sect.

"What should I write on the stupa?" asked Shōhachi. Ashinuma asked for a writing kit and wrote some Sanskrit letters that Shōhachi could not read. Ashinuma explained, "Letters used in the human world are different from those used in the Land after Death. These letters are the *Kōmyō shingon*—True Words of Kōmyo[615]—and those after them are my posthumous name. I have become an official in the Land after Death.[616] You, on the other hand, practiced evil deeds daily, thinking only of yourself. You abused peasants by overtaxing their straw, bran, wood, and bamboo and then pocketing the money. People hate you because you acted against human nature. You have displeased the Heavenly Emperor, who has broken the tablet of your fortune. [The king of] the Land after Death has written off the tablet of your lifespan, which encourages evil demons to bring you misfortune. Sooner or later, you will definitely be bound by black ropes[617] and become the target of swords. Not only will you lose your life, but also your misfortune will affect your wife and children. Because I pitied you, I made you enter the Way to try to prevent this. But you are ungrateful and have not even visited my grave." Thus strongly pressed, Shōhachi could find no words to excuse himself. He took out some sake and urged his uncle to drink. Although Ashinuma accepted, he was unmoved.

Shōhachi asked, "As an official in the Land after Death what are your duties?" Ashinuma replied, "Anyone in this world with talent, virtue, honesty, and sympathy [for others] will become an official in the Land after Death. But no matter how talented, he will fall into hell if, in the end, he proves to be selfish, greedy, and disloyal to his lords and parents. Also, although he anticipates the next life, he will fall into hell no matter how diligent he practices if he is found guilty of *hōbōzai*,[618] adhering only to his sect and disdaining others.

"I was very merciful, pitied peasants, and was faithful to my lord. I avoided avarice and pursued the honest and correct way. I am now one of the eight *shubunrō*[619] in the Land after Death. I keep records of the good

....

615. *Darani* incantations eliminate many kinds of sins when recited.

616. *Jifu* 地府: the land or earth office; translated here as the Land after Death.

617. Black ropes were used to restrain criminals.

618. 誇法罪: the sin of slandering the Way. Here it refers to slandering other sects including Buddhist ones.

619. 修文郎: an official who handles letters and writing.

and evil deeds of the people in this world.[620] I work under Aoto Saemon Fujitaka[621] and Nago Saemon Masakata.[622] Governor Sagami Yasutoki[623] and Saimyōji Tokiyori Nyūdō[624] were in charge of literary matters, while Kusunoki Masashige[625] and Hosokawa Yoriyuki[626] headed the military. But they are now retired and have become Buddhas. So presently no one holds their former positions. Numerous people from Japan have applied, but none is suitable because they, being selfish and greedy, have been disloyal to their lords and parents. Although I know some of them personally, I am unable to intervene and have to send them to hell."

Shōhachi went on to ask several more questions, which his uncle answered: "How different is this world from the Land after Death?"

"Nothing is especially different. But those dead are void, while the living are substantial."[627]

"Why is it that the soul cannot return to the body [after death]?"

"When an arm is cut off, it feels no pain. Once you leave your form [body] after death, you feel nothing because your body has turned to dust."

Shōhachi continued: "This spring many people died in an epidemic. Why?"

"Being courageous and honest, Miura Dōun[628] and his son, Arajirō,[629] remained in the Land after Death as military officials. But later they planned a revolt. To gather the soldiers they needed to carry out their plot, they conspired with disease demons,[630] who caused the

620. *Tenchi-shikai-hakkyoku* 天地四海八極: heaven, earth, the four seas, and the eight extremities, i.e., the whole world.

621. Aoto Fujitaka 青砥藤綱 worked as a consultant to Hōjō Tokiyori 北条時頼 (1227–1265). See *Hōjōkudaiki* 北条九代記, 8.

622. Nagao Masakata 長尾昌賢 was an elder of Uesugi Noritada.

623. HōjōYasutoki 北条泰時 (1188–1242), the third controller of the Kamakura shogunate.

624. Hōjō Tokiyori Nyūdō 北条時頼 入道 (1227–1263) was the fifth controller of the Kamakura shogunate. *Nyūdo* is a Buddhist title equivalent to priest or monk.

625. 楠正成: a celebrated loyal general of Emperor Godaigo (r. 1318–1339).

626. 細川頼之 (1329–1392); assisted Ashikaga Yoshimitsu, the third shogun of the Muromachi shogunate.

627. Unclear. *Jitsu* 実 means true, real, or substantial.

628. See *OT*, 4-1, n.2.

629. 荒次郎. For the revolt by Dōsun and his son, see *Hōjōgodaiki*, 9.

630. Yakujin 疫神.

epidemic. When the North Emperor[631] found out, he caught them and sent them to hell."

"Can those in the Land after Death harm their enemies in this world?"

"In the Land after Death, they protect the living and pity the dead; they do not like killing. So you cannot kill your enemies here while [in the Land after Death]. If you die of fear upon seeing the ghost of your enemy, you must have been a wicked man. [The king of] the Land after Death sent your enemy to kill you in order to punish you. "Now it is already daybreak. Be sure to be firm in your faith, and do not fall into hell by entering the wrong Way." As soon as Ashinuma finished speaking, he disappeared.

It is said that when Shōhachi finally and completely left the secular world, he was delivered[632] because of his constant recitation of Amida Buddha's name.[633]

7-3 Jumping Katō

When Nagauo Kenshin[634] of Echigo lived in a castle on Mount Kasuga,[635] his military prowess known far and wide, a famous *shinobi*[636] magician arrrived from the Akitsu district[637] of Hitachi Province. Skilled in legerdemain and juggling, he surprised and impressed his audiences. Once, while performing magic,[638] he spied a nearby cow and swallowed it. Everyone was immensely impressed and thought the trick most extraordinary. But someone who had climbed a pine tree to watch the performance from above said of the magician, "He only

---

631. Hokutei 北帝; unidentified.

632. *Raikōōjō* 来迎往生. *Raikō*, or *raigō*, refers to Amida's coming to welcome (his devotee). Amida Buddha, accompanied by bodhisattvas, rides on a white cloud during his devotee's last moments and leads him to the Pure Land. *Ōjō* refers to one's successful deliverance.

633. This story, based on the *Reikishi* 霊鬼志 (蘇韶), borrows from historical tales in the *Hōjōgodaiki, Hōjōrokudaiki,* and *Hōjōkudaiki.*

634. 長尾謙信 or Uesugi Kenshin 上杉謙信. See *OT,* 5-2, n.13.

635. A mountain castle in present-day Kasugayama-cho, Kamietsu-shi, Niigata-ken.

636. 窃盗: stealth; the characters refer to stealing or theft. Here I translate it as someone who performs magic tricks.

637. Unidentified.

638. *Genjutsu* 幻術: an illusory technique or performance.

appears to have swallowed the cow; he is really just [standing] astride it." Upon hearing this, the magician became very angry and immediately conjured an evening glory growing out of the ground. A vine gradually appeared from two leaves and a flower began to bloom as the magician fanned it with a fan. Finally, the vine bore fruit. Everyone gathered around the flower, some tiptoeing to get a better look. When it had grown two feet high, the magician cut the base of the flower. As soon as he did so, the head of the person who had climbed the pine tree fell off. Those who witnessed this thought it most extraordinary but remained skeptical.

When Kenshin heard about the incident, he summoned the magician and questioned him about the details. The magician answered, "I have mastered magic. With a foot-long sword I can jump over any wall, no matter how high, and I can steal into any castle unnoticed. That is why I am called Tobi Katō (Jumping Katō)." [Kenshin] pressed him: "Then show us your trick. Tonight you will bring me a long sword from the chamber of Governor Yamashiro Naoe."[639]

The rooms of the governor's mansion were well lit and well guarded. With unblinking eyes, male and female servants kept watch. A famous guard dog called Murasame barked as soon as he saw anyone suspicious. This intelligent dog never slept at night and roamed the mansion. Strong as a wild boar, it was released to patrol the grounds.

Tobi Katō arrived at the governor's mansion near midnight with one or two baked rice balls. [As soon as he gave them to the dog,] it fell down dead. Katō climbed over the mansion wall and entered the compound. The guards did not notice him because they were asleep. [Katō] left the mansion near dawn, taking with him a long sword from the governor's chamber and carrying on his back an eleven-year-old girl, a servant of the governor's wife. Like the guards, the girl slept so soundly she noticed nothing.

Later Kenshin said to the governor, "Tobi Katō may be very useful for destroying our enemies. But if he were to conspire with them, it would be devastating for us. It would be like keeping a wolf—a misfortune. Quickly kill him."

So the governor decided to catch and kill the magician. Katō guessed

639. The author may be referring to Naoe Kagetsuna; see OT, 5-2, n.12.

his intention and tried to escape, but he was too heavily guarded. So he announced to those [around him], "I will show you something interesting to amuse you" and produced a pair of tin sake bottles. Twenty dolls, about three-inches high, popped out of the bottles and began dancing in a line. While everyone's attention was fixed on the dolls, Katō disappeared, and no one could guess his whereabouts. Later it was rumored that he went to the mansion of Takeda Shingen[640] in Kofu to serve Atobe Daisuke,[641] but in the meantime he stole a copy of the *Kokinshū*.[642] It is said that [Kenshin], tired of Katō's thievery, had him secretly killed.[643]

....

640. 武田信玄 (1521–1573): a celebrated warlord who often fought against Nagauo Kenshin.

641. Atobe was an elder of the Takeda family.

642. 古今集 or *Kokinwakashū* 古今和歌集; compiled in 905 by KinoTsurayuki 紀貫之, this work is the first of the imperial anthologies.

643. See *Kōyōgunkan-matsusho-ketsuyōbon* 甲陽軍艦末書結粟本, 9–13. This story is adopted from the *Kengyōden* 検校伝 (崑崙 奴) and a historical tale from the *Kōyōgunkan-matsusho-ketsuyōbon*.

7-4   How a Spirit of Middle Status[644] Changed Her Form and Pledged Herself to a Man

Oyamada Kinai[645] lived in Kiyosu of Owari.[646] One evening, while he was standing by the gate and looking out, he saw an unusually beautiful woman of seventeen or eighteen years of age walking from west to east. The following evening he saw her again. Kinai was known as a good-looking man in the neighborhood, and the woman repeatedly glanced back at him as if interested in him.

After four or five times the woman finally stopped and approached him. Kinai moved closer, took her hand, and said playfully, "Where are you from and where are you going every evening?" The woman did not hesitate and replied, smiling, "My house is to the west,[647] and I am on an errand to a village in the east." When Kinai tried to lead her past [the gate], the woman did not refuse and appeared very friendly. [Once inside] she spent the night and exchanged pledges with him. As she was leaving near dawn, Kinai asked, "When can you come again?" She replied, "I cannot say because I am in a discreet position." She then recited:

naozari ni
chigiri okite ya
nakanaka ni
hito no kokoro no
makoto o mo mimu[648]

Shall I try to
Reveal your true
Feelings for me

....

644. Chūu 中有: the period of time before souls of the deceased are reborn; translated here as "middle status."

645. Unidentified.

646. Present-day Kiyosucho, Nishikasugai-gun, Aichi-ken.

647. The sun sets in the west and is the location of Amida's Pure Land, so the direction is often associated with the souls of the dead. The mysterious woman's home lies to the west, which indicates a connection with death.

648. A similar poem appears in the *Dairingushō*, Koi, 1.

By casually making
A promise?

Kinai thought to himself, "Indeed, she replies with a poem," and
followed with his own:

ii somete
kokoro kawara ba
nakanaka ni
chigira nu sakizo
koishikaru beki[649]

When you change
Your mind
After your promise,
I will miss the time
Before you made the pledge.

At dawn Kinai and the woman exchanged their farewells, wetting
their sleeves with tears and the morning dew.

Four or five days later, the woman returned to Kinai in the evening.
They became so intimate that the strings of their undergarments[650]
appeared to intensify in color as their pledges to each other deepened.
She began to visit him nightly, which made them wary of the watchful
eyes of the guards.[651]

One day Kinai said to the woman, "We have become so close, there
is no need for pretense. You live nearby, so why don't I come to your
place?" The woman answered, "My place is too small and unsightly to
receive a guest for the night. Besides, since my older brother died, his
wife, the widow, has been living there. I would feel uneasy if you were
to visit me." Kinai agreed, so they continued to keep their relationship
to themselves.

Meanwhile, Kinai discovered that the woman was an expert in

....

649. A similar poem appears in the *Dairingushō*, Koi, 1.

650. *Shitahimo* 下ひも implies sexual intercourse.

651. *Sekimori* 関守: barrier guards.

caring for and sewing[652] kimonos. She came every evening to dress Kinai. She wove hemp yarn into beautiful and delicate cloth and used it to make him a kimono. Everyone who saw the cloth praised it: "There is nothing like it in the world! Even the wave flowers of Tsukushi[653] and the snows of Echigo[654] cannot compare." Later the woman brought a handsome young girl with her who was also skilled at handiwork. For six months, the woman stayed at Kinai's during the day, wove silk with the girl, and dressed Kinai in the kimonos she made. She also took care of various household chores. Kinai observed, "Once you stole here at night; now you remain all day. I wonder if your sister-in-law is suspicious and complains about you." The woman replied, "How long have I been taking care of you? I don't know how you feel about it. I have abandoned everything for you." Kinai was most pleased to hear this. It was quite reasonable for him to love and appreciate her.

One night the woman arrived looking sad and tearful. When Kinai asked the reason, she said, "You have been most considerate and I have relied on you. But something has happened and we must separate, so I am shedding tears of sadness." Surprised at this, Kinai asked, "You and I have pledged that our hearts would not change for thousands of years. Why are we to be separated?" Finally, the woman explained, "I have no reason to hide anything from you now. I was a daughter of Shinshichi of Iio[655]and died of illness when I was seventeen years old. Come tomorrow I will have been dead for three years and my middle status will end. After that I will be reborn [as something else] somewhere else according to my bad karma.[656] Tonight is the last time I will see you." And with this, she burst into tears. Despite knowing that she was a ghost, Kinai was unafraid. Given his affection for her, he was full of sadness and regret. They spent the entire night without sleeping. Finally, the woman took out a silver sake cup and a small vase decorated with pearls and gave them to him, saying mournfully, "Please remember me by these tokens." She then recited:

....

652. *Nuihari* 縫張 refers to the washing of kimono cloth, stretching it as it dries, and finally sewing it into a garment.

653. *Nami no hana* 波の花; i.e., the cloth was as white as the "wave flowers" (salt) of Tsukushi in Kyushu.

654. Present-day Niigata.

655. The Iio family served Oda Nobunaga and Nobukatsu. Shinshichi is unidentified.

656. *Gōin* 業因: suffering or punishment resulting from bad deeds performed during one's lifetime.

omokage no
kawaranu tsuki ni
omoide yo
chigiri wa kumo no
yoso ni naru tomo[657]

Remember me
As the moon is unchanged,
Recollect our pledges
Although they are away
Beyond the clouds.

Kinai offered her a white sash and a fine kimono and recited the following as he tearfully lamented their separation:

machi izuru
tsuki no yonayona
sono mama ni
chigiri tayasuna
waga nochi no yo ni[658]

Waiting for the moon
We nightly made
Our pledges,
Don't wipe them out
Even in the world beyond.

They heard a distant bell ringing and birds calling [as dawn approached]. Kinai caught the woman by the sleeve just as she was about to leave and asked, "Where are you[659] buried?"

"Near Jinmokuji Temple,"[660] she answered and disappeared as soon as she left him.

Unable to bear the separation, Kinai went to the temple but found

....

657. A similar poem appears in the *Dairingushō*, Koi, 1.

658. A similar poem appears in the *Dairingushō*, Koi, 1.

659. Here the term *nakikage* (a shadow that has vanished) refers to a deceased person's body.

660. Jinmokuji Temple 甚目寺 is in present-day Jinmokuji-cho, Umibe-gun, Aichi-ken.

no burial mound for her. "I must keep looking," he said to himself, but his search was in vain. That evening he recited with heavy heart:

tanome koshi
sono tsuka nobe wa
natsu fukashi
izuko naru ramu
mozu no kusaguki[661]

I expected to find
The mound in a field
Of profuse summer grasses,
But it had disappeared like a shrike
Hiding among the grass stems.[662]

Kinai missed the woman so much that eventually he became ill. He took no medicine for days, saying, "I will die and see her soon," and so passed away.[663]

7-5 Pledges Made after Death

Sakurada Gengo[664] lived in Yamato in Nara. He was twenty-five years old and had no wife or parents. His uncle, Tsuda Chōbei,[665] had a twenty-four-year-old son, Hikohachi. The two cousins, Gengo and Hikohachi, were quite close.

One day, when Gengo was on his way home from Tōdaiji,[666] he saw a beautiful carriage attended by a man and two female servants stopped near the Sarusawa pool.[667] [Someone] in the carriage was amusing herself by tossing rice cracker crumbs to the fish in the pool.

....

661. A similar poem appears in the *Dairingushō*, Koi, 1.

662. *Mozu no kusaguki.*

663. The Japanese story is based on a tale in the *Reikishi* 霊鬼志 (王玄之) about a man from Kiyosu. In the original Chinese version, the protagonist recovers from his illness after several days.

664. Unidentified.

665. Unidentified.

666. A temple in present-day Zōshi-cho, Nara. It is the headquarters of the Kegon sect.

667. The pool was made for the release of captured fish in front of the South Great Gate of Kofukuji in Nara.

Beautiful white hands, with nails the color of red copper and fingers as lithe as bamboo shoots,[668] could be seen, as well as a pair of equally elegant slim arms. When Gengo stopped to get a better look, the carriage door opened and a woman gazed out at him for a while before the carriage moved on. Gengo followed until he had entered the compound of the Tsutsui house at the end of Sanjō Avenue.

Infatuated, Gengo fell in love with [the woman in the carriage] at first glance. Through his various connections, Gengo learned that the father [of the woman in the carriage][669] was related to Tsutsui Junshō,[670] and died fighting in the battle of Kawachi. The widowed mother was now living alone with her daughter. Gengo knew the daughter's wet nurse, and asked her [to deliver a message]. The wet nurse hoped to match the young couple, as she was impressed by Gengo's good looks and virtuous character.

Gengo thought of writing a letter to the daughter, but instead composed a poem on a thin piece of colored paper.[671]

> *isaribi no*
> *hono miteshi yori*
> *koromode ni*
> *isobe no nami no*
> *yosenu hi zo naki*

Since I took a glance at you
In the fishing torch's light,[672]
Not a single day has passed
Without waves of my tears
Washing the beach of my sleeves.[673]

---

668. This is one of Asai's favorite expressions for describing a beautiful woman.

669. Hereafter referred to as "the daughter."

670. Tsutsui Junshō 筒井順昭, the father of Junkei 順慶 (1549–1584), controlled most of Yamato Province and died in 1550.

671. *Kōyō* (autumn leaf or red leaf) *gasane* (doubled) *no usuyō* (of thin paper) refers to the two sheets of thin paper doubled with the red one in between, which appears soft pink in color.

672. *Isaribi* 漁り火, "the fishing torch's light," appears dim and faint in the distance, and is used here to express Genko's delicate feelings.

673. *Koromode*, "the sleeves of a robe," evokes the poet's tears wetting his sleeves like waves on a beach. *Dairingushō*, Koi, 1.

When the wet nurse showed Gengo's poem to the daughter,[674] she blushed, put the poem into her sleeve and left.

After a while, Gengo's uncle, Tsuda, heard about the daughter, and thought of making her his son's wife. He asked a middleman to approach the daughter's mother. Since the Tsuda clan was wealthy and descendants of samurai, the widowed mother accepted [the proposal].[675] However, the daughter fell ill and refused to take anything, including water. Her mother said to her, "I have agreed that you will marry Tsuda Hikohachi, so collect yourself. You will be sent to him shortly." The daughter appeared even more sorrowful, and confided to her wet nurse, "I wanted to go to Gengo. I would rather die than go to Hikohachi." She continued to refuse any medicine. Then the sad mother, concurring with the wet nurse's concerns, talked with Gengo and arranged for him to take the daughter. Extremely pleased, Gengo left Nara with the daughter and the wet nurse. The three went to Kōriyama[676] and lived there in hiding.

After a while, Tsuda Chōbei came to the mother asking for the daughter. The mother tearfully made excuses, saying, "Someone has kidnapped her. She is missing along with her wet nurse." Chōbei became very angry and said, "I hear my nephew Gengo was interested in her. He must have taken and hidden her." Meanwhile, the mother died and her younger brother arranged the funeral. Grieving her mother terribly, the daughter and Gengo attended the funeral to bid their final farewell[677] to the deceased.

Tsuda Hikohachi happened to notice the couple at the funeral. He followed them to their home in Kōriyama, and reported back to his father, Chōbei. Immediately Chōbei appealed to Matsunaga,[678] the *shoshidai*,[679] to pass judgment.

....

674. *Himegimi*, "princess," is used in the text.

675. The sentence implies that the mother receives betrothal gifts.

676. 郡山, in present-day Yamatokōriyama-shi, Nara-ken.

677. *Nobe no okuri*, "sending off in the field," is a typical ritual performed for the repose of the deceased's soul.

678. Possibly Matsunaga Hiahide 松永久秀 (1510–1577), who ousted Tsutsui Junkei. For years, Matsunaga ruled Yamato Province from Tsutsui's former castle on Mount Shigi, but later committed suicide when besieged by Oda Nobunaga.

679. 所司代, the director of the samurai office in the Muromachi shogunate. The Kyoto *shoshidai* was in charge of administrative affairs, including the security of Kyoto. In Nara, the office was referred to as *Nara shoshidai* or *Nara bugyō*.

[During the inquiry,] Gengo said, "She belongs to me, as I had a previous contract with her." Tsuda insisted that he had sent for her, with the go-between as his witness. The final judgment decreed, "Since the mother of the daughter passed away, it is hard to know which party is right. It is certain that Tsuda asked for the daughter through the go-between. Gengo may have his own thoughts, but keeping her is against the law. So she should be returned to her rightful place." And so Gengo's wife helplessly was taken away to Hikohachi. Both the daughter and her wet nurse became ill on account of these events and soon passed away. [Before her death, the daughter] likely thought of Gengo and recited a poem.

> saritomo to
> omoishi made no
> inochi sae
> ima wa tanomi mo
> naki mi tozo naru

> Strongly I
> Wished to
> Prolong my life,
> But alas, it has become
> Nothing to depend on.[680]

Hikohachi likewise was very sad. He prayed for the repose of the souls of the daughter and the wet nurse as he made their graves together at a temple.

After his wife was gone, Gengo could not forget her, and felt everything was futile. He regretfully thought, "Since I hear hardly anything about her,[681] she must have fallen for Hikohachi and forgotten me," and recited a poem as he gazed at [the beach].

> nabiku ka to
> mie shi moshio no
> kefuri dani

----

680. *Daringushū*, Koi, 2.

681. *Kaze no tayori*, "letters of the wind," suggests something undependable, like a rumor.

ima wa ato naki
ura kaze zo fuku

The smoke of burning seawater
Appeared as it was
Wafting this way.
Tracing it now is harder
When only the wind blows on the beach.[682]

That evening, someone knocked at his door. Gengo opened the door and saw his wife and her wet nurse, who was holding a bag containing a comb and mirror and said, "My mistress has fled here." Gengo happily led them inside [the house]. With her hairstyle unchanged, the wife did not look at all different. The man and wife were overjoyed, and they tearfully joined hands as she explained, "I haven't forgotten you. I've secretly come here since I can no longer stay at the home of Hikohachi. How happy am I to have my wish fulfilled!" Hearing this, Gengo was overwhelmed with joy and the two spent the night in intimate conversation.

Meanwhile, one of Hikohachi's servants went to Kōriyama and happened to see the wet nurse by the gate of Gengo's house. He ran back home and reported this to Hikohachi, whose father had passed away the previous year. Hikohachi became suspicious at his servant's report, and said, "They were truly dead and have been buried. You must be mistaken since there are many who look like them." The servant insisted, "No, I am not mistaken." So Hikohachi went [to Kōriyama] and peeked through the hedge at Gengo's house. He saw the wife at the mirror putting on her makeup while the wet nurse sat before her. Dashing into the house, Hikohachi confronted Gengo, and said to him, "Both of these women passed away last spring and are buried in the same place. How strange that they are living here!" Feeling most extraordinary, Gengo immediately went to his wife's room. There he found her disappearing with her wet nurse. Then the two men said to each other, "So the ghosts of the two must have come here. From now on there is no animosity between us." Soon Gengo and Hikohachi went to the temple, dug up the grave, and saw the two women lying as if alive, with

682. *Dairingushō*, Koi, 2.

no damage to their appearances. After reburying the women, the two men went to Mount Kōya, where they remained, cultivated their faith in the Way, and never again descended from the mountain.[683]

7-6   Sugenoya Kuemon[684]

During the Tenshō era,[685] the governor of Ise, Tomonori,[686] was called Takei *gosho.*[687] Tomotoki,[688] an assistant to the director of the Ministry of Popular Affairs[689] and a nephew of the governor, was living in Kozukuri[690] of South Ise. He had two samurai, Tsuge Saburōzaemon[691] and Takigawa Saburobei,[692] who were renowned for their superiority in military arts and tactics.

Both Tomonori and Tomotoki lived extravagantly by exploiting their people. They surrounded themselves with sycophants and neglected their duties. Recognizing the bleak fate of the province, Tsuge and Takigawa secretly reported the situation to Lord Nobunaga,[693] who in turn destroyed the governor and his nephew. Both Tsuge and Takigawa were rewarded, and their success earned them respect and prestige.[694]

Meanwhile, there was a revolt in Iga Province.[695] Many vagrants from the neighboring villages gathered and made the castle of Takei their headquarters, from where they plundered the people and peasants

....

683. The story is based largely on *Reikishi,* 柳参軍— a romantic ghost tale that includes some *waka* poems.

684. Possibly Sugenoya Nagase 菅谷長瀬 (d. 1582), one of Nobunaga's close retainers.

685. 1573–1592.

686. Kitabatake Tomonori 北畠具教 (1528–1576). The governorship of Ise was traditionally held by members of the Kitabatake clan.

687. *Gosho* 御所, palace. Here it refers to the castle of the governor.

688. Possibly Kizukuri Tomomasa, third son of Kitabatake Harutomo.

689. The *minbu-shō* 民部省 was in charge of civil affairs, including registration and taxation.

690. Present-day Kizukuri-cho, Kui-shi, Mie-ken.

691. A subject of Kizukuri Tomomasa (*Korōgun monogatari,* 6).

692. Takigawa Katsutoshi, a son of Kizukuri Tomoyasu, served Takigawa Kazumasu of Lord Nobunaga and received the family name of Takigawa (*Kōyōgunkan,* 8).

693. They first informed Takigawa Kazumasu, who passed the report on to Lord Nobunaga.

694. Both became elders of Oda Nobukatsu, a son of Nobunaga (*Kōyōgunkan,* 8).

695. The western part of present-day Mie-ken.

in the districts and villages. [When Lord Nobunaga heard of this,] he sent his army to the castle and said, "Unless we subdue them now, they will make more trouble for the armies of other [lords]." But the castle was defended more strongly than expected, and Tsuge and Takigawa[696] lost their lives in combat. An arbitrator was sent and eventually the rebels returned to following Nobunaga.

One year later, when Sugenoya Kuemon, one of Nobunaga's subjects, was heading to Yamada Village[697] on an errand, he met Tsuge and Takigawa along the way. Sugenoya thought, "Surely I am dreaming, for I heard both Tsuge and Takigawa died last year in the fighting." Suspicious, Sugenoya stopped to speak to them. Tsuge said to him, "It's been a long time since we saw each other. How about some sake?" Tsuge gave his *kosode*[698] to his servant and had him go to a shop and exchange it for some sake. Then he took a piece of straw mat and spread it on the grass by the road. The three men—Tsuge, Takigawa, and Sugenoya— sat on the grass and exchanged cups of sake.

Takigawa began, "In the olden days, someone named Shokatsu Chōmin[699] wanted to start a revolt among the soldiers when Ryūki[700] was killed. But he could not decide whether to do it, and said [to himself], 'If you are poor, you wish for wealth. When you become wealthy, you meet some treachery and wish again to be poor, but that is impossible. So, carrying ten thousand coins at your waist, you fly to Yōshū on a crane.' Thus [in this life], nothing unfolds as one wishes. If you are born a warrior but earn no reward, you leave nothing behind but shame. Many such examples are found in the past and present. We need not look far. For example, Oda Kanbe[701] achieved many great things, but in the end he was executed by Hioki Taizen.[702] Sakuma Uemon[703]

....

696. There is a discrepancy in the text concerning the date of Takigawa's death. While Tsuge died in 1579 during the revolt, Takigawa survived the fighting and died in 1610.

697. Present-day Ōyamada-mura, Ayama-gun, Mie-ken.

698. 小袖, a kimono with smaller, short sleeves that was the everyday clothing for non-elites.

699. 諸葛長民, a man of Yōto (Yangdu) during the Shin (Jin) dynasty (403–376 B.C.). He attacked Kakigen with Ryōki and Ryūyū, but was later killed by Ryūyū (*Shinsho* 晋書, 85).

700. 劉毅, a man of Pei during the Shin dynasty who was attacked by Ryūyū.

701. Oda Kanbe, a son of Tsuda Ichian, or Oda Tanbanokami (*Shinchōkōki*, 2), who assisted Oda Nobukatsu and participated in attacking Ōkōchi Castle.

702. Hioki Taizen, a close retainer of Nobukatsu.

703. A close retainer of Nobunaga.

was faithful to Lord Nobunaga in the beginning, but later was shamed and sent into exile [by the lord]. Thus even the most loyal and praiseworthy subjects [of Lord Nobunaga] fell from grace. What happened to others [who were less successful] is not known."

Takigawa continued, "Governor Shimotsuma of Chikuzen,[704] who was allied with Asakura of Chikuzen, confined himself to a castle in Kinometōge.[705] Asakura later attacked it, and Shimotsuma hid himself in Hiraizumi Temple.[706] There he became an enlightened ascetic and recited the following poem.

azusa yumi
hiku towa nashi ni
nogarezu wa
koyoi no tsuki o
ikade machi mimu

Without drawing[707]
The Azusa bow
I prolonged my life.
Without having escaped
How could I watch tonight's moon?

Thus he buried his name[708] and changed his way to the Buddhist Way. It was most noble when Odera Kanbei,[709] a subject of Governor Araki[710] of Settsu, renounced the material world after having failed to admonish his lord's treasonous ideas. He cut his hair to become a priest,[711] and recited in Chinese 'For forty years I plotted to receive

....

704. Shimotsuma worked in Honganji, managing temple affairs on behalf of Lord Asakura.

705. A pass between present-day Tsuruga-shi, Fukui-ken and Konjō-cho, Nanjō-gun.

706. A temple in present-day Hiraizumi-cho, Tsuruga-shi, Fukui-ken.

707. *Azusa-yumi* 梓弓 is a pillow word (*makurakotoba* 枕詞, a poetic device) for *hiku*, "drawing."

708. That is, he renounced fame and reputation and embraced the Way of Buddhism.

709. Kuroda Yoshitaka (1546–1604) was later called Kanbei. He admonished his lord Murashige for committing treason against Nobunaga, but was imprisoned and released a year later.

710. Araki Murashige was attacked by Nobunaga in 1578 on account of treason. Later he asked the Mōri clan for protection.

711. Kanbei converted to Christianity later in life.

military promotions. All my armor is worn and my bows are all broken. No one knows of my priestly robes. I follow the Buddhist way with my solitary recitation of the wonderful sutra."[712] These two men [Odera and Shimotsuma] served treacherous lords, yet succeeded in avoiding misfortune. Surely this was due to their deep wisdom."

Tsuge said with a smile, "I wonder if [the rebels of Iga] would be embarrassed before us, for their tactics were rather weak."

Takigawa retorted, "We should not talk about them now, as it was a most lamentable occasion. Just have a drink, Sugenoya." After having exchanged several more cups of sake with them, Sugenoya finally asked the two, "Now, gentlemen, since you have been living a courtly life of late, how about composing poems for today's entertainment?"

"Now then," said Tsuge thinking, and he recited a poem.

tsuyu shimo to
kiete no nochiwa
soreka to mo
kusaba yori hoka
shiruhito mo nashi

After perishing
And disappearing
Like the dew and frost,
No one remembers me
But the grass and leaves.

Takigawa followed [with his own poem].

uzumore nu
na wa ariake no
tsuki kage ni
mi wa kuchi nagara
tou hito mo nashi

After being buried
The name may

---

712. *Myōkyō* 妙経, referring to the *Lotus Sutra*.

Still remain.
In the shadow of the dawning moon[713]
No one asks of the decayed body.

After reciting their poems, both Tsuge and Takigawa wiped away their tears. Seeing this, Sugenoya felt strange as he pondered the meanings of the poems' words, and asked them, "I wonder that you, with characters full of courage and valor, shed tears when reciting sad and sentimental poems. It is strange." Ignoring his comment, the two men sighed deeply and remained silent. Meanwhile, more cups of sake were drunk and at length the two stood up and said, "That is all for now." They bid farewell to Sugenoya, walked away for half a *chō*, and suddenly vanished with their servants. Greatly astonished, Sugenoya then recalled their deaths at Iga. The sun was tilting to the side of the mountain and the birds were competing for a perch on the branches. Sugenoya sent someone to the shop to bring back the kimono that was exchanged for sake. As soon as he took it in his hands, it crumbled to dust. It is said that Sugenoya then hastened home, secretly invited a priest, and had him pray for the repose of the two men's souls.[714]

7-7   The Bright Deity of Snow White

In the ninth month of the first year of Chōkō [1487], Shogun Yoshiteru[715] led his army to Gō Province,[716] headquartered himself in Sakamoto, and attacked Takayori,[717] the judge of Rokkaku. Unable to defend his castle,[718] Takayori left it and hid deep in the mountains of Kōga District.[719]

....

713. The first two syllables of *ariake no tsuki* 有明の月 (the moon in the dawn) form the word *ari* (to exist). The poem explains that while a famous name may remain, no one will ask about the buried body it belonged to.

714. The story is based on *SS*, 1-3 華亭逢故人記. Asai portrays the sad lives of the warriors around Lord Nobunaga on account of their faithfulness to their lords.

715. Ashikaga Yoshiteru (1465–1489) was the ninth shogun of the Muromachi shogunate.

716. Ōmi Province, in present-day Shiga-ken.

717. Sasaki Takayori (d. 1520), the lord of Kannonji Castle in Omi Province, often invited the shogun's attacks because of dissension within the clan.

718. Kannonji Castle, which belonged to the Sasaki clan, was in present-day Azuchi-cho, Gamō-gun, Shiga-ken.

719. The mountains of the southern part of Shiga-ken were under the control of the Sasaki clan. The local samurai formed the Kōga school of *ninjutsu*, which is famous for its sudden attacks.

Katada Matagorō,[720] a subject of Takayori, was very valorous and excelled in the military arts. He also was very religious, respecting the gods and Buddhas and wishing for his future deliverance. His daily activities included reading the Kannon chapter of the *Lotus Sutra,* reading one scroll of the *Amida-kyō,* and reciting Amida's name one hundred times. After his lord ran away from his castle, Katada, who had been fighting, finally left the army and fled to the mountain near An'yōji.[721] The sun was setting, and he had no idea where to head. He saw a straw hut near him. It stood in a valley and there was no sign of people inside. While hiding in the hut, Katada heard some twenty horsemen passing by talking to each other, "Really, we don't see even his shadow. He might have run down to the Iga Road." At this, Katada immediately realized that they were after him. But the horsemen did not pay any attention to the hut where he was hiding, and finally went away. While thinking, "Now, I am saved," he heard someone coming toward the hut. Stealthily he peeked through the window and saw a tall, thin woman of forty dressed in an old indigo-colored kimono with a beautiful bag in her hand.

She called to him, "Is Matagorō Katada here?" Katada was still hiding without a word. Laughing, the woman said, "Why are you hiding? There is nothing to fear. I am a messenger of the [Bright] Deity of Snow White in the Kurimoto District of this province. The deity sent me to console you. So don't be doubtful. You have been very merciful, respectful of the gods and Buddhas, and have never been negligent about your future life. The Bright Deity of Snow White is moved by your devotion and has protected you." The woman untied the string of the bag, took out some pieces of baked rice cake, and gave them to Katada [who finally came out of the hut]. She also took out some sake, poured it into a small jar and offered it to him. Katada felt completely content and was very grateful. The woman spoke to him again and said, "I will draw a line on the ground below the window. At about midnight, someone will come and threaten you. But don't be afraid and don't move. After this, you will have nothing to fear in your future life." When she finished speaking, she appeared to leave, and vanished.

<hr>

720. Unidentified.

721. The mountain was behind An'yōji, a temple in Kurihigashi-cho, Kurita-gun, Shiga-ken.

Just as the woman had said, around midnight someone came by giving off a strange light. Katada thought, "This is it," as he peeked out the window. There he saw a demon one *jō*[722] tall with disheveled red hair, crossed white fangs, and two horns like flames. His mouth stretched from ear to ear, and glaring eyes shone from a red face that looked as if it were painted. His claws were like those of a hawk. He wore a leopard skin on his loins and was about to enter the hut, but stopped when he saw the line on the ground drawn by the woman. Frustrated and angry, his glaring eyes turned into lightning. The fire-breathing demon stamped his feet with such a frightful roar that all of Katada's hair stood on end and he lost his soul. Unable to cross the line, the demon stood there in frustration.

A score of horsemen galloping back to the hut said to each other, "We hear Matagorō Katada is hiding in this hut. Everyone advance!" Immediately, the demon ran to them, grabbed one, stomped on his horse, and ate it. The rest of the frightened horsemen fled in confusion.

The night passed, morning dawned, and the demon disappeared. Everything became quiet. When Katada came out of the hut, he saw

....

722. One *jō* is about 3 meters.

the horse's bloody head, as well as human hands and feet scattered on the ground amidst pieces of broken armor, helmets, and swords. So Katada had escaped [from the danger]. He went toward Ise, took a boat from Shirako,[723] and finally arrived in Sei Province.[724] Relying on the Imagawa clan, he hid himself, and nothing further is known about his life.[725]

8-1   Land of the Long Beard

A merchant lived in Kitanoshō of Echizen.[726] Every year, he went to Matsumae[727] to do business with Ezo[728] by trading cotton and hemp for seaweed and dried abalone, which he sold at a profit back home.

One year when the merchant went to Matsumae by boat, the wind suddenly changed and the waves grew large. The sails ripped, the mast broke, and the boat drifted to an island. After resting for a while, the merchant left the boat and walked about five chō[729] to arrive at a village. All the villagers had short hair and long beards and they spoke Japanese. When he went to a house and asked the name of the land, he learned that it was called, "Land of the Long Beard."[730] When he asked about the king, he was informed, "He lives a castle about one ri from here."

When the merchant arrived [at the castle], he passed though a great gate and looked back. The building looked like a king's castle with its stylish gates, high earthen wall, and steep rock foundation. When he stood at the gate, the gatekeepers came out and respectfully led him inside. As soon as he was in the compound, a man in unfamiliar attire ran toward him and showed him into the building. It was an

....

723. The port, in present-day Shirako-cho, Suzuka-shi, Mie-ken, had been prosperous since medieval times.

724. Ise Province.

725. The expression implies that no one knows his whereabouts. The story is based on *Hakuishi*, 馬侍中. Asai narrates the downfall of the Sasaki-Rokkaku clan.

726. An old name for Fukui-shi.

727. Present-day Matsumae-cho, Matsumae-kgun, Hokkaido.

728. Matsumae was a trading center in the Ezo area. Ezo is an old name for Hokkaido. Those who lived in the northern part of Japan and did not follow the Yamato imperial court were called the Emishi 蝦夷.

729. One *chō* is about 99 meters.

730. *Chōshukoku* 長鬚国.

indescribably beautiful palace made of hard black *shitan,*[731] red *karin,* and fragrant white *byakudan,*[732] inlaid with gold, silver, and fragrant *jinkō.*[733] A brocade mat was spread on the floor. Soon the king appeared and announced, "A rare guest from the great land of Japan has come here. Isn't it our good fortune to receive him in our rural land?" At the king's order, all the clan members gathered in the palace. They were well dressed but short in stature, with short hair and long beards. They walked with a slight stoop.

As soon as the merchant took his seat, a richly colored persimmon with green leaves, yellow chestnuts, purple lozenge fruits,[734] red lotus stems, blue pears, and tangerines in a red jar were brought in a crystal bowl on a lapis lazuli tray. A food tray was laden with other kinds of foods such as new wild geese from the field, sea gulls from the marshland, quail, and lark. There also were ginger, blue greens, and bamboo shoots from the valley, as well as dropwort from sacred mountain streams. A tasty grape beverage and the famous Shugai[735] drink were

....

731. A black, hard and heavy wood used for furniture.

732. A fragrant yellowish-white wood used for furniture.

733. Petrified tree resin used as *kōboku* or *jinkō* incense

734. *Murasakihishi* 紫菱, a thorny lozenge fruit grown in marshland.

735. A place during the Han dynasty, in the southeastern part of present-day Kainan-shō. The area produced high quality pearls.

served in cups with floating yellow chrysanthemum and *shuyu* petals. The [king] had a most delicious feast prepared with flavors like nothing the merchant had ever tasted. But the merchant wondered why fish and shellfish from the sea and river were not served.

Soon the king said to him, "I have a daughter. I hope you will stay here. I will arrange the marriage for you. It will be most wonderful for us." The merchant was pleased and replied, "I will follow your wishes." While he was enjoying cup after cup, the moon shone as brightly as broad daylight. "Now is the time for drinking and entertaining," the people at the party said as they began to dance and sing. Meanwhile, the princess appeared accompanied by two scores of ladies in waiting, all adorned with flowers and dressed in long skirts. The scent of *jinja*[736] filled the banquet room. When he looked at the princess, he saw that despite her elegant appearance, she too had a beard. He wondered why and was so upset that he composed an old-fashioned poem.

saku totemo
shibe naku hana wa
ashikara me
imo ga hige aru
kao no uruwashi

Even though blooming,
The flower with no pistil
Is not good.
Your face with a beard
Is beautiful.

At the poem, the king roared with laughter while others laughed holding their bellies. The daughter and the ladies-in-waiting appeared embarrassed. From that night on, the merchant was granted the position of Director of the Wind[737] and the ladies in waiting as well as the princess served him well. Enjoying the glory of his advancement and the respect and admiration of all the people in the land, the merchant

----

736. Civet or musk.

737. Husbands of imperial daughters were commonly appointed to the position of *shifū no chō* 司風の長, which entailed superintending the royal stables and carriages.

became used to his bearded wife and became the father of one boy and two girls in three years.

One day, all his family were sad and his wife especially was lamenting and grieving. Everything was quiet in the castle. When the puzzled merchant inquired, his wife tearfully replied, "My father was summoned by the Dragon King and went to the Dragon Palace. We are all grieving because he will never return." Greatly astonished, the merchant said to her, "With planning there must be a way to avoid this fate. How can I offer myself?" The wife continued, "Without your help, it would be impossible for him to return to this peaceful land. I wish for you go to the Dragon Palace and appeal to the king, saying, 'The Land of the Long Beard, the seventh island of the third channel of the Eastern Sea, is about to decline because of a great misfortune. If you mercifully release its leader, then peace will rightfully be restored to the land.' If you make this strong appeal, the Dragon King will not act cruelly and will change this grief into joy. So please go there as soon as possible." Thus his wife pleaded in her tearful voice. The merchant was moved by her appeal and hurried to the Dragon Palace accompanied by ten samurai, five servants, and two guides, all beautifully attired. After traveling by boat for a while, they finally arrived at a beach with golden and silver sand. The people were formally dressed with crowns, and appeared tall like those in India. They passed the gateway and saw the palace decorated with the Seven Jewels like a temple. When the merchant advanced to the jade steps of the main building, the Dragon King appeared and the merchant respectfully bowed. Soon the king asked him, "So you are the Director of the Wind. Why did you come here?" The merchant explained everything in detail. The king summoned the record-keeper of the sea and had him check the records on the matter. Soon the record-keeper answered, "There is no such country in the realm of the Dragon Castle." The merchant repeatedly explained about the Land of the Long Beard, the seventh island of the third channel. The king again had the record-keeper examine the records. He checked the main ledger and reported, "That is the place where shrimp live. Since they are designated to be the Dragon King's food, some of them were caught yesterday."

Laughing, the Dragon King said to the merchant, "The Director of the Wind is truly a human being who was fooled by the shrimp. Although I am the king of the sea, my daily meals, including live fish and birds, are assigned by the Heavenly King, and the amount and number are determined by him. Even a human, if he eats more lives than assigned by the Heavenly King, surely will be punished with misfortune. So we certainly cannot eat freely, but only the assigned amount. But since you have come all the way here, I cannot break your heart. I will reduce the amount of food for today." After saying this, he went inside the palace and told an officer in charge of food[738] to show the merchant to the kitchen.

There the merchant saw intestines of hornless deer, palms of bear, monkey limbs, the water mirror of the rabbit,[739] the five kinds of shavings,[740] the seven kinds of fruit,[741] flower-shaped turtle feet, *hōō*[742] marrow, lion's fat, *seibō*,[743] and white honey. All kinds of rare foods from both sea and mountain were prepared there and the sight was beyond description. The merchant also saw gold and silver cooking pots and a basket filled with several prawns and lobsters. [One of them] was as long as three feet and dark purple with long whiskers. Looking at the merchant, it shed tears like rainfall and constantly jumped up as if begging, "Please save us." The head officer of the kitchen said, "This is the king of them." Hearing this, the merchant shed tears of chagrin. The Dragon King told another officer to release the lobsters and sent the merchant back to Japan.

At nightfall the merchant finally arrived at Cape Suzu in Noto Province.[744] After he went ashore and looked back, the officer who had accompanied him turned into a great dragon, split the waves, and hid itself at the bottom of the sea. When the merchant returned home, he told the story of his experiences and handed it down in writing.[745]

....

738. *Shizen* 司膳, one in charge of trays (food).

739. Unidentified.

740. The shavings of five kinds of dried fish, including eel, octopus, abalone, bonito, and brim.

741. Unidentified, but it might include fruits such as plum, peach, and chestnut.

742. The marrow of the imaginary *hōō* 鳳凰, "phoenix"; refers here to bone marrow in general.

743. Unidentified.

744. The tip of the northeast part of Noto Peninsula, in present-day Suzu-misaki, Suzu-shi, Ishikawa-ken.

745. The story is based on *Dakukōki*, 大足初有士人云々. Asai relates a strange tale about rare foods in the context of trade in the northern province.

8-2 Killing the Evil Deity

Once there was a small shrine in a field in the nKasama District of Jō Province.[746] Behind it was Mount Tsukuba, where the shade of the trees made it dark even in daytime. In front of the shrine, an algae bloom covered the surface of a deep pool. Constantly cloudy and drizzling, the shrine looked intimidating. Everyone in the vicinity was so afraid of the shrine's wild deity that whenever passing by they made offerings of sake, rice, and other foods obtained in the neighboring villages. Otherwise, the deity's curse would be immediate and the thick clouds suddenly would gather [and explode] with violent wind and rain.

During the Meitoku era,[747] Priest Shōkai of Tanikumi Temple in Mino Province[748] came and rested in front of the shrine. Devoted to the Way, the priest thought, "I will travel to the northlands[749] for my practice and go to the Ashikaga School in Sagami."[750] Soon he left his temple, headed to the north, and finally arrived in Jō Province. As a traveling monk he had nothing in his bag. He paid his respects to the shrine's deity by reciting a sutra as his offering, and left. When he had walked about ten *chō*, he lost his way. While trying this and that direction, a great wind suddenly arose, blowing up the sand and pebbles. Dark clouds and fog covered the area and the priest felt like he was being chased. Frightened, he turned and looked back to see about two hundred strange demon-like creatures[751] coming after him. "So I am about to lose my life on account of these demons. I cannot help that," thought the priest. He single-mindedly recited the *fumonbon* chapter, or *Kannon Sutra*,[752] and ran away as fast as possible. Meanwhile the wind ceased as the sky cleared of clouds, and no one was chasing after him. He barely was able to run to the shrine of the Bright Deity of

....

746. Hitachi Province, Ibaraki-ken.

747. 1390–1394.

748. In Gifu-ken.

749. *Hokuriku* 北陸 included Wakasa, Echizen, Kaga, Noto, Ecchū, Echigo, and Sado.

750. The Ashikaga School, in present-day Ashikaga-shi, Tochigi-ken, was famous for Confucian studies during the Muromachi period.

751. *Iruiigyō* 異類異形.

752. The *fumonbon* chapter of the *Lotus Sutra*, also known as the *Kannon Sutra*, extols the merits of Bodhisattva Kannon.

Kashima.[753]

As soon as he sat before the altar [of the shrine's worship hall], he recited the *Hannyashingyō*[754] seven times and the *fumonbon* chapter three times. He prayed, "Was it because the shrine's evil deity chose not to accept my offering that he caused the violent wind and rain? Or was it because of some fault of my own? Please, Bright Deity of Kashima, let me know the reason." After sunset, he lay down [before the altar] and fell asleep in exhaustion.

In his dream, the inner part of the altar opened, the brocade curtain was raised, and the jade screen was rolled up halfway. There, the Bright Deity was sitting flanked by other deities of lesser shrines, who took their positions according to their rank. With tall taper candles inside and outside, the altar was as bright as broad daylight. The awestruck priest went down to the garden and paid his respects by placing his forehead on the ground. Suddenly, a man dressed in red with a tall *eboshi* hat appeared by the steps to the worship hall and said to the priest, "You made offerings to the deity of this shrine, who was pleased to accept them with grace and compassion. What you requested in your prayer will be granted shortly." As soon as he finished, the man entered

....

753. Kashima Shrine in Kashima-shi, Ibaragi-ken was popular among the warriors of the northeast dating back to the Kamakura period.

754. The *Hannyakyō* distills the wisdom of the *Heart Sutra* into 262 characters.

[the altar]. After a while the priest heard a score of men running into the sky and bringing an old, white-haired man wearing a tall black hat and a pair of blue *hakama* trousers. The old man was placed in the garden [before the altar]. Then a voice came from the inner part of the altar, saying, "You are a local deity who has not protected his people. More than that, you have deliberately annoyed and troubled this ascetic traveler, who paid his respects by making Buddhist offerings, superior to all others in this world. But you tried to bother him and even to kill him. You certainly cannot escape from your bad deeds."

An officer [appeared] and warned and pressed him. Putting his forehead on the ground, the old man made an excuse saying, "Even though I am a deity of a rural shrine, long ago I was taken by a great poisonous serpent which robbed me of the shrine. And now I live in the root of a tree by the shrine. Being weak and without a place of my own, I am unable to control the great serpent and have forgotten my job of protecting the world and the people. So in past years, all the evil deeds of bringing rainstorms, creating clouds, and causing fog and violent winds while taking the offerings from visitors, were done by the serpent, and they are not my fault."

The officer further pressed him, "If that is so, why didn't you appeal?" The old man said, "The great serpent has been in this world for a long time. He sometimes changes his form and disturbs the people. Other times, he causes evil deeds. His mysterious powers are indescribable. All the demon deities in the mountain and evil spirits in the fields have joined him, as well as the poisonous snakes. If I come here to make an appeal, he will catch me and not even let me poke my head out of my place. I was able to come here because you summoned me." The voice from the inner shrine said again, "Officers, quickly go there and catch the great serpent!" The old man said again, "Even the officers won't be able to catch him because of his powers and all those who have joined him. Unless you send a great army of divine soldiers, you will not subjugate him so easily." [The voice] replied, "In that case, send a general with five thousand soldiers to the shrine in the field."

About three hours later, scores of soldiers carried the head of a white serpent on large logs into the garden before the altar. The serpent's head was as big as a five-*koku* jar.[755] It had two sharp horns,

---

755. Five *koku* is about 180 liters.

ears as big as *mino* baskets,[756] a shaggy mane, a mouth extending to the back of its head, and fierce-looking red eyes like painted mirrors that were still open after death. The officers said to Priest Shōkai, "The Bright Deity, the first deity of this country, listened to your appeal and judged well. You must be content. Now, quickly [leave]." Saying this, they made the priest stand up and he paid his respects. Then he awoke from his dream. He thought it most unusual that he was perspiring yet the hair on his body was standing on end.

After daybreak, the priest returned to the [shrine in the field]. He saw that the building and the *torii* were burned to ashes, with fallen trees and uprooted grass strewn across the grounds. When he dropped by the neighboring village and inquired, all the villagers said, "After midnight, we heard voices fighting in the violent rain and wind while the thunder crashed loudly. It was most frightening. A fire burning in the black clouds consumed the shrine and reduced the *torii* to ashes. We saw a great serpent as long as twenty *jō* lying dead without its head, and countless dead snakes five to three *jō* long lying on the ground, one on top of another. They smelled terrible." The priest learned that the time of the fire corresponded with the time of his dream. After this, the priest went to Ashikaga in Sō Province and told his story.[757]

8-3 Making a Pledge through Poems

Nagatani Hyobu-shōsuke[758] was living near Ichijō-modoribashi.[759] He was twenty-one years old, very good looking, and amorous. Highly talented, he always was interested in studies and often attended lectures by the Confucian scholar Kitabatake Shōsetsu,[760] who lived in the eastern part of Minami Madenkōji, Sanjō-bōmon.[761]

There was a wealthy family in the neighborhood of the *shingikan*.[762]

---

756. Baskets made of bamboo used to winnow grain.

757. The story is based on *SS*, 3-2 永州野廟記, which extols the superiority of the popular Kashima Shrine.

758. The title for a third rank officer of the *hyōbushō* (military office).

759. "Returning bridge," a bridge at Ichijō-Horikawa.

760. Unidentified.

761. Near Yanagibaba, Chūō-ku, Kyoto-shi.

762. The *shingikan* 神偽官 controlled all the affairs of the local shrines. The neighborhood referred to was in present-day Marutamachi, Nishinotōin, Kamigyō-ku, Kyoto-shi.

The family's ancestor was related to the Yamana clan.[763] He had left the military class and came to the capital, and was leading a quiet life and didn't associate with high-ranking families. The family had a daughter, Makiko, who was about sixteen years old. She was incomparably beautiful and talented in painting and making flowers from silken thread.[764] Although less talented in poetry, she always was inclined to it. With deep feelings, she appreciated flowers and the moon. She consoled her lonely heart by making poems while admiring red leaves in the autumn and snowy evenings [in the winter].

One day, with his book at his breast, Nagatani went out to Madenokōji. He rested by the earthen wall of Makiko's house and looked into the garden through a hole in the broken wall. It was a spring day when he saw the garden's thread-like willow branches mixed with cherry blossoms, and the *hiwa* and *kogara*[765] birds rivaling each other with their singing. The daughter was seated near the edge

....

763. A well-known *daimyō* (feudal lord) family who owned the nine provinces during the Muromachi period.

764. *Hana-musubi*, "flower-tying," is the craft of tying thread into flower shapes, which are then used to decorate furniture. It was a skill widespread among young women of high-ranking families.

765. The *hiwa* is a bluish-yellow bird slightly smaller than a sparrow; the *kogara* has a black head with a white belly.

of the sitting room [by the garden], where she was sewing a *kosode*.[766]
She stopped sewing as she tilted her head and recited a poem.

> *hokorobite*
> *saku hana chiraba*
> *aoyagi no*
> *ito yori kakete*
> *tsunagi todo meyo*

> When the blooming[767]
> Cherry blossoms scatter,
> I should stop them
> By tying the threads
> Of blue willow leaves.[768]

As soon as he saw her and listened to her poem, he was completely infatuated. He was so enthralled that he could hardly walk, and kept staring while filled with unbearable yearning. Without knowing this, Makiko went down to the garden, walked around the earthen wall, and met his eyes. She was so moved by his beautiful looks that she thought she would never share a pillow[769] with anyone but him. And like autumn leaves showing red in a sudden *shigure*,[770] she expressed her feelings by reciting a poem.

> *waga kado no*
> *soto moto ni sakeru*
> *unohana o*
> *kazashi no tameni*
> *oru yoshi mo gana*

> It would be nice
> To break off

---

766. See *OT*, 7-6, n.15.

767. *Hokorobu*, "to tear," here also means "to bloom."

768. *Aoyagi*, young blue or green willow leaves, are used to symbolize youth and suppleness.

769. *Makura o narubi*, "lining up pillows."

770. A type of light rain that falls during late autumn and early winter.

An *unohana*[771]
Blooming outside my gate
To decorate my hair.

Unable to suppress his feelings, Nagatani took out his portable writing kit,[772] wrote two poems on a sheet of rough paper,[773] and threw it into the garden with a stone.

inochi sae
mi no owari niya
narinu ramu
kyōkurasu beki
kokochi koso sene

I wonder
If the end of my life
Might have come.
I don't feel
It will last today.[774]

irisomuru
koiji wa sue ya
tōkaramu
kanete kurushiki
waga kokoro kana

The future
Path of our love
May be farther.
Thinking of that,
My heart already suffers.[775]

....

771. The small *unohana* 卯の花, or *utsugi* flower, which often blooms on hedges in the fourth and fifth months. Here it is compared with the handsome Nagatani.

772. *Yatate* 矢立.

773. *Zasshi*, rough paper for miscellaneous use, was not suitable for writing poems on.

774. The poem suggests Nagatani's anxiety about his new love life. *Dairingushō*, Koi, 2.

775. *Dairingushō*, Koi, 1.

After reading his poems a few times, Makiko's yearning for him increased, and she took out a *tanzaku*,[776] wrote a poem on it, and tossed it [to him] with a stone.

ajiki nashi
tare mo hakanaki
inochi mote
tanomeba kyō no
kure o tanomeyo

Every one
Has a futile life.
If you wish
For something,
Depend on this evening.[777]

Nagatani took her poem home and longed for the evening.

In the evening, he went to the daughter's [house] and walked around the wall. A branch of cherry blossoms was protruding over the wall with a blue sash hanging down like a rope. Getting the idea, he climbed over the wall with the help of the sash and stood [in the garden]. The soft spring moon rising over the eastern mountain cast shadows of the flowers into the garden. As the flowers' wafting fragrance filled the air, he felt as if he were outside the human world, like in tales of the Three and Ten Hermits' Islands.[778] Just like a man facing a secret meeting, he felt terribly anxious.[779] The daughter was waiting for him under a tree and recited a poem as soon as she saw him.

utsutsu tomo
omoi sadamenu
au koto o
yume ni magae te

---

776. 短冊, an oblong card on which poetry is usually written.

777. *Dairingushō*, Koi, 1.

778. *Mitsu no shima* 三の島 and *tō no kuni* 十の州, legendary islands that are the utopian home of hermits and recluses.

779. *Minoke yodachite*, "bodily hair standing up," is usually used to indicate feelings of fear.

hito ni kata runa

Unable to determine
If this meeting
Is real or unreal,
Take it as a dream
And repeat it to no one.[780]

He replied with his poem.

mata nochi no
chigiri wa shirazu
niimakura
tada koyoi koso
kagiru naru rame

Not knowing of
Our future pledge
Of the new pillow,[781]
It may be limited
To only this evening.

At this, Makiko said to him grudgingly, "Having been so close, I thought that our pledge tonight would last for a thousand years. How can you feel so indecisive? I pledge my life to you and would never dream of changing my mind. Even if my parents were to pressure me with their warnings, I would not regret even losing my life for you. Please recall Lord Shunzei's poem,[782] which says:

tanomazu wa
shikama no kachi no
iro o miyo
aisomete koso
fukaku naru nare

....
780. *Dairingusho*, Koi, 2.

781. *Niimakura*, "new pillow," connotes sleeping with someone for the first time.

782. See Fujiwara Shunzei's poem in *Shin zokukokinshū*, Koi, 3.

If you can not rely on
Our relationship
Look at the dark color of Shikama.[783]
It becomes darker
By repeating dying.[784]

Soon she told her maidservant[785] to bring some sake, which she urged him to drink. As the night deepened, it became quieter. He asked in a whisper, "Whose house is this?" She began to explain, "My parents are related to the Yamana clan, but left the military class. They are still quite wealthy, however. Even though there are many *daimyō* lords in the family, they do not associate with any of them. They are living very discreetly, as if hiding from the world. As I am their only daughter, they love me so much that they built this separate garden with a room for enjoying the spring flowers and autumn moon. They live a short distance from here." Hearing her story, Nagatani relaxed a little and recited a poem.

yo ni more mu
nochino ukina o
nageku koso
auyo mo tae nu
omoi nari kere

As I grieve for our
Floating name[786]
Leaking to the future world,
I feel more unbearable
For tonight's meeting.

Makiko responded with her poem.

----

783. *Kachi* or *kasshoku*, a dark indigo dye that was produced in Shikama port (in present-day Himeji-shi), appears darker with repeated application.

784. *Aisome*, "indigo dyeing," contains the words *ai* (love) and *some* (dyeing). The poem suggests that the couple's relationship will deepen as they repeatedly see each other. *Dairingushō*, Koi, 2.

785. *Miyuzukue*, "imperial court service," here refers to a private maidservant.

786. *Ukina*, "floating name," is used to refer to a scandalous love affair.

nagarete wa
hito no tame ukina
tori kawa
yoshi ya waga mi wa
shizumi hatsu tomo

I don't mind
Losing my life
By sinking in the flow[787]
When I exchange
My floating name for you.[788]

Thus talking, they enjoyed themselves by sharing the sleeves of their robes as new pillows. Meanwhile, the day broke. Their conversation was still not exhausted when they heard the temple bell and the early birds' noisy singing. Their tears on parting were the [morning] dew that becomes clouds, and finally rainfall, as on Mount Yōdai.[789] He recited a poem.

chigiri oku
nochi o matsu beki
inochi kawa
tsuraki kagiri no
kesa no wakare ji

After our pledge,
I should wait for another time,
Yet it is most difficult
On the way after

---

787. *Nagarete* (flow) continues the "floating name" figure of speech, and *kawa* (river or stream) plays on *kawasu* (to exchange). Thus, the sense is, "I don't mind if I lose my reputation in exchange for you."

788. *Dairingushō*, Koi, 1.

789. Referring to Mount Miko 巫山, in Shisen-sho, China. The clouds over the mountain frequently produce rain. A legend says that King Jō of So once dreamed of a divine woman from Mount Miko who told him that she would become a cloud in the morning and rain in the evening (*Yōshō* 謡抄, Tōru).

My parting[790] of this morning.[791]

She responded with her poem.

kurabete wa
waga mi no kata ya
masaru beki
onaji wakare no
sode no namida wa

In comparison,
My sadness is more
In the same parting
Of this morning,
With tears on my sleeves.

In the morning Nagatani followed the cherry branch[792] [to get over the wall] and went home. Unable to concentrate on his studies, he longed for evening. Thus he went to see the daughter night after night.

One day Nagatani's father said to him, "I wonder if you have become tired of studying. Leaving home in the morning and returning in the evening is the right way to pursue studies. But these days you leave home in the evening and return in the morning. I am afraid you have been doing frivolous things, like breaking through someone's wall, jumping over a hedge, and behaving improperly. If you are exposed to the world, your life will sink into the mud, your name will be spoilt by the dirt, and you will be completely ignored by the world. If the woman you are seeing is of high birth, her family will be shamed by you. Not only will her life be destroyed, but also your sinful deeds will definitely damage our family. This is most grave. From now on, you cannot go outside." Saying this, his father confined him to a room as punishment.

Meanwhile, every night the daughter was waiting for him in the flower garden, and did not see him for more than twenty days. She

....

790. *Wakare ji*, "parting ways," refers to the fact that he will be sad after parting from her.

791. *Dairingushō*, Kol, 2.

792. He leaves the garden in the same way he entered.

thought, "Just like the unsettled water of the Asuka River,[793] people's minds are changeable. He may have found someone else to see and forgot me. Or he may be very ill." She sent a child[794] to find out about him and finally learned of his situation. She found that [even the child] could not talk with anyone who had seen him [Nagatani] in confinement. At the news, she became seriously ill in bed and would not even take water. At times, her thoughts and speech were deranged. Her looks and complexion soon deteriorated, as she constantly was sad and tearful. Her parents obtained all kinds of medicines and prayed in vain to the gods and Buddhas. Since it seemed that nothing in this life would help her, the grieving parents asked her, "Do you have something on your mind?" But they did not get a proper reply. Finally finding Nagatani's poems [written on the pieces of paper] at the bottom of her box, the surprised parents questioned the child, who told them everything.

"No matter who it may be, when our dear daughter is in love, nothing is impossible," said the parents. They selected a go-between, who explained everything to Nagatani's father. The father said, "My son is talented. He could master his studies, serve as a government official, and succeed me. He should not degrade himself by taking just any woman as his wife. It is not yet too late." Makiko's parents further insisted, saying, "As we heard only lately about your son, he may still be unknown [in the world], but he will be a successful man in the future. If he marries our only daughter, whom else would we seek for our successor? As our son, he will inherit everything we have." They immediately selected a suitable day and received Nagatani as their son-in-law. The excited daughter completely recovered from her illness. Nagatani recited a poem.

> *inochi areba*
> *mata mo afuse ni*
> *meguri kite*
> *futatabi kawasu*
> *kimi ga temakura*

....

793. The expression refers to a poem in the *Kokinshū*, and means that everything in this life is changeable like the flowing Asuka River: Its water may be deep one moment and become shallow the next.

794. *Warawa*, "child," here refers to a young servant.

Having prolonged
For my life,
I come and see you again
As I exchange and use
Your arm as a pillow.[795]

The happy daughter replied with her poem.

mikazuki no
warete mishi yo no
omokage o
ariake made ni
narini keru kana

When I saw you first
It was the night
Of the crescent moon,
But now it has become
The moon in the dawning sky.[796]

Thus the couple now could speak intimately,[797] no longer worrying about a secret guard.[798]

Meanwhile, the Ōnin War broke out because of power struggles between the Hosokawa and Yamana clans. Numerous houses, big and small, were burnt down in the city of Kyoto. Many samurai soldiers came up to the capital, Kyoto, where the atrocities committed by them were beyond description.

Nagatani's wife was captured by the soldiers of Yoichi[799] of Yakushiji.[800] Since she was beautiful, some of them tried to violate her.

....

795. *Temakura*, "hand pillow" or "arm pillow," refers to lying down with one's hand or arm for a pillow.

796. The poem remarks on how time has passed and expresses Makiko's happy feelings. *Dairingushō*, Koi, 2.

797. *Hiyoku*, "a pair of wings," here refers to the couple.

798. *Shinoburu sekimori*, the secret guard that kept watch for rendezvous.

799. Yoichi Motonaga.

800. Unidentified. Possibly a member of Yokushiji Motoichi's family.

At that time, she called out, "Just kill me. I would never surrender to the dirty men of the countryside!" The angry soldiers stabbed her to death.

Meanwhile, Nagatani escaped and hid himself [outside Kyoto]. When he returned to the city after conditions became quiet during the winter, he found that his house was burnt down. He went to his wife's place and found no one. His wife's father, who had belonged to the Yamana clan, had died in battle, while robbers had killed the mother. Sadly and in tears, Nagatani stood alone in his wife's room. That night, as in a dream, Makiko returned home. "What happened?" Calling out to one other, they took each other's hands tearfully. The wife said, "After we were separated, I was caught by the soldiers and lost my life. It was most pitiful that my body was left alone by the roadside with no one to take care of it. The Heavenly Emperor pitied me, who had lost my life on account of my chastity, and was much moved by your feelings for me. He allowed me to come here tonight to see you." Even though sad, Nagatani felt joyful to see his wife again, and tears fell like raindrops. Both talked throughout the night and at dawn he tearfully recited a poem.

omowazu yo
mata meguri au
tsuki kage ni
kawaru chigiri o
nageku beshi towa

I never thought
I would see you again,[801]
Nor grieve for
The change of our pledge
In the shadow of the moon.[802]

His wife replied with her poem.

---

801. The expression *mata meguri au*, "again meeting," can be used with *tsuki*, "moon," to describe the moon completing its cycle and returning again. I translate it here non-figuratively as Nagatani seeing his wife again.

802. *Dairingushō*, Koi, 2.

yuku sue o
chigirishi yori zo
urami mashi
kakaru beshi tomo
kanete shiri seba

Since we pledged
Our future,
We would have lamented more
If we knew
It would be like this.[803]

She tearfully bade her farewell and disappeared like a shadow.

After that, Nagatani became more pious and confined himself to a temple on Higashiyama. But soon he became ill and finally passed away. All the people who heard this [story] thought it most pitiful and extraordinary.[804]

8-4 A Ghost Appeared and Met a Priest

Sumiya Fujikurō,[805] who was descended from the Kusunoki clan[806] and in the service of Hatakeyama Uemonsa Yoshinari,[807] won immeasurable glory in the battle of Dakeyama.[808] In the end, he died fighting and left behind an honorable name. His son, Fujishirō,[809] who also served Yoshinari, was slain by an arrow shot from the camp of Hatakeyama

....

803. Makiko's poem sounds more fatalistic and resigned than Nagatani's. *Dairingushō*, Koi, 2.

804. The story is based on *Kingaoshinwa* 金鰲新話, 2 李生窺墻伝. Asai changes the place and time to Kyoto during the Ōnin War. The original Chinese poems have been replaced by Japanese *waka* poems.

805. Unidentified.

806. This was the clan of Kusunoki Masashige 楠木正成 (1294–1336), a samurai who fought alongside Emperor Godaigo against the Kamakura shogunate. Kusunoki was famous for his loyalty to the emperor (Ōninki 応仁記).

807. Hatakeyama Yoshinari 畠山義就 (1437–1490), the son of Mochikuni, whose dispute with his cousin, Masanaga, over who would succeed as *kanrei* triggered the Ōnin War.

808. In present-day Tondabayashi-shi, Osaka. Yoshinari used the mountain as his headquarters when he fought against Masanaga in 1461.

809. Unidentified.

Saemon Masanaga[810] at Goryō Riding Ground[811] in the first year of the Ōnin War [1467]. Because both father and son had served Yoshinari faithfully, the manor of Kadoma in Kawachi[812] Province was offered to Fujishirō's five-year-old brother, Fujitsugu, and his mother, Fujikurō's widow. The two lived together in the manor.

Around this time, a priest on a pilgrimage happened to arrive in the vicinity. It was after sunset, and the priest was in the village seeking shelter for the night. While stopping to rest on a path between rice paddies near Kadoma village, he heard the faint sound of a flute. As the priest was slowly making his way towards the sound, he happened upon a most beautiful boy of fourteen or fifteen coming from the opposite direction. He was dressed in white, with his hair divided into two loops atop a lightly powdered face with blackened teeth.[813] The boy, with his fair complexion and thinly drawn eyebrows, saw the priest and asked, "Why are you standing there?"

"I am an ascetic on pilgrimage, and have stopped here after sunset to seek shelter for the night." The boy smiled slightly and said, "In today's world of unrest, how will you find anyone willing to let you stay? In these times, everyone doubts the other. You appear to be a priest, but they may suspect you are part of some plot by their enemies. Do not lose your life by acting foolishly and attracting suspicion. Since it's getting dark, why don't you come and spend the night in my room?" Saying so, he led the priest to a house. The boy said, "The front gate keeper may have already retired. Come this way." Then he stealthily led the priest through a smaller gate at the back of the house. "This is the room I usually use," the boy said, and he showed the priest into a room that looked like a Buddhist shrine, with three images, including one of Amida Buddha,[814] and three sutras of the Pure Land school on the dais before them. Twelve taper lights[815] were burning with the faint

....

810. Hatakeyama Masanaga 畠山政長 (1442–1493), a cousin of Yoshinari, was adopted by Mochikuni and later fought against Mochikuni's son, Yoshinari.

811. In present-day Kamigoryō-Baba-machi, Kamigyō-ku, Kyoto-shi.

812. In the northern part of present-day Kadoma-shi, Osaka-fu.

813. Blackening the teeth was a custom among aristocrats starting in the Heian period, and the practice was adopted by married women in the Edo period, mainly to avoid cavities.

814. Amida Budda is often depicted being flanked by the bodhisattvas Kannon and Seishi.

815. *Jūnigō* 十二行, representing the twelve bodhisattvas.

scent of incense. Some offerings had been placed in front of the spirit tablets containing the names of the deceased. Everything appeared very noble. Feeling pious, the priest read the sutras and recited the names of the Buddha for a while.

The boy said, "Since it is evening, I should have someone prepare food for you. But everything is quiet now and I have no means of preparing any food. Therefore I will give you the offerings to satisfy your hunger and fatigue from traveling." The priest said, "It is no matter," and divided the rice offering into two halves and shared it with the boy.

After a while, the priest asked the boy, "Whose house is this? And what is your name?" The boy replied, "My father was Sumiya Fujikurō, a very brave and honorable samurai who died in the battle of Dakeyama last year. Even though my younger brother and I succeeded him, we were both too young and so we live with my mother. My name is Fujishirō. Letting you stay here tonight is not a light karmic relation. Should I lose my life, I do hope you will pray for my future," the boy said, finishing his story in tears.

Hearing the boy's words, the priest said, "Why do you say that? You are still young like a bud that is not yet ready to bloom, and you will be very successful in the future. I am much older than you, and even I don't know that my life will end tonight." But the boy disagreed, saying, "No. Being born to a military family and expected to attain glory and leave my name behind, my life will be as short-lived as the morning dew. Your life may vanish and you cannot wait for the evening. I say this because life is not dependable. Please, write down my name in the *kakochō*[816] you have with you." Saying this, the boy took out an ink box. The priest replied, "You do not understand. You aren't yet grown. Why do you wish to do this when you know nothing? Usually only the names of the deceased are recorded in the register. But it would be too rude to reject your wish. I will pray for your future military success by recording your name while you are still alive." With a smile, the boy said, "Please do. I will leave everything to you." As soon as he finished speaking, the look in his eyes suddenly changed, and his breathing appeared to be difficult. "What do you want now? I understand." Saying this, the boy grabbed the long sword by him, appeared to leave through the sliding door, and vanished. The shocked priest went out of the room, but saw no one and

---

816. 過去帳, a temple register in which the names and ages of the deceased are recorded.

heard nothing. He felt strange, but since he had no thought of leaving and returning on his way, he spent the night in the shrine room.

The following morning, when the family members, including Fujikurō's widow, entered the Buddhist room, they were surprised to see a thin, dark priest sitting alone in front of the Buddhist images. They pressed him, saying, "What kind of old thief are you? Are you some incarnation of the old fox, impersonating [a priest]? Everyone, get him and tie him up." Unperturbed, the old priest began speaking to them calmly, "Please be quiet and listen to my story." He explained everything that had happened the previous night.

"So, the ghost of Master Fujishirō must have appeared." Saying this, the family examined the offerings and found that the half eaten by the priest was gone, but the other half was untouched and set before the spirit tablet. The mother prostrated herself before the tablet and cried out tearfully, saying, "Today is the one hundredth day since my son died, shot by an arrow at Goryō Riding Ground in Kyoto on the nineteenth day of the first month. It sounds to me that his soul still suffers." Saying this, the mother was so overcome with grief that she shaved her head, became a nun with a priest's help, and prayed for the deliverance of her son.[817]

8-5   The Figures on a Screen
     that Danced and Sang

Hosokawa Ukyōdaibu Masamoto,[818] who supported Lord Minamoto Yoshitaka to become the Great Barbarian-Subduing General,[819] obtained great power and prestige.

One day, after having drunk a great deal of sake, he returned home and lay down. A little while later, a strange noise awakened him. Lifting his head from his pillow, he saw next to him a colorful screen depicting beautiful women and young boys amusing themselves. Then the five-inch tall women and boys left the screen and began to sing and

---

817. Asai adapts the original story from *Sangokudenki* 三国伝記, 12-15 and *Sorori monogatari* 曽呂利物語, 2-5 into a Buddhist one by placing it in the context of the Ōnin War.

818. Hosokawa Masamoto 細川政元 (1466–1507), a son of Katsumoto, overcame Hatakeyama Masanaga, who supported Shogun Yoshitane and helped Ashikaga Yoshizumi 足利義澄 (1480–1511) to become the eleventh shogun of the Muromachi shogunate.

819. *Seiitaishōgun* 征夷大将軍.

dance, clapping their hands and tapping their feet. Masamoto carefully listened to their faint voices, which sang:

"In this world, their grudging for spring lingers at daybreak. Like the moon on a spring evening covered by clouds, flowers [are scattered] by the wind,[820] and the shadows [of the flowers] on the jade water are blown [by the wind] and gone."

The doll-like figures repeatedly sang the song as they danced. Raising his voice, Masamoto scolded them. "The deeds of mischievous creatures!" As soon as he called out, the figures climbed onto the screen and went back into the original painting. It was very strange. So Yasukata the *yin-yang* master[821] was called. He predicted, "The women *fūryū*[822] dancing on the screen sang about flowers and the wind. So anything related to the wind should be avoided. This is most serious." These events happened in the sixth month of the fourth year of Eishō [1507].

On the following day, Masamoto bathed and fasted [823] before he visited [the shrine on] Mount Atago,[824] where he prayed to Jizō Bodhisattva of victory for future military success and good fortune.[825] On the way home from the mountain on the twenty-third, his horse collapsed at Sakaguchi.[826] On the following day, the twenty-fourth, while taking a bath, he was attacked and stabbed to death[827] by his enemy, with whom his scribe had secretly communicated.

People wondered whether Yasukata's warning about the wind meant that Masamoto's bath was a bad omen.[828]

....

820. The wind scatters flowers (usually cherry blossoms); that is, the "wind" and "flowers" oppose each other.

821. *Onmyōji* 陰陽師, *yin-yang* masters, practiced divination. Yasukata is unidentified.

822. *Fūryū* 風流, "wind flow" or "water flow," refers to something fashionable or changeable. Japanese commoners would dress decoratively and perform the *fūryū* dance and sing songs for festivals and on ceremonial occasions.

823. Masamoto observes *shōjinkessai* 精進潔斎 before visiting Atago Shrine (*Honchō shōgunki*, 10).

824. 愛宕山, in present-day Ukyo-ku, Kyoto-shi. The mountain is home to Atago Shrine, where the bodhisattva Jizō is enshrined.

825. Military men prayed for victory at the shrine's image of a mounted and armed Jizō.

826. At the foot of Mount Atago.

827. See *Honchō shōgunki*, 10.

828. The first character in *furo* 風呂, "bath," is *fū* or *kaze*, "wind." The first portion of the story is taken from *Dakukōki*, 元和初有一士 人云々 and the latter part from *Honcho shōgunki* 本朝将軍記, 10.

9-1   Foxes Tricked a Man
and Kept Him Company

One day, Adachi Kiheiji, who lived in Sakamoto of Gō Province,[829] was heading home after serving the shogun. Accompanied by two attendants and a groom to lead his horse, he was just passing the mountain path from Shirakawa[830] to Yamanaka.[831] The sun was already setting. Then, east of Kaguraoka[832] and south of his route, he saw a beautiful girl of seventeen or eighteen dressed in a kimono with red-purple lining and embroidered with various birds and cherry blossoms. While she wandered along a thorny path as if she had lost her way, the girl raised the skirt of her kimono. Wondering if she might be the daughter of a high-ranking family, Adachi moved closer to see her better. Hiding her face with her sleeve, the girl was stumbling on pebbles and stones. Adachi dismounted and sent one of his men to ask her, "Who would be wandering alone like this at dusk without any servants?" But she did not reply. Adachi sent another man with his horse to speak with her on his behalf. "It is a pity to see you like this on my way home. Please ride on this horse and I will escort you home." The girl appeared very pleased. Adachi lifted her to mount the horse and she felt as light as a thin silk robe. Up close, her noble eyebrows and elegant features were glowing and beautiful. Everything about her, including her fragrant kimono sleeves, was as exquisite as white jade.[833] He thought he would not mind dying for her. Adachi [and his men] followed the horse and went back about one *chō* toward Kyoto. Suddenly at Tanaka, several young maidservants ran to them, saying to the girl, "What a relief. We are so surprised since you've been missing since this evening, and we've been looking everywhere for you." When they went together along with the horse for about two *chō* to the south, an old man of sixty appeared, and gasped out a few words to the mounted girl and to Adachi. "We have been looking for you. Now I am relieved [to see you like this]. It is most kind of you to let her use your horse." Adachi explained to him, "I felt

....

829. In present-day Ōtsu-shi, Shiga-ken.

830. In present-day Sakyō-ku, Kyoto-shi.

831. In present-day Yamanaka-cho, Otsu-shi.

832. In present-day Kaguraoka-cho, Yoshida, Sakyō-ku, Kyoto-shi.

833. White jade connotes something rare and precious.

sorry for her losing her way so I lent her my horse to bring her home. Now I am going down to Sakamoto." The old man said, "Today when we were amusing ourselves with sake, our princess wandered off from our party by herself and lost her way around Tanaka. It's dark now and you will not arrive at Sakamoto so easily. If you don't mind, why don't you stay at our place for the night?" Adachi thanked him, saying, "You are most kind." So they went on three *chō* to the south until they came to a mansion surrounded with fine trees.

Inside the compound, Adachi saw the stately buildings and the garden with blooming plum, cherry, peach, and apricot trees, wisteria on the Japanese roses along the hedge, and irises and flags blooming in a tasteful pool. Everything made it appear to be the place of someone very wealthy. [In the main building] there were rooms partitioned by *fusuma* and *shōji*,[834] including a *shoin*[835] and a small sitting room that led to a room of paintings depicting Chinese and Japanese birds and flowers.

When Adachi came into the building through the entryway, the mistress of the mansion, a very noble-looking lady of forty, came out with several maids and servants. She greeted him, saying, "Unexpectedly this evening, we are honored to entertain a guest. Our princess happened to wander off today. Intoxicated from the sake, she left the party and lost her way. If she hadn't met you, she could have been tricked by foxes and wolves, or threatened by thieves. We greatly a ppreciate that you brought her safely home. Everyone, do your very best to entertain our guest."

Soon sake and food were brought. The mistress took a sake cup and offered it to Adachi, saying, "You enjoy yourself tonight as a memory of this life. Wet nurse of the princess, come out here and offer him sake." Another lady appeared smiling, about twenty-four or twenty-five and gorgeously dressed. She was another rare beauty. Highly pleased, Adachi wondered, "Have I come to Senkyō[836] or to the realm of heaven? Tonight, nowhere, not even Japan's imperial palace, is superior to here."

As he emptied his cups of sake, the party went into full swing. The

....

834. Types of paper doors.

835. A study.

836. 仙境, the country of hermits; a Shangri-La-like paradise.

mistress suggested, "Why don't you play backgammon with the wet nurse?" She brought in a game table made of black *kokutan* wood inlaid with *shitan*[837] and *binrō*.[838] Paintings of scenes from *The Tale of Genji* decorated the sides of the table. The black and white stones were made of ivory and water buffalo horn and the dice were placed in a *makie*-lacquered cup.

Facing the wet nurse, Adachi rolled the dice for the first move. At times, when [they were] arguing, he took her hands as if he had amorous intentions.[839] The couple reminded others of the scene where Chō Bunsen and Jūrōme play the game in *Yusenkutsu*.[840] When Adachi won, she offered him five *ryō*'s worth of *jinkō*[841] incense, and when she won, Adachi presented his *kōgai*[842] to her as he had nothing else to offer.

Dawn already was breaking and the summits of the eastern mountains were whitening when they heard someone coming inside. Then suddenly the people of the house became agitated, calling out to each other, "A thief is breaking in!" The mistress quickly pushed Adachi out through the rear gate. While wondering if the wet nurse had found a hiding place, Adachi emerged alone from a hole on the eroded side of the mountain. He looked around and saw he was standing amidst *chigaya* grass mingled with blooming violets. He heard the wind passing high above the pine trees and the distant sound of water running through the valley. He realized that he no longer had his small knife and the *jinkō* incense was nothing but a wooden chip.

In the beginning, when the girl lost her way, Adachi had dismounted and followed her and then finally vanished. While his men were searching for him, they found the hole in the ground into which their master had disappeared. They borrowed hoes and plows and be-

---

837. See *OT*, 8-1, n.6.

838. A kind of palm wood used for furniture

839. *Kokoro ariya*, "Is there any heart?" or "Is there any intention?" The expression suggests Adachi's amorous intentions towards the wet nurse.

840. 遊仙窟, a Tang dynasty fiction describing the romance between Chō Bunsen 張文潛 and Jūrome 十郎女. The book was introduced to Japan during the Nara period and greatly influenced Japanese literature. The original work circulated in China and appears in the Japanese *Manyōshū*.

841. See *OT*, 8 1, n.8.

842. A small knife attached to the sheath of a sword.

gan to dig into the hole. Then they heard a surprised voice say, "A thief is breaking in!"

When they asked [the people in the vicinity], "Where is this place?" [they replied,] "It's behind Kaguraoka." Certainly the whole incident must have been the trickery of the foxes.[843]

9-2   The Underground Senkyō[844]

Long ago, Ōta Dōkan[845] built a castle in Edo of Bu Province. It was difficult to obtain good water in that area. A wealthy man called Funaki Jinshichi tried to build a well. He hired a *kanehori* and some workmen, who dug nearly one hundred *jō* deep and a half-*chō* wide, but did not find water. While resting quietly at the bottom of the hole, the digger heard faint sounds of dogs barking and chickens crying. Feeling strange, he dug four to five feet more and saw a rock gate off to the side. When he went through the gate, it was too dark to see anything, but he felt surrounded by a wall. After he groped along for about one *chō*, suddenly it became bright. When he looked up, he saw the blue sky of a bright day and a succession of mountain summits below him. He went down to one of the peaks and looked around. It looked like an entirely different world with its own sun and moon. He descended the mountain into a valley, climbed up to another summit, and walked about one *ri*. He saw that all the rocks were colored blue like lapis lazuli. Many palaces and tall buildings stood on the mountain and were decorated in gold and jade, with lapis lazuli tiles and agate pillars, all of it beyond imagination and description. Many big trees with purple blossoms grew there. They had stems with joints like bamboo and palm-like leaves as big as wheels. Five-colored butterflies with wings like fans were playing among flowers while five-colored birds as big as geese were flying above the trees. Other plants and flowers such as he never had seen were blooming and fruiting. There were two waterfalls between the rocks; one looked as clear as a polished mirror and the other as white as milk.

....

843. The story is based on *Reikishi*, 嵯書生. Asai narrates how a subject of the Muromachi shogun was tricked by foxes. The tricky foxes have replaced the princess who was buried in an old mound in the Chinese version.

844. See *OT*, 9-1, n.6.

845. Ōta Dōkan (1432–1486) built Edo Castle in 1456–1457 in present-day Tokyo. It was the headquarters of the Tokugawa shogunate and later the imperial palace.

The digger finally went down the mountain and walked for one *chō* until he came to a tall gateway topped by the sign, "The Mountain Palace of the Heavenly Pole." Two guards at the gateway, each standing five feet tall, were surprised to see the digger. With red lips, white teeth, and hair like dark blue thread, and dressed in green robes with black *eboshi* hats, they looked as beautiful as jade. One of the guards ran to the digger and asked, "Who are you and why are you here?" The digger explained everything. Then, twenty-some gorgeously dressed men with complexions as luminous as Chinese lanterns entered the gateway and demanded of the guards, "We smell something bad and strange. What happened?" So the scared guards explained in detail, "A digger from the human world lost his way and unexpectedly arrived here." Then another man dressed in bright red with a gold hat appeared and said to everybody, "The Great Hermit orders that the digger be taken around for sightseeing." The twenty men respectfully complied with the order.

The guards brought the digger to the waterfalls and washed his body with the pure water, and then rinsed his mouth with the milky water, which tasted as sweet as honey to the digger. Drinking as much as he wanted, at first he felt drunk but soon was very refreshed. Then the guards took him around the mountain where a profusion of palaces and buildings lined every valley. They only saw the outside of the buildings. After half a day's walk, they arrived at a castle at the foot of the mountain. Above the gateway the digger saw a golden sign on which was written, "The Palace of the Great Hermit Emperor." The entire castle was made of crystal with gold and silver walls, hedges of turtle shell, amber railings decorated with white jade at the corners, screens of *shako* shell, and railings embellished with pearls. Five colors of jade [pebbles] were spread like sand throughout the garden, where rare plants grew and exotic birds flew. The castle's opulence was beyond description. Since he could not go inside the castle, he imagined, "How beautiful it must be inside." He asked the guard, "What kind of place is this?" The guard replied, "This is the place where the hermits who have mastered the Hermit Way come and practice for seventy thousand days. After that, they ascend to heaven, some to Horai Palace[846] and others to Ha-

---

846. A legendary palace for hermits in the Eastern Sea.

koya Mountain or to Kyokei-konron,[847] where they receive their proper work and titles. After they master the *furokuinju-yakujutsu*,[848] they acquire the power to fly freely." The digger asked again, "If this is the hermits' country, why is it below rather than above the human world?" The guard answered, "This is the hermits' underworld country. There is another one above the human world." The guard looked around and said, "You, quickly return to your country," then brought the digger to the white waterfall, had him drink its water, escorted him to the summit of the mountain [where the digger first had appeared] and on to the first great gate that the digger had seen. The guard called out and went inside to obtain a jade tablet and gold sign. Taking these, the guard took the digger to the entrance of the rock hole. All the gates were open and the guard finally said to the digger, "You may think that you spent only half a day here, but several scores of years in the human world have passed." Then the digger went back into the hole, where it was so dark that he could see nothing of his way and only could hear the sound of the wind. Finally he happened to come out of the cave at the foot

....

847. The residence of the Heavenly EOmperor in Taoism
848. The secret incantations and hand gestures in Taoism

of Mount Fuji. Quite surprised and feeling extraordinary, the digger returned to Edo, where he asked about Ōta Dōkan and learned that everything had happened a hundred years ago. No one knew about his digging a well and the site was gone. The people had built new houses while [Edo] Castle had become enormously prosperous. He went to see his house but it also was gone and he heard nothing of his people.

He pondered, one hundred years had passed since the construction of Edo Castle in the first year of Chōroku to the present, the second year of Kōji. The digger no longer wished for anything from the human world.[849] He stopped eating the five cereals, only drank water with nuts, and engaged in the practice as he traveled on foot. Several years later someone saw him on Mount Fuji. After that his whereabouts became unknown.[850]

9-3　Making Pledges with a Ghost in the Gold Pavilion

Twenty-six-year-old Nakahara Mondo no Kami[851] was known for his good looks. He was unmarried and very amorous. Yearning for spring blossoms and loathing the wind [that scatters them], he admired the autumn moon and detested the clouds [that cover it]. He held a government office, but [instead of concentrating on his work], he often went wandering without a care in the world.

In the spring of the fifth year of Taiei [1535], while lamenting spring's passing he wandered northeast along a mountain path. He visited the Higaki grove of Kitashirakawa,[852] Sakurai Village,[853] Iwakura Valley at Mount Himuro,[854] Fox Slope,[855] Yashio Hill,[856] the

....

849. The expression suggests that he wished to become a hermit.

850. The story is based on *Hakuishi*, 陰隱客. Asai places it in the context of Dōkan's construction of Edo Castle.

851. Unidentified. Hereafter referred to as "Mondo."

852. In present-day Sakyō-ku, Kyoto-shi.

853. In present-day Matsugasaki, Sakyō-ku.

854. 氷室, a room where ice for the imperial palace was stored. The mountain is in present-day Himuro-cho, Kamitakano, Sakyō-ku.

855. In present-day Matsugasaki, Sakyō-ku.

856. In present-day Iwakura, Sakyō-ku.

Demon Castle[857] of Kataoka, Yokawa of Mount Hiei,[858] Ōhara,[859] the Otonashi Waterfall,[860] Shizuhara,[861] the pure water of Oboro,[862] the field of Ichihara,[863] Mount Kurabu,[864] and finally Rokuon'in,[865] popularly called Kinkakuji, the Gold Pavilion. At one time Shogun[866] Minamoto Yoshimitsu built a house and lived there. The house became a temple not long after he passed away.[867] As in olden times, it was a very beautiful place with its mounds and rock fountain.

When Mondo wandered into [Kinkakuji], it was already dark and the spring moon[868] was rising in the east. He thought of [the old saying], "Who would not pay one thousand gold coins for this [passing] moment on a spring evening?" Thus thinking, he was unable to move from beneath the tree. He took shelter for the night at a nearby village, but he could not sleep. [So he went out] walking around the garden and stepping on the moss, and finally came to Kinkakuji. One hundred and eighteen years had gone by since Lord Yoshimitsu passed away in the fifteenth year of Ōei. While he was alive the place bustled with people, but visitors were fewer after he departed. Meanwhile the building's foundation had begun to settle and tilt, and the pillars were decaying, but the temple structure retained its character. Mondo stood under the eaves near the railing, thinking of olden times and reflecting on the present era. Looking at the moon of the deepening night and the sparse blossoms of the old cherry tree, he recited a poem.

....

857. A rock chamber in Yase, Sakyō-ku where the demon Shutendōji hid after being expelled from Mount Hiei. Finally he was killed by Minamoto Yorimitsu on Mount Ōe in Tanba.

858. Yokawa is one of three pagodas on Mount Hiei, in present-day Ōtsu-shi, Shiga-ken.

859. In present-day Ōhara, Sakyō-ku.

860. In present-day Ohara-Raigoin-cho, Sakyō-ku.

861. In present-day Shizuichi-Shizuhara-cho, Sakyō-ku.

862. A famous stream running southeast of Jakkōin Temple, in present-day Ohara-Kusao-cho, Sakyō-ku.

863. In present-day Shizuichi-Ichihara-cho, Sakyō-ku.

864. A part of Mount Kurama north of Kyoto-shi.

865. 鹿苑院, a temple of the Rinzai sect in present-day Kinkakuji-cho, Kita-ku.

866. Ashikaga Yoshimitsu 足利義満 (1358–1408), the third shogun of the Muromachi shogunate, received the title of *seitaishogun*, "Great Barbarian-Subduing General."

867. Present-day Kinkakuji.

868. *Oborozuki* 朧月, the misty spring moon, in contrast to the clear autumn moon.

sakura bana
iza koto towa mu
haru no yo no
tsuki wa mukashimo
oboro nariki ya

Cherry blossoms,
I would like to ask you,
If the moon was
Misty in the spring night
Of olden times?[869]

Then a young woman of seventeen or eighteen appeared with a female servant. Her thin eyebrows curved like *katsura* leaves[870] and her hair was as voluminous as clouds. Her elegant features were beyond description. As he looked at her and secretly wondered [who she was], the woman said, "The Gold Pavilion and the garden are not different from days long ago. Only the times and the world have changed. It is so sad to remember the olden days." Saying this, she rested by the fountain and recited an old poem by Tsumori Kunimoto[871] about going to Hanayama[872] and seeing cherry blossoms fall and scatter. The tree was planted by Abbot Henjō [when the temple was built].

aruji naki
sumika ni nokoru
sakurabana
wware mukashi no
haru ya koi shiki

The cherry blossoms

---

869. A similar poem appears in *Isemonogatari*, 9.

870. The leaves of the *katsura* tree are thin and curved like the crescent moon. The expression is typically used to describe beautiful eyebrows.

871. Tsumori no Kunimoto, a poet of the Heian period who wrote the anthology *Tsumori Kunimotoshū* 津守国基集.

872. Referring to Gangyōji, in present-day Kita-Hanayama-Kawara-machi, Yamashina ku, Kyōto-shi. The temple was built by Sōjō Henjō 遍昭 (816–890), a well-known poet. He was popularly known as Hanayama Sōjō, Abbot Hanayama.

Still remain at
The place without the master.
Do you miss the spring
Of old times?[873]

Hearing her recitation, Mondo became so agitated that he felt as if he were losing his mind. In his confusion he recited a poem.

saku hana ni
mukashi o omou
kimi wa taso
koyoi wa ware zo
aruji naru mono

Who are you?
Recalling old times
By seeing the blossoms,
Tonight, I am
The master of this place.[874]

When he faced the woman, she did not seem surprised to see him and said in a small voice, "Since I knew you were here, I have come to meet you." Immensely surprised, Mondo asked her name. The woman replied, "I haven't been seen by humans for a long time. You will be most surprised and frightened if I tell you about myself." Mondo thought, "So she is not human. Is she an echo from the nearby mountain? The trick of a fox? A ghost?" Her beauty completely infatuated him and he was not at all afraid of her. He asked her again, "Why would I be surprised and afraid of you? Just tell me exactly what happened to you."

So she began, "I was born in the Hatakeyama clan and served Lord Yoshimitsu, who had confined himself here. I died at the age of twenty and was buried in this temple thanks to the mercy of Lord [Yoshimitsu]. Tonight I came for the memorial service of Nun Yoshiko of the first rank, the mother of Lord Yoshimitsu. I was away for a long time, but finally I have returned." Saying this, she told her servant

....

873. *Zokukokinnshū* 続古今集, Aishō.

874. *Heike monogatari*, 9, Tadanori.

to bring a carpet. Some sake and fruit were brought in. Sitting and facing the eaves of the building, she said, "We can't waste this evening's flowers and moon, can we?" and amused herself with drinking and talking. Meanwhile, as the number of sake cups increased, the servant began to sing. Tilting her head,[875] the woman tearfully recited a poem.

ake yuka ba
koishikaru beki
nagori kana
hana no kage moru
atara yo no tsuki

When the dawn breaks
I will miss the remembrance
Of tonight's moon
That escaped through
The blossoms' shadows.[876]

....

875. The expression shows that the woman is thinking.

876. The poem suggests that the woman will miss Mondo, whom she compares with the moon. *Fukishō* 夫木抄, Spring, 4.

Hearing her recitation, Mondo pensively recited his poem.

izure o ka
hana wa ureshi to
omouramu
sasou arashi to
oshimu kokoro to

I wonder which
The blossoms
Would be pleased with,
The alluring storm
Or the heart that misses them.[877]

When she heard his poem, the woman joined her sleeves to collect herself, and said to him, "I think the poem you recited shows your true feelings. It's been a long time since I left this life but I feel that I am back again. If I make a pledge with you, [my heart] will not perish even if I die." Saying this, she began to talk more intimately with him. Meanwhile, the moon disappeared behind the western summit as stars gathered in the northern sky. They moved to [a room] by the building's western eave. The woman grew more expressive in showing her feelings and the couple moved their pillows together.[878] As happens on a spring night, time passed quickly and the couple soon heard the rooster crow three times.[879] The clouds sidled along the western summits like white flowers.[880] Finally the couple bade each other a tearful farewell.[881]

....

877. The poem compares the two: he is a storm that scatters the blossoms away, and she the heart that misses or holds a grudge against the scattered blossoms. The poem projects Mondo's indecisive feelings onto the blossoms and compares them with the woman's pledge. *Mikishō*, Spring, 4.

878. The expression suggests that the couple lies down together with their pillows side by side.

879. *Tori*, "bird," here means "rooster."

880. *Yokogumo*, "side clouds," referring to clouds that often float sideways in the early morning.

881. *Kinuginu* (silk robes or robes in general) *no wakare*, (separation) describes a separation where tears are dried with the sleeves of one's robes. The expression is used for parting lovers.

During the day, Mondo looked around the temple compound and found an old, decrepit stupa. A smaller one beside it on a mossy mound was for the maid. She died from grieving for her mistress, and sympathetic people later buried her near her mistress. Mondo felt distraught. Forgetting his home, he stayed there until evening. When he walked around the building, again the woman appeared. Taking his hands she tearfully said, "Moved by your feelings, I cherish the pledge made to you last night. But sadly, like the gods of Kazuraki, I must avoid the daytime."[882] Mondo replied by asking her, "What is it you avoid?" He continued, "Would you say that there is no way to meet unless it is in the evening? It is truly painful to wait until nightfall. To avoid attracting the guard's attention,[883] I will grieve quietly and my lamentations will accumulate secretly."[884] Saying this, Mondo saw the woman every night, and twenty-some days later he even saw her during the daytime. Since he had a government job, he returned to his home in Kyoto and traveled each day to the temple. Finally one rainy day, he saw her during the day and brought her to his home to live together.

With her modest and refined manners and speech, the woman was easily accepted by Mondo's family. Anyone who associated with her never failed to become her friend. She was kind to her young maidservants at home and outside her home, and attentive to the old woman next door. She was skillful in sewing and writing, as well as discreet in her relationships. People envied Mondo and said, "Truly, he has obtained a good wife."

In this way, three years passed. On the fifteenth day of the seventh month, the woman said to Mondo, "I left my maidservant to look after my old place. She must be waiting for me. I will visit her tonight at the Gold Pavilion to find out how she has been." So Mondo and his wife went to the temple with some sake. The sun already had set and the moon had just risen over the eastern mountain. Lotus flowers were blooming in the southern part of the pool, while willow leaves hung with dew and bamboo swayed in the breeze. Soon the servant appeared

---

882. An old legend tells that the gods of Mount Kazuraki only appear at night because of their unsightly looks.

883. *Sekimori*, the guard that kept watch for secret meetings of lovers.

884. *Nageki* 嘆き, "lamentation," can also mean *nageki* 投げ木, "throwing logs [onto a fire]." So the sentence also could be translated as, "I will accumulate logs to throw [onto the fire of our passion]."

and said to the woman, "It's been three years since you returned to the human world. Did you forget your old home while you were enjoying yourself?" The couple and servant went to the west of the building.

The woman tearfully said to Mondo, "Attracted by your deep feelings, the three years flew by as quickly as the shadow of a running horse. Our pledge is unexhausted, but I have to leave you tonight. I am from the Land after Death and I returned to this world thanks to a deep karmic relation. Now that my karma is extinguished, I must leave you. If I resist and stay here longer, I am afraid that punishment from the Land after Death would come soon and harm you." Both Mondo and the woman shed tears and dried them with their sleeves. After a while it was dawn and they heard the morning bells echoing and the [rooster] crowing eight times.[885] The woman stood up, placed an incense burner in a *makie*-lacquered box, and offered it to Mondo, saying, "Please take this as a token from me." She tearfully bade him farewell and walked to the mound. She appeared to turn back but then vanished like smoke. The grief-stricken Mondo felt as if his heart were on fire and his tears were of blood. He tried in vain to follow her.

After returning home, Mondo called a priest, had him recite the *Lotus Sutra* for the repose of the woman's soul, and wrote a vow on a sheet of paper for the dedication.

The vow read, "She was born with a good soul and the fine qualities of mountain people.[886] The beauty of flowers and jade took form in her soul. Once she served in a court with golden doors,[887] now she is buried in a ruined mound. She endures the fox and rabbit trampling the pampas grass above her. Scattered flowers cannot return to their branches, or flowing water to its spring. The sun sets and the moon returns. The spirit does not perish and the soul lasts forever.[888] Although a spirit cannot return [to this world], it might have enough merit to reappear [in this world].[889]

....

885. *Yakoe*, the eight crows of the rooster in the early morning.

886. The meaning is unclear. "Mountain people" may connote mountain-dwelling ascetics, who seek the Way with pure hearts.

887. *Kogane no tobira*, "golden doors," is a reference to a high-ranking place like the imperial court.

888. The meaning is unclear.

889. The meaning is unclear. I understand it to mean that although a soul cannot return to this world, it can reappear as a ghost if it is courageous enough and has accumulated enough merit.

"Her jade comb and crimson robe were beautiful and her fragrance still lingers here. I shared pleasures and made a pledge with her, which like the evergreen tree should remain unchanged for a thousand years. I thought we would live together until our old age, but alas, we met and are now separated. You have become clouds and rain and I grieve in the morning and evening, yearning for you and lamenting that you have vanished. Even when I face the mound [that bears traces of your remains], I hear nothing of your voice. When will I see you again? The crying geese and the faint light of fireflies are slight consolation for my grieving heart.

"Since you disappeared, a heavy mist shrouds the starry sky, making it dark and empty. My heart is like tangled thread and my tears are dyed crimson. Beset with such grief, I recite sutras and offer flowers. Please receive them. Oh, how sad and pitiful it is! Please, I beg you, accept my offerings.

tomosu hi ya
tamukuru mizu ya
kouge o
tama no arika ni
ukete shire kimi

The taper light,
Water, flowers, and incense
For the offerings to you,
Please accept them
At the place of your soul."[890]

After completing his vow, Mondo left his government job and lived alone with a grieving heart. Her memory never left him. He did not take another wife. After he retired to Ōhara, nobody ever knew what became of him.[891]

....

890. *Fukishō*, 19, Fire.

891. The story is based on *SS*, 2-3. Asai turns a romantic tale with old *waka* poems into a Buddhist one about the futility of life. It is interesting to see how the young man, who is unattached to anything in the beginning, becomes deeply attached to the woman's spirit by the end of the story.

9-4   The Scab with a Human Face

A farmer of Ogura in Yamashiro Province[892] was suffering from an illness for a long time. Sometimes he felt cold with a high fever like a bout of malaria, and other times his whole body ached as if he had rheumatism. He tried all kinds of medicines and cures, but to no avail. Six months passed and a scab appeared on his left thigh that looked just like a human face with eyes and a mouth but no ears or nose. After that he didn't feel pain anywhere except for the scab, which pained him beyond description. Just to try it out, he poured some sake into the scab's mouth, and its face reddened [like a drunk's]. When he put some rice and rice cakes in, the scab moved its mouth, swallowed, and ate the food like a human. When the farmer fed the scab, he was relieved of his pain, but it returned whenever the scab was not fed. Because of this, the sick farmer became very tired and thin. He lost weight, becoming just skin and bones, and was ready to die. All of the doctors from other provinces heard of him and gathered to try out their medical and surgical cures, but they had no effect.

One day, an ascetic who was traveling through various countries on pilgrimage came to the farmer and said to him, "Your scab is quite rare and those who suffer from it usually die. But there is one way to cure it." The farmer replied, "If I can be cured of it, I don't mind at all selling my land." So the farmer sold his land and rice paddies and gave the money to the ascetic. After gathering all kinds of herbs, gold, stone, and earth, the ascetic fed everything to the farmer's scab, which ate it all except for the *baimo*.[893] When the *baimo* was brought to its mouth, the scab closed its mouth and eyes and refused to take it. So the ascetic made the *baimo* into a powder, [forcefully] opened the scab's mouth, and inserted the powder into the mouth using a reed stalk for a straw. The scab closed up and the farmer was cured within a week. They called [his case] the Scab with a Human Face.[894]

....

892. In present-day Ogura-cho, Uji-shi.

893. 貝母, a perennial plant belonging to the lily family.

894. The original tale is from *Dakukōki*, 許卑山人云々, but similar versions appear in *Biyōhonzō* 備用本草, 8 and *Jichinhonzō* 時珍本草, 13.

9-5   A Human Demon

Yotsugu, who lived in Nonokuchi of Tanba Province,[895] had a grandmother who was one hundred and sixty-some years old. As her hair had turned completely white, Yotsugu made her into a nun with the help of a priest.

Ever since her youth, the grandmother was very wild and riotous. Yotsugu was already about eighty years old, with many children and grandchildren. The grandmother always treated Yotsugu like a little boy and scolded and pressed him about anything she did not like. But since she was his grandmother, Yotsugu dutifully looked after her.

The grandmother had reached a very old age, but her eyesight was still so sharp that she could thread a needle and her hearing so keen that she could hear a whisper. She lost all her teeth when she was around ninety years old, but they all came back after she turned one hundred. People around the world thought it most extraordinary, and they came to serve her and ask her to name their young children, hoping that they would live as long as she. The grandmother worked at home during the daytime spinning hemp thread, but went out at night. No one knew where she went. Her children and grandchildren thought this strange, so one night they followed her. But when she returned home, she scolded them with a loud voice. Despite her walking stick, she walked as if she were flying. So still no one in her household knew where she went. Meanwhile, she lost so much weight that her large bones stuck out, and soon the whites of her eyes changed to blue. Although she did not eat much for her morning and evening meals, her spirits were as high as those of a young person.

One day, just before she left home, she called together all the people in the household, including her grandchildren, great-grandchildren, and daughters-in-law, and said to them, "While I am gone, don't open the door to my room. And don't peek into my room through the windows. If you do, I will hold a grudge against you." The family members thought this strange.

Sometimes she went out during the day and returned home very late at night. One time Yotsugu's youngest son got drunk and thought, "Why did our grandmother tell us not to open the door to her room?

895. Near present-day Sonobe-cho, Funai-gun, Kyoto-fu.

How strange. Maybe I should look into her room during her absence." So he opened up her room. There he saw a dog's head, chicken feathers, a young child's wrist, a skull, and countless limb bones all piled up and hidden under a bamboo board. Horrified, the son ran out of the room and reported this to his father. The household was gathered and discussing what to do about the situation when the grandmother returned and saw the door to her room was open.

Greatly surprised and furious, her shiny eyes grew large and round while her mouth opened wide with a roar, and she ran out of the house and disappeared. It was terrifying.

Some time later, a woodcutter saw her near Mount Ōe.[896] She was clad in a white one-layered *katabira* kimono with its skirt tucked in up to her waist. She was climbing to the summit of the mountain with a walking stick. She was moving so fast it seemed like she was flying. The woodcutter remembered having seen her catch and force a wild boar down to the ground, and he said, "I was so scared that I felt all my hair stand on end. I ran down the mountain to my home." When he finished speaking, everyone thought it must have been the grandmother. They were sure that she had become a demon while she was still alive.[897]

10-1 The Apparitions of the Imori[898]

There was a castle ruin[899] in the inner part of Yunoo of Echizen Province.[900] Overgrown thorn bushes and roots of old pine trees covered the grounds of the ruin. All that one could hear were the faint cries of birds and the frightful din of water rushing through the valley. At

896. 大江山, in present day Ōe-cho, Kasa-gun, Kyoto-fu, is known for the *oni* 鬼 (demons) subjugated there by Minamoto Yorimitsu. Refer to the tale of Shutendōji in *Otogizōshi*.

897. The story is based on *Danen* 談淵, 太原王仁裕家遠祖母云々. Asai adapts the original story's demon theme to the demon tradition of Mount Ōe.

898. The name of the *tokage* (lizard) that appears in the latter part of the story is pronounced *imori* (newt) but is written and actually refers to *yamori* (gecko).

899. Soyama Castle, in present-day Akuwa, Nanjō-cho, Nanjō-gun, Fukui-ken. See "How the Uryū Raised the Banner" in *Taiheiki* 太平記, 18.

900. Present-day Konjō-cho, Nanjō-gun, Fukui-ken was an important lodging place for the military and those traveling and transporting goods along the northern route.

this very place Jingai Shuso,[901] a Zen monk of the Sōtō sect clad in a *hensan*,[902] built a grass hut and enjoyed practicing meditation and studying. He picked *warabi*[903] in the spring to satisfy his hunger and waited for the leaves scattered by autumn storms to use as firewood. The people of the nearby village visited him and brought food for his daily meal. Other than that, he had hardly any visitors. When he opened his books, it was as if he were talking with people from olden times, and when he sat down on the floor to meditate, he entered into the *samādhi* state of exaltation and never felt lonesome.

One night when he was leaning against his desk and reading the *Dendō no roku*[904] (Should this be *Dentō roku?*) in candlelight, a tiny man four or five inches tall wearing a black hat appeared with a thin stick, and said to him in a voice as spare as a fly's buzz, "I have come here tonight, but the master is not here and I feel lonely with no one to talk with." Nothing surprised Shuso, who had mastered the Way of the mind. Soon the little man became angry and jumped over to the desk, saying, "I have come here as your guest, and it is most impolite for you to remain silent." So saying, he jumped up onto the desk. Taking his fan, Shuso tried to hit him. But he instantly jumped down from the desk, shouting, "Remember your insolence!" The man left through the gateway and disappeared.

Soon after that five women appeared. Some were young, some old, and they all were four or five inches tall. One of the old women said to Shuso, "My lord said to our scholar, 'The priest is studying alone under the candlelight. Go and console him by asking questions about the profundity of Buddhist teachings.' But you hit our man and shamed him. My lord will be here shortly to learn the details."

Then about ten thousand men, all five to six inches tall with sleeves rolled up to their elbows, came running like ants and hit Shuso, which felt very painful despite his trance. Soon a man in red with a black *eboshi* hat sat down near Shusho's [feet] and said to him, "You, priest, quickly leave here. Otherwise your eyes will sting with

....

901. *Shuso* is the term for the sixth and highest rank of a Zen monk, or one who has mastered ascetic practices. Hereafter, I use the term as Jingai's personal name.

902. A short robe worn by ascetics.

903. Bracken.

904. 伝灯録 (*should this be* 景德傳燈錄 [The Records of the Transmission of the Lamp]?), the biographical records of eminent Zen monks.

tears." Meanwhile, several of the men jumped up onto Shuso's shoulders and began biting his ears and nose. Brushing them off, Shuso ran out through the gateway and climbed the hill to the south. He saw a gateway and approached it thinking, "This is strange. But I will drop in here to spend the night." When he came near the gateway, the ten thousand small men caught him, pushed him down, and dragged him into the gateway, where several thousand tiny men filled the compound. The lord-general also returned [to his headquarters inside the gateway] and said to Shuso, "I pitied you and sent someone to entertain you, but you harmed him. You must atone for your sin by having your limbs cut off." Several hundred men with swords in their hands began to press him. Greatly confused and frightened, Shuso apologized to the lord, saying, "Being ignorant of your kindness, my mistakes were great and it is too late for regrets.Now, I only wish that you forgive me."

"Now that you regret your deeds, you should not be harassed any longer about your sins. Release him," said the lord. Shuso felt he was being pushed out of the gateway and found himself in front of the small gate of his own hut. When he went into his hut, the candle was almost burnt out and light was beginning to fill the eastern sky. Completely puzzled, he looked around the gateway but found no trace [of the night's events]. He finally found a hole on the small hill to the east. Many geckoes went in and out of the hole. Feeling very suspicious, Shuso hired villagers to dig into the hole, which was quite wide under the ground. When they dug down about one *jō*, they saw some twenty thousand geckoes gathered at the bottom of the hole. Among them was a red one as long as a foot that looked like their king. An old villager stepped out and told Shusho a story, saying, "Long ago, valorous Uryū Hogan[905] lived in the castle and controlled its surroundings. He later sided with Nitta Yoshiharu.[906] Priest Gikanbō,[907] the younger brother

---

905. Uryū Tamotsu 瓜生保 (d. 1337) followed Nitta Yoshisada 新田義貞 (1301–1338) and died in battle attacking Kanasaki Castle in Echizen.

906. Nitta Yoshiharu 新田義治, or Wakiya Yoshiharu (b. 1323), followed his father and participated in attacking Kanasaki Castle.

907. Gikanbō 義鑑房 was described in the *Taiheiki* as a man of righteousness who helped his brother Uryū.

of Uryū, fell in love with Nitta,[908] who was an incomparably beautiful boy. Later he urged his brother to raise an army[909] [to attack their enemy]. Unfortunately Gikanbō died in battle before he attained his purpose. Since then Gikanbō's soul has remained in the castle, where it became a gecko and has lived for a long time in the [well of the] castle compound. It is said that after many years the well was destroyed. Undoubtedly it must have been an evil trick of the gecko. Unless we get rid of it now, it may cause further misfortune."

Shuso wrote a message [to the gecko] on a sheet of paper, saying, "You are a kind of four-legged lizard called *kōkai* with a head like a toad's and a long tail. Your black back is covered with small scales. You are a lizard of the *yamori* family of gecko. Sometimes you hide in muddy water and other times gather in the ruined well. But now you live underground in this hole and have freely multiplied your descendants so that they number a hundred thousand. For months and years, you have committed evil deeds by changing your form to distract and annoy the souls and minds of humans. Why do you do that?

"You were born with the status of the insect[910] but your form is of a kind of snake. Your name is among the Twelve-Hour-Insects,[911] but you are not among the Thirty-Six Animals.[912] Because you often catch sawyers and flies, people call you a beautiful name, *katsuko*, newt-tiger.[913] You change your colors during the day, and may be called a lizard, but Chōka[914] records you as *imori* [newt], and Ōsei[915] writes in his book about your amorous deeds. That is because of your jealous nature and strong sexual desire. I hear that once you were a Buddhist monk, but suddenly you were deranged by lust for a boy and finally left your [ascetic] practice. Then valor inspired you; you

....

908. The *Taiheiki* mentions that thirteen-year-old Yoshiharu was entrusted by his father to Gikanbō's care.

909. Uryū originally sided with Ashikaga Takauji 足利尊氏 (1305–1358) but later changed his mind and helped Nitta, who supported Emperor Godaigo 後醍醐 (r. 1318–1339).

910. That is, with limbs.

911. *Imori*, the newt, changes its color twelve times a day.

912. The thirty-six kinds of birds and animals used in divination to determine the right direction and tell fortunes.

913. *Katsuko* 蝎虎 includes *ko*, "tiger," which makes the name sound prestigious.

914. A Chinese naturalist of the Shin dynasty, who edited the 400-volume *Hakubutsushi* 博物志.

915. A Chinese author of the Ming dynasty, who wrote in his book about the lasciviousness of geckos.

suffered because of it, died, and finally were reborn as an insect. Alas, the monk who loves *so*[916] becomes an insect of *so,* while one who loves *tachibana*[917] becomes an insect of *tachibana.* I have heard of this since olden times. So because of your love [while a human], you were reborn as an insect and your nature is to make love. That is what the people hate and what the world warns you against. Why, without regrets and repentance, have you done such strange and evil deeds? Reform quickly, turn to the correct path, and return to your original goodness." As soon as he finished reading what he had written, maybe being moved by it, all at once the tens of thousands of geckos died. The villagers felt most strange and could not leave the situation as it was. So they piled firewood and burnt [the dead geckos] to ash, which was collected to make a mound as a memorial. After that, no more strange things happened.[918]

10-2 A Jealous Woman Becomes a Water Deity

A district[919] of Yamashiro Province was east of Uji Bridge. Kuse District was west of the bridge. The shrine of Princess Hashi[920] was on the western side of the bridge at the northern end.

Tradition said that since Princess Hashi was very ugly she never had a male suitor. The shrine of Rikyū Bright Deity[921] was south of the bridge. The deity came each night to see the princess. When he crossed the river to visit her, the water of the Uji River rose terribly high with white waves and it was most frightening. So they said that the deity composed a poem.

....

916. *So* is condensed milk. Once there was a Buddhist monk who loved *so* and always was concerned about love. Because of this he was reborn as an insect (*Gisorokuchō* 義楚六提, 19, So, 11).

917. Similar stories about *tachibana* tangerines appear in *Hosshinshū* 発心集, 8-8 and *Sangokudenki* 三国伝記, 3-21. In these stories the protagonist is a nun instead of a monk.

918. The story is based on *Dakukōki,* 太和末荊南云々 Asai transforms the original story into a didactic Buddhist one by adding the message about the *imori* in the last part of the story. The story of Gikanbō also appears in *Inuhariko* 狗張子, 5.

919. Possibly Uji District, east of Uji Bridge. Kuse District was on the west side of the Uji River. Both are in present-day Uji-shi, Kyoto-fu.

920. The shrine was moved to its present place, Ujirenge, Uji-shi because of a flood in 1688.

921. A branch of Uji Shrine, or Mataburi Shrine, in present-day Mataburi-Uji, Uji-shi.

yo ya samuki
koromo ya usuki
katasogi no
yukiai no ma ni
shimo ya oku ramu

I wonder whether
The night is cold or
My robe is thin,
Or was the frost placed between
The openings of the *katasogi*[922] gables?[923]

So it was said that if a bride and groom traveling between Kuze and Uji passed in front of the shrine of Princess Hashi, the couple surely would be separated in the near future. Because of that, couples would take a boat from Makinoshima[924] north of the bridge to cross the river and ensure a good marriage. It was said that the unsightly Princess Hashi grieved for being unmarried and was jealous of anyone who was going to be married. But this was not so.[925]

Long ago, there was a rich man called Okanoya Shikibu in Uji District. His wife was a daughter of Murase Heie, the lord of Ogura Village.[926] The wife was intensely jealous of everyone, even of her young servant girls. If a girl appeared remotely normal,[927] she drove her away. She only kept physically disfigured female servants in her household. When she heard about romances between other men and women, she got so jealous that she could not eat a thing. As for her husband, she was so jealous that she harassed him and would not let him go outside the gateway. The helpless husband tried to divorce her and send her back to her family. But she violently threatened him, saying, "If you

....

922. A crossbeam in the *hafu* gable of a typical *gasshozukuri*- (合掌造り, "joining-palms") style Japanese shrine that was rough-cut on the end and projected towards the front of the shrine.

923. *Shinkokinshū*, Shingika.

924. West of the river, in present-day Akishima-cho, Uji-shi.

925. The expression, *sore niwa arazu*, "that is not so," suggests a different explanation, as presented in the following story.

926. In present-day Ogura-cho, Uji-shi.

927. *Hito gamashii*, "like a human."

divorce me and send me back home, I will die and become a demon to eat you up." Thus they spent many years without any children.

Meanwhile, the husband consoled himself by reading collections of tales.

One day he said to his wife, "*In The Tale of Genji*,[928] examples of jealous women include Lady Miyasudokoro of Rokujo, who became a demon after her death, and the wife of the Black Bearded General,[929] who was possessed and became deranged. These ladies are known to later generations for their jealous nature. Although they were frightful, they were all described as beautiful women. [I could bear your] jealousy if you were good looking. So don't be so violently jealous." This enraged the wife and she replied, "So you hate your ugly wife and might want to give your heart to another woman. Men hate me because I am ugly. I will change my life[930] and punish indecisive men[931] as I wish." As soon as she finished, her hair stood on end and her mouth turned red and widened. Shedding bloody tears from her bulging eyes, she ran out of the room and jumped into the river. Expert swimmers were hired to look for her body, but to no avail. The shocked husband held various Buddhist services at Byōdōin Temple.[932] On the seventh night [after her death], the wife appeared in his dream saying, "I died and became the deity of this river. If anyone crosses the bridge because of a relationship, I will certainly break it up in the future." Then he woke up.

After that, they said that any couple crossing the bridge to get married surely will separate later. Nothing happens when an ugly woman crosses the river in a boat [to be married]. But when a good-looking woman crosses, the wind blows up large waves and makes the boat dangerous. So when a bride crosses the river and there is no wind or waves, everyone knows that she's not a beauty.[933]

....

928. *Genji monogatari* 源氏物語, written by Lady Murasaki in the mid-Heian period.

929. The wife throws ashes from an incense burner at her husband for being in love with another woman, Tamakatsura.

930. She will change her status to *irui*, "nonhuman"; that is, she will turn herself into a demon.

931. *Kokoro sadamaranu*, "unsettled hearts," here refers to flirtatious men.

932. West of the Uji River, in present-day Ujirenge, Uji-shi. The temple was built by Fujiwara Michinaga in 1052.

933. The story is based on *Dakukōki*, 妬婦津相. Asai introduces the Hashihime legend, which appears in various other poem-tales such as *Shūchūshō* 袖中抄, *Ōgishō* 奧義抄, and *Dekisai-kyōmiyage* 出来斎京土産 (1677), as well as in a local Kyoto journal.

10-3 Pledging with a Ghost by Prayer

Uesugi Norimasa[934] lived in Hirai Castle[935] of Kozuke Province. Hōjō Ujiyasu attacked the castle and Norimasa fled to Nagao Kenshin[936] in Echigo, where he planned to rebuild his fortune. Now Hōjō Shinrokurō[937] was the new castellan. The castle had a very beautiful room with a screen decorated in silver and gold and paper doors painted with a variety of plants, flowers, and birds. In the garden next to the room, the stones and rocks were placed skillfully around a mound and spring. The flowers in the garden next to the mound bloomed continuously from spring to autumn.

This was the room of fifteen-year-old Iyako, the daughter of Norimasa and an incomparable beauty with a kind heart. Everyone who saw and heard about her was attracted by her appearance and gentle heart and entranced by her. Norimasa thought about matching her with a man from a high-ranking family, which would bring prosperity to his clan, and he cherished her by making the special room for her. Meanwhile Shiroishi Hannai,[938] a close young servant[939] of Norimasa, fell in love with her at first glance. Unable to contain his strong desire for her, he wrote a letter.[940] But the letter was discovered and he was secretly decapitated. About a hundred days later, the daughter suddenly became frightened one evening, and in the end she died. People said it must have been the deed of Hannai's soul.

Hearing the story, Shinrokurō [the new castellan] thought, "Even though she's a ghost, if I could meet and talk with such a beauty, I would be most happy. Nothing in this life could be better than that." Thus thinking, he secretly nourished his desire for her and prayed for [her soul] by offering flowers and incense in the morning and evening.

....

934. Uesugi Norimasa 上杉憲政 was attacked by the Hōjō clan in 1551 and fled to Echigo.

935. In present-day Nishihirai, Fujioka-shi, Gunma-ken.

936. Referring to Uesugi Kenshin 上杉謙信 (1530–1578), who controlled Echigo Province (present-day Niigata-ken) and often fought against the Hōjō clan and Takeda Shingen 武田信玄 (1521–1573).

937. Unidentified.

938. Unidentified.

939. Kōshō 小性, a close servant in a samurai household, who looked after the various private affairs of his master.

940. *Kaze no tayori*; see *OT*, 7-5, n.18.

One evening, a young servant girl appeared from somewhere and said to Shinrokurō, "Since you started living here, my mistress has been impressed by your heart, and now will come out here. Would you please meet her?" Saying this, the girl then disappeared. After a while, a pleasant fragrance permeated the air and a beautiful lady appeared behind the mound accompanied by the servant girl. Her beautiful features were not of this world. He wondered if a divine lady had descended from the heavens. She appeared as radiant as a deity-hermit from the realm of the *shinsen*.[941] He thought, "This must be the ghost of Iyako that I have heard of. Maybe she has come here today in response to my daily prayers. People speak of a lord of demons,[942] but I don't feel any fear [of someone from another world]. Although a human and a ghost are not the same, if we exchange our pledges and thoughts, there should be no difference between the dead and the living as far as our feelings are concerned." Thus thinking, he took her hands, led her inside, and talked with her for some time. When she was about to leave, she had him make a promise to her, saying, "Don't tell anyone about my coming here. Please wait for the evening." She then recited a poem.

soko fukaki
ike ni ouchou
mikurina wa
kuru towa hitoni
kataribashi suna

Relating to the *mikurina*[943]
Growing in the depths
Of the pool,
Do not tell the people
About my coming.

As soon as she finished, she seemed to leave the garden and then disappeared. She returned the following evening. Thus, her leaving at

....

941. *Shinsen* 神仙, "gods," "saints," or "hermits"; referring here to divine beings in general.

942. That is, something terribly frightening.

943. A type of water grass said to look like floating ropes when it drifts on the water's surface.

dawn and returning in the evening continued for about sixty days.

One day, Shinrokurō gathered the people in his household and told them various stories. Forgetting his promise to the lady, he began to talk about her. Now feeling curious, the people in the household peeked into his room through a hole in the wall the next time the lady came and talked with him. Strangely, they saw no one except a *togibōko* doll[944] in the place of a female servant.

One evening the lady came looking very sad and grudgingly said to Shinrokurō, "Why did you break your promise and tell your people about me? Because of that, our pledge is broken and we cannot see each other any more. This is the last time I will see you." After saying this, she tearfully recited a poem.

> *shibashi koso*
> *hitome shinobu no*
> *kayoiji wa*
> *araware somete*
> *taehate ni keri*

> The path for
> Our secret meeting
> Lasted for a while,
> But now it was found
> And is perished away.[945]

In tears, he recited his poem.

> *sashimo waga*
> *taezu shinobishi*
> *naka ni shimo*
> *watashite kuyashi*
> *kume no iwahashi*

> Although I have been
> Always bearing for

....

944. See *OT*, 3 3, n.16.

945. *Dairungushō*, Koi, 2; *Shingoshūishū*, Koi, 4, by Gonijōin.

Our secret love-path,
I regret to span
The Rock Bridge of Kume[946] [to break it].[947]

Now the woman tearfully took out a gold incense case and gave it to him, saying, "If your heart is unchanged, please look at this as my token." Shinrokurō took out prayer beads made of silver, gold, amber, and coral as he said to her, "This is nothing special, but take it to your place in the Land after Death as a memento of me." He placed it in her hands and asked her, "Will you set the time when we see each other again beyond this world?"

"Will you wait for the year of *kinohene*?"[948] Saying this, she disappeared like frost and snow melting away. The sad Shinrokurō missed her so much that a terrible depression exhausted his heart and body. The doctor gave him some medicine, and he recovered a month later.

Sometime later someone said, "Norimasa's loving daughter lived here and suddenly died from fear. This was done by the soul of the deceased Shiraishi Hannai, who fell in love with the daughter and was killed. While Norimasa was living here, Hannai's ghost appeared whenever it was cloudy and rainy. But lately, it stopped appearing and no one has seen it." Hearing this, Shinrokurō felt terribly frightened.

One cloudy and rainy evening, an emaciated and exhausted twenty-year-old man stood alone by the spring. He was dressed in a white silk kimono and *hakama* trousers, had disheveled hair, and was carrying a black stick.[949] When Shinrokurō faced the ghost and drew his large sword, it disappeared. After that, he invited a priest to perform the seven-day *suiroku*[950] service for the soul of the deceased. Perhaps the service softened the grudge, for the ghost never appeared again.[951]

....

946. *Kume no iwahashi*, referring to the legendary bridge in Kume that ruins the love affair of any couple who crosses it together.

947. *Dairingushō*, Koi 2; *Zokugoenshū*, Koi, 5 by Abbot Jichin.

948. That is, twelve years into the future since the end of the first *kinohene* (span of sixty years) after the fall of Hirai Castle in 1552 would be in 1564.

949. It is implied that the young man is the ghost of Hannai.

950. *Suiroku-saie* 水陸斎会, a Buddhist service during which a variety of food is offered to all living beings on land and in water.

951. The story is based on *Saikiki* 才鬼記, 魯季衛. Asai modifies the story, which reminds us of *OT*, 3-3, by adding historical facts about the Uesugi and Hōjō clans.

10-4 The Art of Shinobi[952]

Takeda Shingen of Kai Province[953] was close to his son-in-law, Imagawa Yoshimoto. After Yoshimoto was defeated by Lord Nobunaga, Shingen despised Yoshimoto's son, Ujizane, who was inferior to [Yoshimoto], and treated him disrespectfully. One time Shingen forcefully borrowed the *Kokinwakashū*[954] compiled by Lord Teika, which was a treasure of the Imagawa clan, and he hid it in his bedroom. Then one day, it was gone.

It was most strange that only the anthology was missing. Especially since no one except several of the subjects' children and female servants, who had served Shingen for generations, were permitted to peek into his bedroom. The room was full of famous swords, including a shorter *wakizashi*[955] decorated in gold and silver. Greatly surprised, Shingen secretly sent his men to search for it in the neighboring provinces, including Kai and Shinano. The infuriated Shingen said to his men, "No strangers could come here. Someone among my close attendants must have stolen it. The anthology is not something I need to worry about, but rather the fact that we allowed some *shinobi* to come in and steal it. That is most unsafe." Saying this, Shingen furiously jumped up and down as he inquired into the situation. Under this strong pressure, his close and distant attendants clenched their fists in fright.

Iitomi Hyōbu had a lowly servant called Kumawaka. He was nineteen years of age. By nature he was smart, brave, bold, and undaunted. When Shingen sent his men to the battle at Warigata Pass in Shinano, Iitomi too participated in the battle, but he had forgotten to bring the bamboo pole for the banner. He was planning to make a second attack at the Hour of the Rabbit [six o'clock in the morning] on the following

---

952. The Japanese title is "Shinobi no jutsu," the arts or techniques of *shinobi*, "stealthiness." The stealthy arts or the techniques of moving fast were later developed into the arts of the *ninja* or spy, who is also called *shinobi no mono*, "stealthy person."

953. See *OT*, 5-2, n.5.

954. There are discrepancies in the text. The *Kokinwakashū* 古今和歌集, the first imperial anthology of *waka* court poetry, was compiled by Ki no Tsurayuki in 914. According to *Kōyōgunkan* 甲陽軍艦, 11-1, the drunken Shingen took *Ise monogatari* (*The Tales of Ise*) from the Imagawa clan. Fujiwara Teika 藤原定家 (1142–1241) compiled the *Shin-kokinwakashū* 新古今和歌集 but not the *Kokinwakashū*.

955. 脇差し, a shorter sword used with the longer *katana* 刀.

day. The sun had already set and everyone was anxiously discussing what to do. Then Kumawaka advanced and said to them, "I will go and get it," and started to run. No one could believe him. About four hours later, he returned with the pole. When they asked him, "How did you do that?" he replied, "Since I was in a hurry, I did not take my certificate with me. When I arrived at Kōfu, all the gates were closed to stop communication among the people. So I climbed the wall, jumped over the hedges, and stealthily opened the door unnoticed by anyone. Soon I sneaked into the mansion, and brought the pole here."

Hearing him, Iitomi thought, "It is nearly one hundred *ri* from here to Kōfu on the eastern route. He went and came back under heavy guard but no one noticed him. He might be the one who stole the anthology. It would be a serious matter if this was found to be so." Thus thinking, he called Kumawaka to his side and asked him, "I didn't know you were so fast and good in the art of *shinobi*. Is it you who stole the anthology by Teika from Shingen?" Kumawaka replied, "I was only able to run fast and do *shinobi* well. I have served my lord since my youth, and I don't even know how my parents are in my old hometown. If you allow me to return to my old home, I will reveal the thief."

Iitomi replied, "That is easy. You may take a leave of absence. And don't report back until you catch the thief." So saying, after the battle at Wariga Pass, Iitomi sent Kumawaka to search [for the anthology]. During the search, Kumawaka saw a man in the western district[956] walking alone and as fast as the wind. When he stopped the man to speak to him, his men captured him from behind. The man said, "I am sorry to be tricked by Kumawaka. The reason I stole the anthology was to see inside Shingen's bedroom. Alas, if this had been found twenty days previously, we could have defeated Shingen. He is truly fortunate [to escape our attack]. I have been serving Lord Nagano,[957] the castellan of Minowa, Jōshū,[958] and am a former disciple of the *shinobi* expert Kazama[959] of Odawara. Since Shingen is my lord's enemy, I plotted to kill him. But I could not attain my purpose. Now quickly kill me." Thus

956. Referring to the area west of the Kamanashi River.

957. Nagano Narimasa, who opposed Shingen for a long time.

958. In present-day Misato-cho, Gunma-gun, Gunma-ken.

959. *Korogun monogatari*, 4-6 says that Kazama Saburō, a *shinobi* expert, served Lord Hōjō Ujizane of Odawara castle and harassed the Takedas, including Shingen.

he confessed and was killed. It is said that the anthology was sold in the capital, and Kumawaka took his leave and returned to his hometown.[960]

10-5 The Kamaitachi and Daibakaze[961]

Once some strange *kamaitachi* incidents occurred in the eight provinces of the northeast.[962] A man met a strong whirlwind and one of his thighs split open vertically as if sliced with a razor blade. He didn't bleed or feel much pain. The cut healed overnight after *josuiso* grass[963] was applied to it. No one knows who causes [the whirlwind]. They say it does not happen to well-mannered samurai, but can affect persons of lowly status, even if they are wealthy.

The people of Owari, Mino, Suruga, Tōtomi, and Mikawa Provinces experienced a similar case called *daibakaze*. It occurs when a mounted villager or someone walking a horse meets a whirlwind. Made of whirling sand, this whirlwind gradually becomes larger, rotating like a wheel in front and then above the horse. The horse's mane stands straight up with a red light running through it like a thread. The horse neighs violently, rears high on its hind legs, and falls down to die. Then as if nothing had happened, the wind instantly stops. No one knows whose deed this is. It is said that once when a whirlwind was passing above a horse, someone drew his sword and brandished it over the horse while reciting the *Kōmyō-shingon* incantation.[964] With this, the wind stopped and the horse was saved. This is called *daibakaze*.[965]

....

960. The story is based on the Chinese *Kengyōden* 剣侠伝. Asai adds the Japanese story of the stolen anthology from *Kōyōgunnkan* 11-1. In the original Chinese version, the protagonist steals a white jade pillow from the bedroom of Emperor Bunsō of the Tang dynasty. See *OT*, 7-3.

961. Both of these phenomena, *kamaitachi*, "the sickle-weasel," and *daibakaze*, "the bank-horse wind," are associated with whirlwinds. They have these names because contact with the vacuum caused by the whirlwind's air pressure slices open the skin.

962. These were Musashi, Sagami, Abō, Kamifusa, Shimoosa, Kamitsuke, Shimotsuke, and Hitachi.

963. Unidentified.

964. See *OT*, 7-2, n.4.

965. The story is based on *Dakukōki*, 上部員外張周封言今年云々. Asai introduces the Japanese phenomenon of *daibakaze*.

10-6 Impoverished Ryōsen
and the Way of the Tengu

Priest Ryōsen was from Kako District of Ban Province.[966] After losing his parents at a young age, he confined himself in a [Buddhist] grass-roofed hall, took the tonsure, and went to the Ashikaga School in Sō Province.[967] There he studied and accumulated merit for more than thirty years. He was familiar with both Buddhist and non-Buddhist classics, as well as the way of Shinto[968] and poetry. He was known for his wide knowledge, and he enjoyed staying at various *danrin*,[969] where many priests gathered for studies and ascetic practices. His eloquent speeches impressed his listeners and no one could compete against him. However, he was eccentric by nature and his career suffered because he was too poor to afford a paper robe. The sleeves of his robe were worn out and his daily meals were sparse.

Because of [his unfortunate circumstances], he did not become a high-ranking priest like a *chōrō* or *shōnin*, but rather remained an ordinary monk. However, for years he had aspired to fame and wealth. Lamenting his misfortune, he said to himself, "Oh, Ryōsen, Ryōsen, you are talented and learned. Your heart and mind are righteous and your name is well known. Why can't you be the master of a temple instead of struggling just to get by?" He tried to understand his situation and thought, "Priest Annen[970] died of hunger under the temple eaves while Kanshun[971] prayed at shrines. Were they lacking in morality? En no Shōkaku[972] was exiled to Izu Province while Kakuban suffered in

966. In present-day Kako-shi, Hyogo-ken.

967. The Ashikaga School, in present-day Ashikaga-shi, Tochigi-ken, used to teach Confucian studies and *ekigaku*, 易学, "fortune-telling."

968. See *OT*, Preface to Otogibōko (Kana), n.7.

969. 壇林, temples where monks study.

970. Annen 安然 was a scholarly priest of the Tendai school. His biography is incomplete. The reference to him dying of hunger is unidentified (*Zōdanshū*, 5).

971. Kanshun 桓瞬, a scholarly priest of the mid-Heian period, prayed for miraculous powers at the Inari shrine (*Kokonchomonjū*, 1; *Shasekishū*, 1; *Genkōshakusho*, 5).

972. En no Shōkaku 役の小角, a mountain ascetic of the Yamato and Nara periods, lived on Mount Kazuragi in Nara, and is regarded as the founder of *shugendō*, the way of the mountain ascetics. In 699 he was exiled to Izu.

Negoro.[973] This is not because their conduct lacked virtue. Kyōin[974] was blessed with a fief while Ankai[975] did not attain any priestly rank. This is not due to differences in their intelligence or ignorance. One ascetic was well dressed and ate to his content while Priest Shuon[976] suffered from hunger. This was not because of a lack of talent. It all depends on karmic relations from previous existences. This is called *tenmei*,[977] heavenly fate, in Confucian teachings. Ryōsen is an unfortunate victim of causes. Why are you vainly wishing for fame and wealth while suffering from a karmic cause?"

Thus he went back and forth in his mind while consoling his heart. However, he was so proud of himself and conceited about his knowledge and learning, and he was so angry about his place in this world that he finally became sick and died in Kamakura in the last year of Tenbun [1555]. He was buried by Kōmyōji.[978]

For a long time Eishun, a leader of the ascetics, was closely associated [with Ryōsen] as a fellow scholar. One day he met Ryōsen on the way to Fujisawa. Carried in an *urushi*-lacquered palanquin borne by eight men in white, Ryōsen looked quite different from the olden days when he was alive. Accompanied by several of his colleagues all beautifully dressed, his men in white were carrying a pair of ceremonial shoes with pointed toes, a chair with a back supporter, and a red umbrella. Ryōsen's splendid procession with a servant at the front was like that of a *kokushi*[979] or *sōjō*.[980] Dressed in the priest's vestment of nine folds,[981] and seated on a ceremonial carpet, Ryōsen called, "Aren't

....

973. Kakuban 覚鑁, a priest of the Shingon school in the late-Heian period, lived in Denpōin on Mount Kōya, but moved to Negoro Temple because of a boycott by his colleagues. He died there (*Mitsugonshōnin gyōjōuki*, 2).

974. Unidentified.

975. Ankai 安海 was a scholarly priest of Enryakuji in the late-Heian period. He was talented and died young.

976. Shuon 主恩, a scholarly priest of Kofukuji in the mid-Heian period, was exiled to Kyushu.

977. *Tenmei* 天命, "heavenly decree," referring to the way that heaven determines fate.

978. 光明寺, a scholarly temple in present-day Zaimokuza, Kamakura-shi representing the Jōdo, or Pure Land school of the northeastern area.

979. An imperial master.

980. An abbot.

981. A ceremonial robe made of nine pieces of cloth sewn together horizontally. It was one of the Six Articles or possessions of a priest.

you Eishun?" as he held out a cedar fan. Dismounting the palanquin, he took Eishun's hands and tearfully began to tell him about his past. Eishun said to him, "It's been only half a year since we were separated. During that time, you have climbed as high as the blue sky,[982] with a high priestly rank and abundant fiefs, while mixing with noblemen of the red gates.[983] Judging from your fabulous clothing and you being carried on a palanquin accompanied by colleagues, you must have attained the highest rank thanks to the excellence of your learning. I am truly envious of you." Ryōsen replied to him saying, "I have a position and have nothing to hide. Just look at what I am now. Come this way." Saying this he took Eishun into the hall of Kōmyōji. There was no one around to see them. The night was already deep, and Ryōsen continued, "I was always conceited but never committed anything against the Way. Although I knew it was all because of my past karmic relations, I constantly bemoaned my poverty and was angry and confused. After I died, I fell into the Way of the *tengu*.[984] I was appointed [to the position of] head of learning. I prepared documents by explaining their meanings and reasons, and transmitted the writings to others. Although the Way of the *tengu* is a way of demons, there is no evil in their conduct or deeds. [In the Way of the *tengu*] one is placed in a position according to one's abilities. [On the contrary], the human Way is mere sycophancy. Humans take bribes and hold flattery in high regard. Considering only outer appearances while ignoring what is inside, they appreciate people for being praised rather than for their abilities. Because of this tendency, the noble, military, and priestly classes are content with their official positions and fiefdoms and [their inferiors'] superficial and sycophantic attitudes. If a person is good and promotes the right way while refusing flattery, he dies with his deeds ignored by the world.

"The *kirin*[985] is sometimes splashed by the cart carrying night soil

....

982. The expression refers to high-ranking court officials.

983. The residences of high-ranking noblemen had red gates.

984. *Tengu* 天狗, "the heavenly dog," traditionally is associated with a mountain ascetic, who holds a huge maple leaf as a fan and wears a pair of high wooden clogs and a *tengu* mask, which has a long, high nose and a red complexion. The *tengu*'s demonic appearance frightened people. *Tengu* is still used to describe a conceited person.

985. The *kirin* 麒麟 is an imaginary horse that like the phoenix is said to appear in a politically ideal world. Its reference here suggests that in the present degenerate age, people do not recognize the kirin when it appears.

and hungers amidst grasses and plants, while the foolish donkey tires of bean gruel.[986] The phoenix lives in the thorny *karatachi* trees, while the common owl hovers amidst fragrant orchids and chrysanthemums. The wise men among the noble, warrior, and priestly classes, with their thin necks and hair, could fall into a ditch without anyone noticing. But flattering fools are recognized by the world and prosper. Thus manners and culture become degraded, and days of confusion outnumber days of goodness.

"But in our *tengu* Way, there are no mistakes in matching people with positions according to their talents and abilities. In general, regardless of rank and status, those who are conceited fall into the status of demons. Those who are unfaithful to their lords or unfilial to their parents definitely suffer from great pain, while those who accumulate merit and virtue are blessed with happiness. The logic of the karmic cycle tells no lies. Those among the emperors, warriors, and priests who obtain fame in this life become generals in our [*tengu*] Way, while the others become their subjects. Depending on their nature, some become obstructive and others are protective. The supreme ones uphold virtue, those in the next station accumulate merit, and the third kind excel in speech and language. Their status is preserved for a long time, even after death. With neither virtue nor merit, I excelled in delivering speeches. But now I am nothing. Just look at the result of my conceitedness."

Saying this, he jumped into the garden, and transformed himself into a fearful form with two wings, an uplifted nose,[987] and eyes full of flying sparks. Meanwhile, a cauldron containing molten iron descended from the sky. A monk descended after it and placed some molten iron into a jar. Then he transferred the contents into a cup and handed it to Ryōsen. As soon as the frightened Ryōsen drank it, his burning intestines burst out of his body as he fell down and rolled on the ground, and then vanished. Meanwhile, all of his colleagues and those who were accompanying him also disappeared.

It was already daybreak and Eishun found himself sitting alone at Enoshima Beach instead of in Kōmyōji hall. After he returned to his place [in the hall], he faithfully followed the Buddhist Way. He stayed

....

986. Here a common donkey is contrasted with the noble *kirin*. In the following sentence, an ordinary owl is contrasted with the legendary phoenix.

987. A turned up nose symbolizes conceit and arrogance.

away from worldly affairs and prayed for the repose of the souls of the deceased while traveling on pilgrimage from place to place.[988]

11-1 A Hidden Village

Utsumi Matagorō lived in Inami of Ban Province.[989] He was familiar with the military arts, and was especially good at archery and horsemanship. He was brave and courageous by nature.

One day he thought, "My name will never be known in the countryside. By relying on Lord Akamatsu in the capital and by serving the shogun, I may succeed during this time of change." Thus thinking, he went to the capital, where he found that the lord already had passed away. Again he thought, "I can't help it about Lord Akamatsu. I hear Gotō Kamon[990] lives in Uji. I should ask him for his help." So he began to make his way [to Uji].

The sun already had set and he lost his way. After traversing a small slope and grassy fields, finally he came to Kurusuno.[991] Heavy clouds darkened the sky and it began to sprinkle. He saw no one to ask the way and heard faint cries of monkeys as he spotted sporadic flashes of foxfire.[992] Finally he saw a *daigen* hall,[993] where Daigensui[994] was once worshipped to make it rain. The place was dilapidated with decaying pillars and slanting hedges. Piles of fallen leaves [in the garden] and broken eaves gave the place a frightful appearance. But since he could find no way to continue ahead or go back, he climbed up to the veranda and decided to spend the night in the hall.

....

988. The story is based on SS, 4-3 修文舎人伝. Asai introduces the *tengu* folk belief and tells of a Buddhist monk who became a *tengu* after his death because of his conceitedness.

989. A town on the east bank of the Kako River, in present-day Kakogawa-shi, Hyogo-ken.

990. Unidentified.

991. In present-day Yamashina-ku, Kyoto-shi.

992. *Kitsunebi* 狐火, or *onibi* 鬼火, flashes of phosphorus light often seen at night in fields and in the mountains.

993. 大(太?)元堂; possibly Hōrinji, a temple in present-day Kitaya-cho, Ogurusu, Fushimi-ku, Kyoto-shi.

994. Daigensui 太元帥, originally a child-eating demon, he was converted by the Buddha and became a protector and helper. Priest Jōgyō 常暁 was an orphan in Ogurusu and went to China in 834. He brought back a cult that had rituals to make it rain. The rituals, which were performed at Hōrinji, started on the eighth day of the first month and lasted for seventeen days (*Genkōshakusho*, Shaku Jōgyō).

At about the Hour of the Wild Boar [ten o'clock at night], he heard the sound of footsteps advancing from the mountain's eastern side. The footsteps gradually approached the hall and were accompanied by torchlight. He thought, "Coming to an old place like this at this hour, they must be either demons or a band of thieves." Feeling suspicious, he stealthily climbed up to the ceiling, held his breath, and kept quiet. Soon he heard the clamor of two scores of them coming into the hall, lighting it up [with their torches].

The one who was dressed gallantly and was first to sit down looked like the band's chief. Then the rest sat down as they lay down their spears, long swords, and bows and arrows. They seemed very attentive and looked like monkeys. Matagorō thought, "They are undoubtedly some kind of demonic creature. I will shoot one of them." He took out his bow and released an arrow with a forked head. Not missing its mark, the arrow squarely hit the chief's elbow. The shocked chief shouted out, "Oh, no! What happened?" At that the rest [of the band] extinguished their torches and fled in confusion. Soon all became quiet.

At dawn, Matagorō looked around and found bloodstains on the floor. "I will look to see where they end," he thought as he began to track the blood around the south side of the mountain. Walking farther to the west, he finally stopped at a large hole in the ground. Feeling strange, he walked here and there around the hole. Then he slipped on the ground, which was slightly damp from the early morning rain, and fell into the deep hole. It was too deep for him to climb out. "There is nothing for me to do here but die," [he thought as] he groped around in the dark and found a passage through a hole in the side. He quietly walked through the passage about one *chō* until he came out at a place as bright as day. There was a rock chamber with a stone gate that was guarded by several scores of men. They looked no different from those he had seen at the *daigen* hall. Surprised [to see him], one of the guards asked, "Who are you and why are you here?" Matgorō answered, "I came to the capital from Ban Province. I earn my living as a doctor. I went to the mountain to collect medicinal herbs, lost my way, fell into a hole, and have arrived here. Will you tell me the way to the capital?" Listening to him, the guards were pleased and said, "Heaven grants us good fortune. Yesterday our lord left the castle to amuse himself, and happened to be hit by a stray arrow. Now he is lying down because of the injury. Please come and treat him." They invited him in. The palace had a roof of polished tile. They took him to the inner part of the palace, where their master lay behind a hanging screen. The chief begged him in a strained voice, "I happened to leave the palace to amuse myself, and unfortunately was shot by a stray arrow. The poison already has penetrated to my bones. It is very painful and my life is in danger. Please cure me with your medicine so I can recover and enjoy life's pleasures. This will be a great favor." He was a big bald monkey. No one knew how old he was but he asked this favor while lying down and groaning with pain. Two very beautiful women attended him. Matagorō stood up, moved closer to the old chief, and took his pulse. While touching his wound, he said to him, "Don't worry. You will be fine soon. I have a famous medicine with me. If you take this, not only will you be cured but also you will live for a long time. Since it is a mar-velous medicine, it rejuvenates and prolongs your life as long as heaven and earth last." Saying this, he took a pill from the flint pouch on his waist and gave it to the chief. All the other monkeys were very pleased, especially when they heard that the medicine ensured longevity. They asked Matagorō, "We rarely meet any *shinsen*.[995] Please give us the pills too." So he tilted his pouch and gave pills to all of the other monkeys. They fought among themselves over the pills. Since the pills were made of a poison to kill animals when hunting, the monkeys soon fell to the ground, suffering and vomiting blood. Matagorō took the big sword by the pillow and slew them all. The poison caused those who tried to get up to stagger. In the end, he killed a total of thirty-six monkeys, large and small.

He said to the women, "You two must be the same kind of demonic creature. I will kill both of you." The two begged him through their tears, "We are not demonic creatures. One of us is the daughter of a man in Namiura of Daigo,[996] and the other is the daughter of Hirata in Fushimi Village.[997] Unexpectedly tricked by those fearful monsters, we fell into a deep hole. Not knowing the way home, we wanted to die here

....

995. 神仙, "gods" or "hermits," referring to those who have followed the Taoist Way and obtained special powers of flying and longevity.

996. Present-day Daigo, Fushimi-ku, Kyoto-shi.

997. In present-day Fushimi-ku, Kyoto-shi. Fushimi Village was a prosperous center for communications and transportation on the route to Osaka. It declined after the castle built by Hideyoshi was emptied in 1623.

but were unable to do so. So we have been in a most dismal situation serving these debased ones for sixty days and nights. Now you have killed them all. You have allowed us to return to the human [world] to meet our parents again. We greatly appreciate your favor."

Matagorō wondered, "I have killed all the demonic creatures, but I have no idea how to return to the human world. What shall I do?" Then a score of old men in white with *eboshi* hats appeared from nowhere and said to him, "We have been living here for a long time. But since those monkeys robbed us of our houses, treasure, and food, we have lost our livelihoods and lived far away, grieving our misfortune with our wives, children, and grandchildren. Without the power to overcome our enemies, we have consoled ourselves with waiting for an opportune time. Now you have destroyed them. Thanks to you, we have regained our homes. We have the highest appreciation for your good deed." Saying this, each one handed a wrapped package of gold to Matagorō. They too appeared non-human, and some were strange creatures with round eyes, pointed mouths, and long beards and eyebrows. Matagorō asked them, "You seem to have lived here for a long time and acquired mysterious powers. Why were you tricked by the monkeys and robbed of your homes? What [kind of beings] are you really? And where is this place?" An old one answered, "We are five hundred years old and changed ourselves once [to be in this present state]. The monkeys were eight hundred years old and changed themselves once. This is why we could not compete against them. Originally, we were the spirits of the Kyosei constellation[998] and messengers of the deity Daikoku.[999] This dwelling of mice is known as a hidden village. We don't harm the residents. Having accumulated merit and accomplished good deeds, we had flown to heaven, freely coming and going from Senkyō[1000] and enjoying the pleasures of mysterious powers. Meanwhile, the monkeys gathered and for years did bad deeds, taking young human girls for their own amusement and causing misfortune and harm to others. Their sins were finally exposed and they all were destroyed at the same place. Heavenly fate destroyed them through your hands. Without heavenly help, how could you have destroyed them? Close your eyes for a moment. We will return you to the human world."

When Matagorō closed his eyes, they carried him and the two girls on their backs. While moving along, he heard a violent rain and wind mixed with noisy voices. When he opened his eyes, he found himself riding on the back of a huge white mouse as large as a pig. It was running and followed by fourteen or fifteen others, who dug a hole in the ground. Soon Matagorō and the two daughters came out into a field. When he asked passers-by, "Where is this place?" they replied, "At the foot of Mount Kohata."[1001]

He took the two girls to their parents and the parents were so pleased and appreciative that they made him the groom of both girls. After that, he left the military and lived comfortably enjoying his wealth. Later he looked for the hole [which he had emerged from] at the end of the field at the foot of Mount Kohata, but only found overgrown grasses like *kaya*.[1002] Matagorō had no children and nothing is known of his later life.[1003]

....

998. 虚星, one of the twenty-eight constellations. Its direction is north and its animal is the mouse.

999. Daikokuten 大黒天, one of the Seven Lucky Gods, is revered in Japan as the god of wealth and especially of food. As a statue, its image often includes a mouse.

1000. See *OT*, 9-1, n.6.

1001. Kohatayama 木幡山 included present-day Kohata, Uji-shi and later Mount Fushimi.

1002. A Japanese pampas grass used for thatch roofs.

1003. The story is based on *SS*, 3-3 申陽洞記. Asai introduces the Akamatsu clan, which was closely associated with the Ashikaga clan. He sets the story in Fushimi-ku, Kyoto-shi.

11-2 The Inukami[1004] of Tosa Province and the Kinsan[1005]

For generations the people in Hata of Tosa Province[1006] believed in the *inukami*, or dog god. When an *inukami* owner went to a place and wished to have someone's treasure, like a *kosode*[1007] or musical instrument, the *inukami* would possess the person and place a curse on him. The possessed person would suffer from a high fever and feel pains in the chest and stomach. The pain was as excruciating as being pierced by a gimlet or run through by a sword. When this happened, the victim immediately had to go to the owner of the *inukami* and give him everything that he wanted. Then the illness would be cured. Otherwise the victim would suffer for a long time before inevitably dying.

Some time ago, when the provincial governor[1008] heard about this, he had the whole area surrounded by a wall and hedges and set a fire to kill everyone, men and women. Since then, the *inukami* was said to have been exterminated. But a clan that managed to survive the fire inherited the *inukami* and it is still alive today. Someone watched the *inukami* being transferred by its owner on his deathbed to the heir. It was a dog as small as a grain of rice and white, black, red, and mixed-colored. It left the dying person and jumped into the bosom of the heir. The new *inukami* owner hated his situation and could not help but regard it as a chronic illness.

The foreign land of Minkō[1009] often had visitations of the accursed *majimono*.[1010] The natives who had the chronic disease called *kinsan*, the golden silkworm, would transfer it to others by placing treasures like gold, brocade, hair ornaments, and other valuables at the left side of the road. Whoever picked them up and brought them home would suffer from the illness. The insect was shaped like a silkworm and gold in color. If a few of them took possession of a human, they increased

....

1004. 狗神, "dog god," the dog spirit or cult of the dog spirit (*Kiyūshōran* 嬉遊笑覧, 8, Hōjutsu).

1005. 金蚕, "golden silkworm," a legendary poisonous insect that eats brocade and human stomachs (*Honzōkōmoku* 本草綱目, 42).

1006. In present-day Hata-gun, Kochi-ken.

1007. See *OT*, 7-6, n.15.

1008. Possibly Chōsokabe Motochika, who unified the Tosa area in 1574.

1009. Possibly Koko or Binetsu, in present-day Fukkensho 福建省.

1010. Evil spirits sent to disturb people.

in number and soon filled the house and harassed the person. It is said that the victim is gradually cured of the illness only when the gold and other valuables that were picked up become exhausted.[1011]

11-3 A Pledge in a Changed Life[1012]

Toyoda Magokichi lived in Matsura Village[1013] in Matsura District of Hizen Province. He lost his parents during his youth and lived alone without a wife. His parents loved their only child and [left him some means and property]. He did not engage in farming or business, and was especially interested in Confucian studies. His daily activities included attending lectures.

One evening when he went out his gate, he saw a young girl of sixteen or seventeen walking from the south. Although she was not wearing a *kosode* over her other kimono, she did not appear to be of humble origins. Instead, her figure and manners appeared refined. Toyoda ran towards her and held one of her sleeves as he talked to her. Unlike a heartless rock or tree,[1014] she did not refuse him. Soon they became intimate, sharing their sleeves as they lay down together. After spending the night talking and making pledges to him, the girl lingered as she departed at dawn. She returned in the evening after sunset. When he asked her about her home and family, she did not answer him directly. When he pressured her to answer, she smiled as she said, "Since I am always dressed in a kimono dyed dark indigo-blue with a *tsuta*[1015] design, I am called Tsutako."[1016] Toyoda thought, "She might be serving a high-ranking family, and comes here secretly. Exposing her could bring her great trouble." Thus thinking, he did not question her further. Meanwhile their relationship became much closer as their intimacy increased like two birds aligning their wings on linked branches.[1017]

....

1011. The story borrows from *Honzōkōmoku*, 42. Asai introduces the traditional Japanese belief in the *inukami* of Tosa and a similar Chinese folk belief in the *kinsan*.

1012. The expression means that one makes a pledge after changing one's life, or after being reborn as another person.

1013. In present-day, Hamatama-cho, Higashimatsura-gun, Saga-ken.

1014. *Iwaki naranu*, "not to be a rock or tree," is used to describe a sympathetic person.

1015. Vine.

1016. Vine child.

1017. *Hiyoku-renri* is a typical expression used to describe intimate couples.

One night a drunken Toyoda playfully said to the girl, "I don't think I can open my heart unless you tell me about your family. I think of you like this." After saying this, he read a poem.

temakura no
ue ni midaruru
asanegami
shita niwa hito no
kokoro tokezu mo

Your hair in the morning[1018]
On my arm is
Very loose,
Yet your heart
Is not relaxed.[1019]

The lamenting girl replied to his poem with a poem of her own.

temakura o
kawasu chigiri ni
shita himo no
tokezu to kimi ga
musu bobore tsutsu

Although sharing
Your arm as a pillow,
Your heart is uneasy
Like the untied string of
My lower garment.[1020]

She finally began [to tell] her story. "Why should I hide anything from you now? I have known you since long ago. Otherwise, why

1018. *Asanegami*, the disheveled hair one has after sleeping.

1019. *Dairingushō*, Koi, 1; *Senzaishū*, Koi, 2 by Monk Saijū.

1020. *Shita-himo*, "lower-garment string," is a poetic expression (*kago* 歌語). The poem connotes that their relationship is intimate since she is using his arm as a pillow, but his heart is uneasy because she keeps secrets from him. It suggests his anxiety and frustration. *Dairingushō*, Koi, 1; *Zokushūishū*, Koi, 3, by Fujiwara Michitsune.

would we have established such a close relationship? I am not someone from this world. I don't mean to fool you, but I wonder if our karmic relation from our previous lives was very deep.

"Once there was quite a bold *daimyō* called Ōtomo Saemonsa[1021] in this Matsura Village. I was from Kishima District[1022] and was so good at making poems and playing *go* that no one could beat me. Because of [my talents], at the age of seventeen I was invited to serve the lord. I served him in the morning and evening and received much favor from him. At that time, you were also serving him as a *koshō*.[1023] I was so attracted by your good looks that I was always thinking of you. Unable to contain my feelings for you, one evening in the darkness before the lights were lit, I slipped my poem into your sleeve. The poem read:

yoso nagara
me niwa kakaredo
amagumo no
hedatsuru naka ni
furu namida kana

Seeing you at a distance
I am weeping.
My sad tears are
Like rain
Across the clouds.[1024]

The following evening you slipped your poem into my sleeve. It read:

yoso ni nomi
mine no shirakumo

1021. Unidentified. The area was governed by the Ōtomo clan, and Ōtomo Sōrin (1530–1587) controlled the six provinces of Kyushu. The name Saemonsa appears in a passage in the Ōtomoki, but the period does not correspond with the story.

1022. In the southwestern part of present-day Shiraishi-cho, Kishima-gun, Saga-ken, near the Ariake Sea.

1023. See *OT*, 10-3, n.6.

1024. *Amagumo no hedatsuru*, "spaced across rain clouds" or "separated by rain clouds," suggests a future hindrance to her love affair. *Dairingushō*, Koi, 1 by Lord Kimitada.

kiekaeri
taezu kokoro ni
furu namida kana

The white clouds
On a distant summit
Appearing and disappearing,
The tears in my heart fall like
The incessant rain.

Being the same age and working at the same place, we thus shared our feelings. But the household's rules were so strict that our only means of making pledges to each other was by exchanging [our poems]. Later, one of my colleagues found out about us [and reported it to our lord]. He was so angry that you and I were tied up and beheaded on the shore of the Matsura River. Since then, you already have been reborn as a human, but I was left alone in the Land after Death. My feelings for you are strong enough to survive over a hundred years. And now my spirit appears here and makes a pledge with you. Recollecting the past, my grief was incomparable," said the girl as her tears fell like rain.

Having listened to her, Toyoda also felt very sympathetic, saying, "Truly thanks to our relation over two generations [past and present], we have met like this. We should talk more and reminisce to our hearts' content. Who are you afraid of now [such that you] visit me in the evening and leave at dawn? You should live here and we will be man and wife." So saying, Toyoda kept the girl at his house and they became more intimate. Even though he was associating with a ghost, he never was afraid of her. Since he was not familiar with *go*, she taught him all the game's secret strategies. Soon he became such a *go* expert that no one in the area could beat him.

Meanwhile, she often talked about Saemonsa. "I remember everything as if seeing it before me. One time, our lord went to the river to amuse himself and was accompanied by his ladies. Two good-looking, beautifully dressed men were walking past on the other side of the river. One of his ladies said, 'Such beautiful men! I wish I could have [one of them] as my sweetheart.' When the lord heard her, he asked, 'Would you like to be his wife?' The lady did not say anything but just blushed. After a while a new wooden bucket with a lid was brought to the ladies. [A note] said, 'This is a gift for the men [whom the lady had noticed]. Open it and look at it.'

"When the ladies removed the lid, they saw the head of the lady who had praised the men. Many of them felt dizzy, their hands and feet trembled, and some lost consciousness and passed out.

"At another time, the lord did not allow the private sale of salt in his province, but bought it himself for the lowest price and sold it in the capital[1025] [at a higher price]. Someone posted a *rakusho*[1026] on his gate [criticizing his deed], saying:

sanakida ni
karaki okime o
saemon ga
kuni no shio yaki
nigari hate keru

With the stricter rules,[1027]
Salt making
Has become
Bitterly hard
In Saemon's province.

"When he heard this he said, 'This must have been the work of the salt makers.' He caught the three leaders of the salt makers and crucified them at a place facing the beach.

"Every spring, the lord lent money and rice[1028] to all the people in the province. He lent more to the wealthy and in the fall he demanded return of the principal at a high rate of interest. When the people could not repay the loan, some rich men in the area were taxed to pay it off. Others had to sell homes and property and send their wives and children away. Thus

----

1025. The *shioza* 塩座, a salt merchant group, monopolized the sale of salt in Nara and Kyoto during the middle ages.

1026. 落書, a note criticizing social conditions that commonly was posted in public places.

1027. *Okime* 置目, regulations controlling the sale of salt. Provincial governors made these regulations because salt was collected as a form of tax.

1028. *Senmai* 銭米.

each year the interest was extracted and the population of the province continued its steep decline. Again, someone read another poem that said:

> *muri ni kasu*
> *risen no kome no*
> *kazu yori mo*
> *kobosu namida wa*
> *itodo ootomo*

Our tears are much[1029] more
Than the rice and
The interest
Forcefully loaned
To us.

"Hearing about this, Lord Saemonsa said, 'The poor peasants could not have done this. This must have been done by the rich.' So he expelled more than ten rich men in the town and took all their wealth for himself.

"At one time, Lord Saemonsa gathered all of the monks in the province and held a memorial service for his deceased father that included meals.[1030] One of the monks arrived late. His robe was very old and worn. As no one invited him inside, he was left alone by the gateway, where he sat and ate his meal. When he finished, he placed the empty bowl upside down on the tray and left. Later when the servants tried to pick up the bowl, it would not move. They gathered and tried to lift it, but like a great mountain it could not be moved. The lord came out and moved it easily. When he lifted the bowl, he saw two poems [written on a piece of paper] under the bowl that read:

> *hana chirite*
> *kozue ni tsuwaru*
> *kudamono no*
> *ima ikuka arite*
> *ochin to suramu*

1029. *Ootomo*, "much," is a pun on Ōtomo.

1030. Buddhists offer *toki* 斎, (meals) to all the participants at the service, including the priests.

As the flowers scattered,
The fruits on the top
Of the tree,
How many days[1031]
Do they last before falling?

ware hito ni
tsuraki urami o
ootomo no
ie no kaze koso
fuki yowari kere

So much hardship
Given to others
Is declining
As the Ōtomo[1032] house's wind[1033]
Is becoming weaker.[1034]

"Even after reading the poems, the lord was not concerned and heartlessly continued to abuse his people. He killed them as if mowing a field of grass, and wantonly committed bad deeds. Finally, two years later, he had a misfortune and lost his life and family because everything is fated by the law of heaven. When one's conduct goes against the law [of heaven], one definitely meets misfortune.

"Now, thanks to our past relationship, I have become very intimate with you. But in one year, my leave of absence from the Land after Death will come to an end."

Days and months went by quickly. One year already was gone as time passed as quickly as light and dark.[1035] Before long the girl did not feel well. A doctor was called in but she would not take any medicine.

....

1031. *Ikuka* 幾日, "how many days," is associated with another expression, *ikuka* 幾果, "how many fruits."

1032. See n.18.

1033. *Ie no kaze*, or *kafū* 家風, "family tradition," here means the prosperity or prestige of the clan.

1034. Both *kyōka* 狂歌, wild or satirical poems, criticize the province's social conditions and suggest the impending downfall of the Ōtomo clan.

1035. *Kōin* 光陰, "light and shade" or "light and dark," is a typical expression used to describe how time elapses.

Taking his hand, she said to Toyoda, "Reminiscing about our past and our deep pledge as man and wife are coming to end. I revealed myself in the form of a spirit of the Land after Death. As I was closely pledged with you, in return I was blessed with your affection.

"Recollecting the old times, I was caught by the attachment of love and fell into unexpected unhappiness. Although the sea becomes *higata* and a rock boils in hot water, my grief would be hard to wipe away.[1036] Even if heaven and earth collapsed, our feelings would never be forgotten. We made a pledge for our future life by forming an intimate relationship in our past life. From now on, I am returning to the Land after Death. One hundred years passed since we were killed, and our present relationship lasted for one year. After waiting such a long time, I met you again. The clouds in my heart finally have cleared away.[1037] So do not lament any more." Tearfully the girl finished speaking. Toyoda, also in tears, said to her, "Please stay here for a while. What will you think about me after your departure when I am left alone?" In tears the girl recited a poem.

nagori o mo
oshimade isogu
kokoro koso
wakare ni masaru
tsura sa narikere

Nothing is harder
Than separation
To the pounding heart
When dreading
A hurrying departure[1038]

1036. *Higata* 干潟, "mudflat" or "tideland," here suggests a salt pan. *Nanji*, "you," could have been used mistakenly instead of *umi* 海, "sea." I use "sea" here. The sentence may be describing the suffering and frustration she felt while her spirit waited for its appearance in this world. This shows why Buddhists perform elaborate funeral services—so that departed souls do not return to this world but rather settle in another.

1037. *Omoi no kumo*, "clouds of thinking," likens fulfilling the wish to see the beloved to clouds clearing away.

1038. *Dairingushō*, Koi, 2.

After reciting the poem, the girl fell on the floor facing the wall. "What happened?" Calling her name, Toyoda found that she had expired, leaving her lifeless body on the floor. He grieved and lamented in vain. Then picking her robe up off the floor, he recited a poem.

utsuri ka ni
nani shimini ken
sayogoromo
wasure nu tsuma to
omoishi mono o

Why is her fragrance
On the night robe?
I only wish to
Remember my
Unforgettable wife.[1039]

When her body was placed in the coffin and sent to the burial ground, he discovered that the coffin was very light. He opened it to see that only her robe remained inside. Toyoda took the coffin to a temple, buried it there, gave a generous funeral service, and never took a wife again. He took the tonsure and traveled around Shikoku and Kyushu. Finally he sailed to China aboard a merchant ship and nothing more was known about his life.[1040]

1039. The term *tsuma* in *wasurenu tsuma*, "unforgettable wife," is associated with another term, *sayogoromo* 小夜衣, "night robe" or "bedclothes." The edge of the long night robe is also called *tsuma*. The poem can be interpreted, "Why has her fragrance so permeated the bedclothes? It makes me even sadder when I recall her." *Dairingushō*, Koi, 2.

1040. The story is based on *SS*, 4-5 緑衣人伝. Asai introduces material from a local tradition about Princess Sayo of Matsura.

11-4 The Demonic[1041]
Seven-Step Snake[1042]

Middle Councilor Okazaki[1043] had an old villa south of Okazaki,[1044] at the western foot of Mount Higashi in Kyoto. For a long time the villa was dilapidated and nothing was alive there except profusely growing grass. Someone named Urai bought the land and built a house. The people [in the neighborhood] said, "No one lives on this lot because of the demonic snakes." Urai did not believe these words, built a house, and began living there. [As soon as he did], several snakes three to four feet long appeared and were crawling on the ceiling. He told his servants to get rid of them. The snakes stared at the servants with glaring eyes and raised heads and scales. The frightened servants retreated. Feeling most strange, Urai hit the snakes with sticks, put them into a wooden bucket, and threw them into the Kamo River.

On the following day, fourteen to fifteen snakes appeared and were taken away. On the next day, about thirty of them appeared. The more of them that were taken away, the more that came out. Later two to three hundred snakes appeared. They were five to seven feet long, speckled white, black, and blue, and had two protruding ears. With their red mouths and feet they looked like dragons. Their number increased each day. Despite being taken away and abandoned, there seemed to be no end to them.

Feeling very strange, finally Urai burnt incense, offered *hei*,[1045] and held the ceremony for the Earth Deity.[1046] He wrote his wish on a piece of paper, saying, "I obtained this lot with some thousand *ryō* and this is the lot where I should live. Why are strange things that bother me happening, like the snakes? Among the earth deities, the

---

1041. *Yōkai* 妖怪, something strange and mysterious.

1042. The poisonous bite of the *shichifuja* 七歩蛇, the seven-step snake, is so strong that the victim cannot walk more than seven steps before collapsing.

1043. Unidentified.

1044. In present-day Okazaki, Sakyō-ku, Kyoto-shi; aristocrats used to own villas there.

1045. Strips of white, gold, or gilt-colored papers inserted in a wooden stick and offered to gods as gifts.

1046. *Chimatsuri* 地祭, a ceremony dedicated to the earth deity conducted before beginning construction of a building.

Five Dragon Kings[1047] have their own duties and positions. Why do they annoy the owner of this lot? If the Dragon Kings knew about this, they would quickly dispel the strange happenings. Otherwise, they are violating their divine positions[1048] and will be unable to avoid punishment by the Heavenly Emperor." Having written it, he then read it aloud.

That night, he heard terrible noises under the ground. In the morning he saw that all the grass [in the garden] had withered overnight and there was a huge stone partly broken and tilted [in a corner of his garden]. The servants felt this to be most strange so they walked to the green grass[1049] [by the stone] and dug up the ground around the stone to get rid of it. There they saw a snake four to five inches long running away. The green grass immediately died as the snake passed over it. The servants were striking and trying to kill it. The snake was only four inches long. It was crimson red with two ears and four legs. With

....

1047. Unidentified.

1048. *Shinshoku* 神職, "divine position" or "divine occupation," here referring to the work of the Dragon Kings, who serve the Heavenly Emperor Tentei 天帝 and control everything under the heavens.

1049. The grass near the stone did not wither the previous night.

its scales, it looked like a little dragon. The color of the skin between the scales was gold. The people [in the neighborhood] said, "We have never seen or heard of any snake like this." A priest of Nanzenji[1050] came and said, "This is called the seven-step snake. When people are bitten by it, they die instantly. The poison is so strong that the victim can walk just seven steps [before falling]. It appears in a Buddhist sutra."

Thereafter, no snakes appeared in Urai's lot. People said that all of the other snakes were incarnations of the seven-step snake.[1051]

11-5 A Wandering Soul

A smith called Tomokatsu lived in Yuge in Kawachi Province.[1052] One day he went to Kōriyama in Yamato on an errand and started home in the evening. Since he was very tired, he rested by the side of the mountain. There he saw someone riding a horse and leading another saddled one. Tomokatsu spoke to the rider, "If you are heading to Kawachi, please lend me your horse. I am very tired. Since you are taking the extra horse with no rider, I hope you can let me ride it."

"Surely. It's easy to do that. Please cross the river and dismount on the other side," replied the owner of the horse. So Tomokatsu happily crossed the river and returned the horse, saying, "I'm very appreciative of your favor." The horse owner whipped his horse and drove away.

Late that night Tomokatsu finally arrived home, where his wife, children, and siblings all were gathered around the table happily eating and chatting. They paid no attention to Tomokatsu. He called the names of his children, brother, and sister, and they completely ignored him. They were amusing themselves, laughing, drinking, and chatting as before. The angry Tomokatsu raised his voice and shouted at them, but no one reacted. Then he punched them. But nothing happened. They said to each other as they continued drinking, "If

1050. 南禅寺, in present-day Sakyō-ku, Kyoto-shi. The temple was the headquarters of the Rinzai sect. It was very prosperous and prestigious, but declined after the Ōnin war. It was revived with the assistance of the Toyotomi and Tokugawa clans.

1051. The story is based on *Tetsuisandansō* 鉄囲山談叢, 劉器之安世元裕臣云々. Asai sets his version of the story of the poisonous seven-step snake in the Okazaki area.

1052. Present-day Yao-shi, Osaka-fu. Yuge was the headquarters of Mononobe Moriya, who was an opponent of Prince Shōtoku.

Tomokatsu were here, we would be much happier!" Finally Tomokatsu thought, "So, I must have lost my life and only my soul is here. My wife, children, and other family members cannot see me." Since no one paid him any attention, he tearfully left home and rested outside the village.

Then he saw a very noble man wearing a crown passing by on a black horse with many attendants. The nobleman was dressed in a pair of loose ceremonial *sashinuki* trousers and a purple ceremonial *naoshi* robe with a large crest. He pointed to Tomokatsu with his whip and said, "That is the soul of a man whose life is not yet ended. The soul must be wandering, as it was involved in an unexpected event." A man appeared in red with a tall *eboshi* hat, prostrated himself before the horse, and said to the [nobleman], "He is Tomokatsu Yuge, whose life is not ended. But he met the Water Deity and borrowed a horse from him. To amuse himself the deity took Tomokatsu's soul. I have come here to return the soul to his body." The nobleman slightly smiled as he said, "It is not proper that the Water Deity, for no reason and just for amusement, fooled with the life of a man. The deity definitely should be punished tomorrow." The man in red appeared frightened, quickly stood up, and called Tomokatsu, saying, "The mounted nobleman is Prince Shōtoku,[1053] who has come out of Shinaga Mound. The prince always goes around the country and protects the people by punishing evil deities and demons. I come here as a relative of the Water Deity. I must return you to the human world. Close your eyes for a while." Saying this, he came behind Tomokatsu, who felt someone pushing his back, and as if waking up from a dream, he instantly revived on the west bank of the Yamato River. Tomokatsu got up and went home to find his wife and children happily welcoming him, saying, "Today all our family members are gathered here. You have come home late." When they heard Tomokatsu's explanation, they were all amazed and felt it was very strange.[1054]

....

1053. Prince Shōtoku 聖徳太子 (574–622), propagated the teachings of Buddhism as Empress Suiko's regent and rode around the country on a black horse that could run and fly (*Shōtokutaishiden* 聖徳太子伝, 6).

1054. The story is based on *Shuiki*, 翡拱. Asai introduces Prince Shōtoku, who helps the protagonist.

11-6 The Mystery of the Fish

Ōshima Fujigorō Morisada was wandering around the country during the Ōnin era[1055] and finally settled down near the cape of Suzu in Noto Province[1056] to wait for his time [to succeed in the world]. By nature he liked raw fish, especially *namasu*.[1057] If he didn't eat it daily, he lost his appetite. So he said to his people, "Among all the delicious foods from the mountains and sea, nothing is better than the taste of *namasu*. I never tire of it."

One day he invited five or six young friends to the beach to amuse themselves.

It was a windless day with a calm sea. A fisherman had caught many kinds of fish in his net and brought his boat back to the beach. Seeing this, Morisada said to his friends, "Let's buy the fish, make *namasu*, and prepare food as a memory of this day!" So saying, he bought five or six baskets of fish and went to the fisherman's house to borrow some cooking utensils. Then he spread straw mats on the beach, made the *namasu*, piled it high in large bowls and barrels together with other cooked fish, and began to enjoy the food with his friends. After he finished eating a bowl of *namasu*, suddenly he felt something stuck in his throat. He immediately vomited it out. It was a fish bone as small as a pea. The color was slightly pink like a pearl. He put it into a small rice bowl with a lid and placed it by his side. Then he picked up his chopsticks and resumed eating the *namasu*. Before everyone finished eating, suddenly the rice bowl tipped over on the straw mat and the lid fell off. Now the small bone inside the rice bowl had grown into a moving human form one foot tall.

He was very amazed, and all his friends felt it very strange and were staring at it. After a while it became a naked man five feet tall, and he began to attack Morisada. Grabbing his large sword, Morisada unsheathed it and swung it at the man, who evaded it as fast as lightning and flew around Morisada like a dragonfly. He hit Morisada's head with his fist, catching him off guard. While fighting, the man hit Morisada's back and blood fell onto the sand. Finally, as soon as

1055. 1467–1469.

1056. In the northeast part of present-day Noto Peninsula, in Ishikawa-ken.

1057. 膾, thinly sliced seafood marinated in vinegar and sake.

Morisada slashed at the man's wrist, the man vanished. Morisada's friends rushed to help him, but could see nothing because of a sudden thick fog. They only heard the noise of fighting. When the fog lifted, they saw Morisada covered with blood, saying, "Everyone, look at this. I cut off the enemy's wrist. The monster is now gone." When the people looked, they saw it was the fin of a large fish. Morisada passed out. Various medicines finally revived him, but he remained unconscious as if dreaming. When his injuries were healed, he finally regained consciousness. Asked about the incident, Morisada replied, "I don't remember a thing." Only his friends who were there knew the details of the incident. So [they concluded that] the spirits of the fish must have gathered and revealed themselves to display their mysteriousness [in the form of the naked man].[1058]

12-1 The Plum Blossom[1059] Spirit

The plum tree at Kaizenji[1060] in Inago District of Shinshū Province[1061] was famous for its plum blossoms. It bloomed in the early winter[1062] and the blossoms' fragrance permeated all four directions. People of the neighboring villages and those who appreciated tasteful things went to the temple every day to view the blossoms.

In general, Shinshū was a dark and cold province. During winter, fresh snow fell before the old snow melted away. Violent storms blew in and all the plants and grasses bloomed late, except for this temple's plum blossoms, which withstood the winter and began blooming early. Who would not admire such blossoms?

Hanishina Bunji, a subject of Murakami Yorihei,[1063] was a very

....

1058. The story is based on *Dakukōki*, 和州劉禄事者云々. Asai narrates a strange incident on Suzu Beach in Noto during the Ōnin era.

1059. *Sōbaika* 早梅花, "early plum blossoms," referring to blossoms that appear early in the winter season, like in the second month. They are highly appreciated precisely because they bloom in spite of the cold weather.

1060. A Zen temple of the Rinzai sect in present-day Kamikawaji, Iida-shi, Nagano-ken.

1061. The southern part of Shinano Province.

1062. The beginning of the second month.

1063. Murakami Yorihei, or Murakami Yorihira (d. 1520), was the lord of Kuzuo Castle, in present-day Sakashiro-cho, Hanishina-gun, Nagano-ken. He fought eleven battles in a single day against Nagao Tamekage in Echigo (*Koyōgunkan*, 5).

sensitive man. Besides practicing the military arts, he cultivated the way of poetry. To his companions' amusement, whenever he saw a tasteful scene while out camping, he composed a poem to express his feelings. No one thought ill of him because he was a man with such a sensitive heart.

At that time, the Takeda clan[1064] of Koshū and the Murakami clan of Shinshū were fighting one another and each set up their own military headquarters. Once while he was in camp, Bunji heard that the blossoms in the temple were at their best. So he secretly left with a servant and made his way to the temple by following the fragrance [of the plum blossoms]. While viewing the blossoms, he recited an old Chinese poem. "The branches facing south [appear] warm while those to the north cold. The spring breeze [wafts] through both branches."[1065] The moon already had risen over the mountainside. Deeply touched by the blossoms, Benji recited a Japanese poem.

hibiki yuku
kane no koe sae
niouramu
mume saku tera no
iri ai no sora

The echoing sound
Of the temple bell
Carries the fragrance
Of the plum blossom
Under the evening sky.[1066]

A strange woman about twenty years old appeared accompanied by a young girl. She was wearing a white *kouchi*[1067] over her plum-blossom-colored undergarment. Her beauty was otherworldly. Gazing at the moon with the blossoms before her, she recited a poem.

....

1064. The Murakami clan fought against Takeda Nobutora in 1522. In 1548, Murakami Yoshikiyo finally defeated Takeda Shingen at Uedahara, in present-day Ueda-shi, Nagano-ken.

1065. *Jibungoshū* 事文後集, 28, Baika.

1066. A similar poem appears in Fujiwara Teika's *Shūigusō* 拾遺愚草.

1067. An everyday kimono with a shortened skirt worn by noble women.

naga mureba
shiranu mukashi no
nioi made
omokage nokoru
niwa no mume ga e

While gazing at
The blossoms in the garden,
I recall even the fragrance of
The unknown old days
That remains on a plum branch.[1068]

After this, she rested for a while. On hearing her poem, Bunji became so overwhelmed with mysterious and unbearable feelings that he
approached the woman, held her sleeve, and playfully spoke to her, "I
wonder if it's only the beauty of the blossoms that is competing under
tonight's moon? Your sleeves are just as fragrant as [the blossoms]."
The woman did not seem to be at all surprised and replied, "Allured
by the plum fragrance, I came here to view this evening's moon. I am
happy to meet someone as sensitive as you."

....

1068. *Mume ga e*, "plum branch." A similar poem appears in *Shūigusō*.

The woman's quiet manners and the way she spoke to Bunji were very fascinating. He immediately told his servant to go to a sake shop, and as soon as the drink arrived, he and the woman sat under the temple eaves and exchanged several cups. Intoxicated by the sake, he became friendlier, and recited a poem.

sode no ue ni
ochite wa nioeru
mume no hana
makura ni kiyuru
yume ka tozo omou

The plum blossom falls
And lends its fragrance
To my sleeves.
Was it just dreams
Disappearing on my pillow?[1069]

The woman replied with her poem.

shikitae no
temakura no no no
mume naraba
nete no asake no
sode ni niowamu

If it is the plum
Of the old[1070] Temakura Field,[1071]
Its fragrance will
Stay on my sleeves
After I awaken at dawn.[1072]

1069. *Makura* "pillow," suggests the couple sharing the same pillow while lying down. *Fukishō*, Spring, 3.

1070. *Shikitae* refers to something old that people used to have or remember, such as customs and traditions.

1071. *Temakura no no*, "Temakura Field," is an *utamakura*, a poetic place. It is also associated with the term *temakura* 手枕; see *OT* 8-3, n.37.

1072. The poem implies her consent to share an arm pillow with him, a response to his suggestive poem. *Fukishō*, Spring, 3.

As she recited her poem, they became so intimate that they made a pledge to each other. Intoxicated after exchanging several more cups, they lay down until dawn, when the clouds began to rise in the eastern sky.

Finally Bunji awoke from his dream and found that he was lying alone at the foot of the plum tree. He saw neither the woman nor her young maid. He heard only the crows crying in the dawn sky. The moon had sunk into the west while the lingering [image of the woman] stayed with him.

Long ago in China, Saigo[1073] saw some peach blossoms inside a palace gateway. Two women appeared and sang with him as they enjoyed drinking. They promised to see each other again the following spring. When Saigo returned to the place in the spring, he saw no women. But a poem was written on the left door of the gate. "Inside this gate on this day last year, women as beautiful as the peach blossoms [appeared], but disappeared. And no one knows where. As in the olden days, only the blossoms smile in the spring breeze."[1074]

That was an example in China and this was in this country. What future did Bunji pledge with the woman? And how did he pledge it? If she were a human being, he might be able to see her again. But he was convinced that she and the young girl were spirits of the blossoms. It was very unusual that the fragrance on his sleeves was that of the blossoms [in the temple garden]. Even after returning to his quarters, Bunji could not forget her. In the evening he missed her so badly that he cried [as he recited a poem].

mume no hana
niou tamoto no
ikanareba
yūgure goto ni
harusame no furu

Why every evening
Does the spring rain

1073. 崔護, a Chinese man of the Tang dynasty.

1074. *Jibungoshū*, 11.

Fall[1075] on my sleeves,
Leaving the fragrance of
The plum blossoms?[1076]

Bunji felt everything in this world was futile. Under the moon at dawn,[1077] his powerful yearning [for her] left him brokenhearted.

The following day he died on the battlefield, as if preferring death to a life of inexhaustible grief and lamentation.[1078]

12-2 A Letter from a Ghost to Her Parents

Tatsuko was a daughter of Masaki in East Sakamoto[1079] of Gō Province. She was a talented child. Her wealthy parents raised her with love and taught her the ways of poetry and literature. Thus Tatsuko grew up with her beautiful features and gentle heart.

Kazuma of the Ashizaki lived next door to Tatsuko. Being the same age, Kazuma and Tatsuko played together during childhood. People teased them saying, "These children of the same age will surely be married in the future." The two believed the people's words. They thought, "During my life I will love only this person." And they opened their hearts to each other. As time passed, they no longer played together. Kazuma went to a mountain [temple][1080] to become a *chigo*[1081] [and study] while Tatsuko remained in her room deep inside her house.[1082]

One day on his way home, Kazuma sent two poems to Tatsuko.

....

1075. *Harusame no furu*, "spring rain falling," suggests the protagonist's sad feelings; his falling tears are implied by the spring rain. Spring is here associated with the plum blossoms.

1076. *Fukishō*, Spring, 3.

1077. *Ariake no tsuki* 有明の月, "the dawn moon," is here related to *tsukinu*, "inexhaustible" (like the protagonist's grief). The dawn moon also contrasts with the evening's spring rain in the previous poem, suggesting that the protagonist's grief continues from morning to evening.

1078. The story is based on the tale of Saigo Kassui, in *Jibungoshū*, 28, Baika. Asai created a romantic tale by introducing some Japanese *waka* poems.

1079. The eastern part of present-day Sakamoto, Otsu-shi, Shiga-ken.

1080. Enryakuji, on Mount Hiei.

1081. A boy attendant at a temple, usually trained in manners and basic reading and writing skills.

1082. *Mado*, "window," is related to *shinsō* 深窓, "deep window," meaning the inner part of the house. It refers to girls who live deep inside the home and are unexposed to worldly affairs.

hito shirezu
musubi kawase shi
waka kusa no
hana wa minagara
sakari sugu ramu

The fresh grass
On which we made
Our secret pledge,
Has it now passed
Its prime?

shira rume ya
yado no kozue o
fuki kawasu
kaze ni kake tsutsu
kayou kokoro o

I wonder if you know
The breeze on top
Of the tree in my garden
Carries my heart
When it blows toward you.

Very pleased, Tatsuko responded with her poems that expressed how much she missed him.

tsukihi nomi
nagare yuku yuku
yodogawa no
yodomi hate taru
naka no ause ni

Days and months
Flow and pass away,
But our meetings[1083]

....

1083. *Ause*, "meeting water rapids," implies the protagonists' meeting.

Are like the static flow
Of the Yodo River.[1084]

ina wa kaku
taenishi mama no
ura ni ouru
mirume o sae ni
nami zo tadayou

Only the *mirume*[1085]
Grows and floats
On the waves
By the now-deserted
Mama Beach.[1086]

When Tatsuko turned seventeen, her parents planned to find a husband from a respectable family. But she would not accept anyone. Finally she became bedridden from her endless weeping. When she was secretly asked, she confided to her parents, "I have promised myself to Kazuma next door. Unless I marry him, I will die. I will not marry anyone else." The parents contacted their neighbor using a proper go-between. The Masaki family was much wealthier than the Ashizaki and [Kazuma's] parents repeatedly declined the proposal for their son, saying, "Even with his good looks and talents, our Kazuma is no match for her." But the Masaki family insisted, saying, "It is our daughter's wish. If he marries her, he will have much treasure of gold and silver. But talking about treasure during marriage arrangements is the vulgar way of barbarians. We are arranging the marriage based on the personality and talents of our groom." Thus saying, Tatsuko's parents decided on a good day [for the wedding]. All the arrangements were taken care of by the bride's family. When the day arrived, Tatsuko and Kazuma were finally married, and their rejoicing was limitless for

....

1084. A similar poem appears in *Dairingushō*, Koi, 2.

1085. *Mirume*, "seaweed," also means "to see," implying the protagonists' rendezvous.

1086. *Taenishi*, "to become extinct," is translated as "deserted" in connection with *mama no ura*, Mama Beach, a poetic landscape in Shimofusa Province. The poem suggests the couple's estrangement and frustration with their thwarted relationship.

they had no more guards[1087] interfering with their rendezvous. Tatsuko recited a poem.

hitori ne no
mado ni sashi iru
tsuki kage o
morotomo ni miru
yo wa zo ureshiki

The moon shadow
Slipped through the window
Of my solitary sleep.
Now I watch it with you.
What a happy night this is![1088]

Kazuma replied with his poem.

yonayona wa
kakochite sugishi
mado no moto ni
tomo ni nagamuru
ariake no tsuki

Night after night
I watched the moon
Passing by your window.
Now together we watch
The dawn moon.

Thus their deep pledge to each other was comparable to birds flying side by side in the sky and intertwined branches of a tree.[1089]

Only a half year later, Lord Oda Nobunaga attacked Gō Province

....

1087. See *OT*, 9-3, n.33.

1088. *Dairingushō*, Kol, 2.

1089. See *OT*, 11-3, n.4.

and Enryakuji stood against him.[1090] On the twelfth day of the ninth month of the second year of Ganki [1571], Lord Nobunaga burned down all the buildings on Mount Hiei[1091] and Hiesanō Shrine.[1092] Because of that, many homes in Sakamoto [at the foot of Mount Hiei] were plundered and families scattered in all directions. Tatsuko was first captured by Sakuma Nobumori,[1093] a subject of Lord Nobunaga, and her whereabouts became unknown. After the Asai[1094] and Asakura were destroyed, Gō Province regained peace. People finally returned home in relief.

Kazuma left his parents and started seeking out his wife. He was determined not to return unless he found her. When he came to the crossroads of Hiei, the people said to him, "Masaki's daughter, Tatsuko, was caught by Sakuma in the camp." He went to the castle of Takaya[1095] in Kawachi Province, where the people told him, "After the castle of Katano[1096] fell, she went to the castle of Odani[1097] in Gō Province." In Gō Province he heard that she went to Kyoto. He went here and there because her whereabouts were uncertain. Finally, in the first month of the eighth year of Tenshō [1580], he heard people saying, "Sakuma is now in the Tennōji camp[1098] with the forces of the seven provinces[1099] since Priest Kennyo[1100] is confined in the castle." So he went to the Tennōji camp in Osaka in Settsu Province. While traveling through

1090. The monks of Enryakuji fought against Nobunaga. Some sided with the Asai and Asakura (*Nobunagaki*, or *Shinchōki* 信長記, 4).

1091. Twenty-one buildings on Mount Hiei were burned down, including a bell tower and a building storing the sutras (*Shinchoki*, 4).

1092. Hiyoshi Shrine, in present-day Sakamoto, Otsu-shi, Shiga-ken, protects Enryakuji and is another example of the amalgamation of Buddhism and Shinto.

1093. Sakuma Nobumori (1527–1581) assisted Nobunaga in attacking the Ishiyama Honganji.

1094. Asai Nagamasa died in 1573 during Nobunaga's attack.

1095. Takaya Castle, in present-day Furuichi, Habikino-shi, Osaka, fell to Nobunaga's force of over thirty thousand (*Honchō shōgunki* 本朝将軍記, 12).

1096. Katano Castle, also called Kisabe Castle, in present-day Kisabe, Katano-shi, Osaka, fell in 1572 (*Shinchōkōki* 信長公記, 5).

1097. Odani Castle, the castle of Asai Nagamasa, in present-day Ibe, Kohoku-cho, Higashiasai-gun, Shiga-ken, fell in 1573 to the Sakuma, the vanguard of the Nobunaga force (*Shinchokoki*, 6).

1098. The camp was set up in order to attack the Ishiyama Honganji in Osaka.

1099. These were Mikawa, Owari, Ōmi, Yamato, Kawachi, Izumi, and Kii.

1100. The eleventh abbot of the Ishiyama Honganji.

various provinces for months, Kazuma's robe became as tattered as a crane's broken wings. His features were changed. He was now emaciated and [his complexion] dark from sleeping in deep thickets of fields where his sleeves were constantly wet from dew and tears. When he came to the camp, he saw soldiers on guard, who frightened him so much that he did not ask any questions. While he was waiting for an opportune moment, some foot soldiers became very skeptical about him and shouted to each other, "He must be an enemy who is spying on us. In that case, don't let him set even one foot in the camp. Catch him, cut his head off, and leave the head in Abeno Field for a lesson!" Thus saying, they ran out of the camp, caught him, tied him up, and reported to General Sakuma about him. "Bring the prisoner here. I will question him and decide what to do with him." Saying this, Sakuma sent Kazuma to the main camp, where Sakuma investigated by asking Kazuma, "Are you one of the confined men of Osaka Castle? Why are you here in this camp? If you confess, you will be free from the water and fire tortures." Kazuma replied to him without showing any fear, "I am not here to make any excuses. I never dreamed of coming from your enemy to spy on you. I am Kazuma of the Ashizaki, a native of Sakamoto in Gō Province. At the time of the disturbance on Mount Hiei, all my family members were scattered and finally they have returned to their native place now that things are quiet. But my younger sister[1101] Tatsuko, has not yet returned. I hear that she is in your camp. I have been looking for her in various places and finally arrived here. Please let me see her once and then I will not regret dying afterwards." Saying this, Kazuma shed tears. "How old is she?" Kazuma answered, "She was seventeen at that time. Nine years have passed since. So she must be about twenty-six years old now."

Immediately [Sakuma had] Tatsuko searched for throughout the camp, and a woman of the same age and name was found. Since she was intelligent and good at calligraphy and reciting poems, she was one of Sakuma's favorites. "She is the one. There is no doubt about it." So saying he untied Kazuma, brought him into a yard with white sand,[1102] and had him meet Tatsuko. As soon as she saw him she cried

....

1101. Since Tatsuko might be one of Sakuma's concubines, Kazuma cannot identify her as his wife.

1102. The *chōba* office here refers to a yard covered with *shirasu*, "white sand," where criminals were investigated.

out, "It's my brother!" She uttered the question, "Is it really he?"[1103] and kept crying. Sakuma said to them, "He has been going around to many places and enduring suspicion at the barriers. He must be exhausted physically and mentally. Let him rest for a while in this camp." Saying this, he gave Kazuma a kimono set and let him stay at a hut in the camp.

On the following day, Sakuma asked Kazuma, "Your sister reads booklets and composes poems well. You also must be good at reading and writing." Kazuma replied, "In my youth I went to a mountain temple, where I was not negligent about learning Buddhist and other writings. As for my calligraphy, I am not so good but better than most people." Hearing this greatly pleased Sakuma and he made Kazuma a proposition. "I have been familiar with military arts since youth and have spent days going around camps, but I never had any interest in the way of letters. Now when I receive letters and poems from other lords, I have no means to reply to them. No one among my men can do that. But now, fortunately, I have you who are familiar with the ways [of reading and writing]. So stay in this camp and take the position." The pleased Kazuma replied, "I would be glad to follow your orders." Kazuma received a fief of two hundred *kan*,[1104] took orders from his lord and handed them down to lower officers, and took care of all writing for his lord. All those in the camp thought that Kazuma held an important position, but no one despised him.

Kazuma was not happy at all. He had come all this way through many difficulties. He had seen her only once and now was separated from her as she lived inside and he outside the compound.[1105] They passed the months only by thinking of each other and hiding their tears with their sleeves. Finally Uzuki, the Month of Changing Robes[1106] arrived and Kazuma took off his soiled kimono. He asked someone to take it to his "sister" [to exchange it with the summer kimono]. He wrote a poem [on a piece of paper] and folded it inside the collar of his old kimono. The poem read:

1103. Her question implies her surprise at seeing her husband's changed appearance.

1104. That is, a parcel of land that annually produced rice equivalent to two hundred *kan* of copper coins.

1105. She lives in the private part of the camp while he is in a public office performing his duties as Sakuma's scribe.

1106. The first day of the fourth month.

iro mienu
kore ya shinobu no
suri koromo
omoi midaruru
sode no shira tsuyu

The color may not show
In this *shinobu*-dyed[1107] robe.
My thoughts[1108] of you
Are in the white dew
On the sleeves.[1109]

Tatsuko received Kazuma's robe and opened the tear on the collar to find his poem. Enduring her tears and saying, "I am sending you the summer robe," the sad Tatsuko wrote her poem on a small piece of paper and sewed it inside the collar of the summer robe. Her poem read:

ika ni shite
yuki te midaremu
michi no ku no
omoi shinobu no
koromo he ni keri

How am I to send you
My enduring love and
Troubled feelings
Through the *shinobu* robe
Dyed in the north?[1110]

....

1107. *Shinobu no suri koromo*, "*shinobu*-dyed robe," refers to a robe dyed with *shinobu* grass, popularly used in Shinobu District, Fukushima-ken. *Shinobu* here means to bear, withstand, or endure the hardships or frustrated feelings of unfulfilled love.

1108. *Omoi*, "a thought" (here meaning love), and *midaruru*, "confused" or "disturbed," can be translated together as "frustrated love"—that is, the love Kazuma must bear or endure. The phrase is repeated in the poem sent by Tatsuko.

1109. The *shira tsuyu* (white dew) in the patterns on the sleeves implies Kazuma's tears. *Dairingushō*, Koi, 4.

1110. *Michinoku*, the northern country, refers to Shinobu District. The poem shows Tatsuko's frustration at not seeing her husband as often as she wanted. *Dairingushō*, Koi, 4.

After seeing her poem, Kazuma's heart was so broken with grief that he became seriously ill. He was at his last moments when Tatsuko finally learned of it. She tearfully asked Sakuma for permission to see him, "My brother's illness is so grave that he may not last long. Please, let me see him one more time to remember him in this life." She was given her lord's permission.

She hurried to Kazuma's hut, where she found her husband lying and groaning. Standing near his pillow, she said to him, "I am here now." Suddenly Kazuma raised himself, took her hands, and sighed deeply. With eyes full of tears, he could not say anything and only moved his mouth. Soon he took his last breath. Feeling sorry, Sakuma buried him in the mountain behind the temple in Tennōji and hired some priests for the funeral. Tatsuko tearfully returned to her place, and lay down with a coverlet over her face. She took neither hot nor cold water. That night, she fell seriously ill from grief and refused any medicine. She only sighed and looked up and down. The following evening she said to Sakuma, "Since I left home, I have served you for years. While traveling to other places, I found no one close to me. Fortunately my brother visited me, but he is also gone. My sadness will be unforgotten even if I change my life. And now my life has come to an end. When I die, please bury me next to my brother so that at least I will see him in the Land after Death, and talk with him about our grief and hardship over the past years, and console ourselves for being outside our home province." So saying, she took her last breath. Sakuma felt utmost pity, buried her next to the mound for Kazuma as expressed in her dying wish, and held a good funeral service as he donated all her clothing to the temple.

In the sixth month of the same year [1580], peace was made between [Nobunaga] and Osaka Castle. After [Priest Kennyo] left the castle, Sakuma also left the camp at Tennōji, and things became quiet. Yagorō, one of the servants of Tatsuko's family who had served the family for a long time, was then a merchant. One day he was on the way from Osaka to Sakai in Izumi.[1111] Coming near Tennōji, he was passing by a newly built house at the foot of the mountain in the east. He saw Tatsuko with Kazuma by the gateway and they spoke to him, saying, "Oh, you are Yagorō. Why don't you drop by and tell us the

....

1111. In present-day Sakai-shi, Osaka-fu.

news of our families." The surprised Yagorō walked back to them and told them, "At home, Master Kazuma's parents have been gone for a long time and Lord Gonshichi, Kazuma's uncle, succeeded [as head of] the family. Lady Tatsuko's parents are still fine, but they sadly look for you and pray to the gods and Buddhas from morning to evening. So please return to them as soon as possible. "I know, I know, but being in the service of my lord, I haven't been able to contact my parents, even though I have been thinking of them," replied Tatsuko. When Yagorō said to her, "I have to return in a hurry, but will you write a letter [to your parents so that I can take it to them]?" Tatsuko said, "Please stay here tonight." She brought some drinks and food and talked with him throughout the night. When dawn came, she wrote a letter explaining everything in detail and gave it to Yagorō, who then left the couple. As soon as he returned to Sakamoto, he gave it to the Masaki couple, while telling them everything about their daughter. Her parents were pleased and quickly opened the letter to find that the words and sentences were undoubtably in Tatsuko's handwriting.

The letter said, "It has been a long time since I saw Yagorō, who told me about things at home. I have missed you very much. Every cloud and the mist that rises in the sky in your direction in the morning and evening remind me of you. I lament that the geese in the autumn sky could not bring me news of you, and my sleeves are now ruined from wiping my tears. At such a time, seeing Yagorō was such a pleasure and I wonder, how can I hide my happy feelings? I was born to my parents, who raised me so affectionately. Their favor has been deeper than the sea, while their care for me is as high as a mountain.

"It is a custom in this life that a man leads while his wife follows him. In the olden days, a mountain collapsed, and the base of the mountain declined. Daylight was covered by smoke, while waves in the lake were aflame.[1112] Grieving people were separated from dear ones in the effort to prolong their lives. They were scattered everywhere like hail and no one knew in which direction. I myself was caught by the fearsome warrior Sakuma. One time I was frightened to be in the camp at Katano, and at another time I was frightened by the battle of Nakanoshima.[1113] I traveled to various provinces following my master,

1112. The sentence suggests Nobunaga's destruction in the Sakamoto area.

1113. Present-day Yodogawa-ku, Osaka-shi. See *Shinchōki*, 3 for information about the battle.

hiding my tears of grief in the ups and downs of my frightening life. Gazing at the misty moon in the spring while bearing the violent winds of autumn, I could not dream unless I turned my night robe inside-out[1114] over my pillow. The times changed as the years passed. I had a visitor [my husband]. Lamenting for the late spring, we tied ourselves to each other like mending a broken willow branch before the gateway, or repairing a broken string. Meanwhile, I and [my husband] gained positions thanks to my lord and spent days working hard to forget our private affairs. Please forgive me for not contacting you until today as if I were neglecting my obligation to repay your kindness." There was a poem inside her letter.

tazuno iru
ashibe no shio no
iyamashini
sode hosu himamo
nakunaku zo furu

Like the cranes
On the reed beach
At high tide,
My sleeves never dry
From the tears for you.[1115]

Reading the letter, her parents were tearfully happy, saying to each other, "We have not heard from her since we were separated. We have been sad thinking that she was not alive. Now we find that she is alive, thanks to the gods and Buddhas to whom we have prayed for her." The father said, "Quickly, we will bring her here and make up for our sad days of the past." He urged Yagorō to hurry [with them] to Tennōji. But when they arrived there, they saw no house with a fine gateway, and only two mounds among thick grass with a trace of rampant foxes. In vain they looked here and there to find the house. There was a temple

....

1114. She could dream of her loved one if she slept with her night robe inside-out. The same expression is found in a poem by Ono no Komachi in *Kokinshū*, Koi, 2.

1115. The rising water of high tide is here compared with the incessant flow of tears. *Dairingushō*, Koi, 4.

one *chō* to the west. When they went to the temple, a priest explained, "These are the mounds of the brother and his sister, whose funerals were held by Lord Sakuma. There is no house around there."

The surprised father opened his daughter's letter to find it a piece of white paper with no letters or any trace of ink. He collapsed by the mounds and cried unashamedly while raising his voice to lament his daughter. "I came here to see you one more time. It is very sad that you are hiding yourself under the mound. If you know the heart of this old father, show yourself and console your sad father." Saying this, the father spent the night there. At night, he dreamed of Kazuma and Tatsuko, who tearfully explained what had happened and asked him, "Please pray for our future deliverance." The father said while still in his dream, "I have come here to take you back to our old place. I will take your relics." The daughter was against him and begged "No, you cannot do that. Since we were buried here, we have to follow the rules of the local Earth Deity.[1116] It will be better for us to settle here quietly. If you move us, you will cause more suffering. Now that we are buried in these mounds, you should not move us. Because of the Earth Deity's anger, some evil spirits will torture you later. So please, please leave us here alone and pray for our deliverance." So saying, his daughter cried as she held and begged him. Then he woke up.

So the father engaged a priest, offered some food to the mounds, had the priest recite the sutras, and tearfully looked after everything properly. Those who saw and heard about the father never failed to be reduced to tears. Some time after returning to Sakamoto, Tatsuko's parents passed away, maybe due to their grief.[1117]

12-3 Atsusa's[1118] Retribution

Sue Harukata,[1119] the governor of Owari Province, plotted against the elder of Ōuchi Yoshitaka, expelled Yoshitaka, took the castle in Yamaguchi, and usurped various fiefs assigned to other *daimyō* lords.

1116. *Jifu* 地府, here referring to the office of the Land after Death.

1117. The story is based on *SS*, 3-5 翠翠伝. Asai reconstructs a romantic tale using Nobunaga's attack on the Ishiyama Honganji as the setting.

1118. Atsusa was also the name of a place in Nagato Province, in present-day Asa-gun, Yamaguchi-ken.

1119. Sue Harukata (d. 1555) plotted against his master, Ōuchi Yoshitaka.

He was so strong that he thought there was nothing in this world to fear, since the great forces [of other lords] followed him. All the generals and samurai of Suō and Nagato [showed they] followed him by lowering their bows and arrows and taking off their helmets. Among them were the Yoshiki and the Oshima of Suō Province. The Mine and Mishiki in Nagato Province did not follow Yamaguchi at first, but later they all surrendered, saying to each other, "It would be better to go along with the trend now. Who would destroy himself because of a sense of loyalty? We better follow him rather than be constrained by the useless sense of loyalty." Thus thinking, many samurai surrendered to Sue. Among such samurai was someone called Danjō Atsusa,[1120] who once had received Yoshitaka's favor. Someone slandered him, saying, "Atsusa has given in temporarily. This must be his plot." Believing the slander, Sue caught Atsusa, chained him to a pole, and set a fire around him. Sue watched him suffer and heard him shout, "I already surrendered to you. But you torture me in this way. If I die here, there should be retribution." Then Atsusa died at the stake. Laughing and joking, Sue said, "Atsusa [burning] at the stake serves him right." He threw Atsusa's corpse into a field.

Six months later, Atsusa was always seen at the right side of Sue, who had hated him. At the battle of Miyajima in Aki Province,[1121] Sue lost to the Mori clan. At that time, some soldiers closely attending Sue saw Atsusa, dressed in armor on a brown horse. He was running straight toward Sue and grabbing his chest to pull him from his horse. It is said that since then, Sue never won any battles again. He always lost.[1122]

....

1120. Unidentified.

1121. Sue sent his army to Miyajima to subdue the Mori in 1555. Later Sue committed suicide after a sudden attack by the Mori.

1122. The story is based on 撥車志, 紹興初福建冠乱賊云々. Asai sets the story against the historical background of the decline of the Ōuchi clan.

12-4 No Success Due
   to the Sin of Lust[1123]

Shiraishi, the director of the *kamon* department,[1124] was serving the Uesugi clan as the general of the foot soldiers. His son Uemon was twenty-three years old and hoped to serve the lord after his father.

From time to time, [the father] appealed to his lord for his son's employment, and a date for the interview was set.

There was a good-looking daughter of seventeen or eighteen at the house Shiraishi was renting. Uemon tried very hard to get her attention, but the father was very strict with his daughter and the slightest noise at night made him very wary. Thus, it was not easy for Uemon to see her. Being so infatuated with her and frustrated, Uemon could not concentrate on his duties, and only looked for moments to see her.

Finally the day before his job interview arrived, and Uemon's father was pleased to prepare for it. That night, the master of the household, the daughter's father, was out for the night on account of an errand for the family. The pleased Uemon stealthily slipped into the daughter's room and attained his aim. He was very happy and went to his room to sleep. That night, he dreamed that a man dressed in a blue hunting robe with an *eboshi* hat was running toward him with a piece of folded paper,[1125] saying, "Tomorrow you will receive a fief of one thousand *koku* of rice." Then he dreamed of another man in red with an erect *eboshi* hat,[1126] saying to Uemon, "The Heavenly Emperor is greatly angered because Uemon committed a private sin, and he has taken back the fief." Then Uemon woke up from the dream.

The following day the splendidly dressed Uemon and his father attended the interview accompanied by samurai guards.[1127] When the

....

1123. One of the five Buddhist sins, which also include killing, theft, lying, and drinking alcohol.

1124. Since the Heian period, the *kamon* department controlled ceremonial affairs and the cleaning of the imperial palace.

1125. The horizontally folded paper used for official documents in the Muromachi period.

1126. Referring to a *tate-eboshi*, as opposed to an *ori-eboshi*, which has a folded top.

1127. *Tōsamurai*, the samurai who were stationed in the samurai office away from the main buildings of a mansion.

kanrei[1128] of the government appeared, something happened to Uemon. Unaware that the director had arrived, he fell into a deep sleep. "Such a careless man will be useless," said the many attendants, and Uemon was not employed. The discouraged father took leave and entered the priesthood.

Without any official employment, Uemon wandered around throughout his life. The one who cannot get what is wished for should not blame life and other people. Just look at oneself. Heaven hates the person who does something he should not, and an official appointment with a fief does not come to him.[1129]

12-5 A Sympathetic Blind Woman Receives a Reward

In the twelfth month of the eleventh year of Eiroku [1568], Takeda Shingen[1130] led his soldiers to Suruga Province to attack Imagawa Ujizane. He burnt the houses around the castle, drove Ujizane out of the castle, and took the province. The confused people fled with their belongings. Meanwhile, the great army of Shingen came, sacked the houses, and looted the valuables. They attacked those who were fleeing, snatched whatever was in their hands, struck them, and knocked them down. The crying of men and women mixed with war cries made it sound as if heaven and earth had collapsed. After a while, everything was burned down and then things became quiet. Ujizane left the castle and no one knew where he went. The victorious Shingen enforced [new] rules in the province and the people finally returned to their homes.

Meanwhile, a young girl of seven or eight years was in a ditch along the street and was crying and shouting, "Mother, father, sister, why are you leaving me alone? Aren't you going to give me food and hot water?

1128. Here referring to the Kanto *kanrei* 関東管領, who assisted the *kubo* 公方, the superintendent of the shogunate in the northeast. The system was set up in 1363 to control the samurai government in the Kanto area, in northeastern Japan. The Uesugi clan traditionally inherited the position.

1129. The story is based on *Hatsushashi*, 竜予人劉観云云. Asai narrates a didactic tale warning about the consequences of wrongdoing, which can prevent one from obtaining a position and promotion.

1130. See *OT*, 5-2, n.5. Shingen attacked Imagawa in 1568 (Koyogunka 甲陽軍艦, 11).

How sad and frightened am I! I am hungry and thirsty. How painful this is!" It was a blind girl. The widow next door heard her crying and went to her, saying to herself, "What a pity! She suffered from smallpox when she was three and lost sight in both of her eyes. Her parents loved her. Since she was smart by nature, they taught her the chapter on the medicinal herbs[1131] and the Kannon chapter[1132] of the *Lotus Sutra,* and had her recite them by heart. While they were tenderly raising her, her father fell out of favor with Miura Uemon,[1133] was imprisoned without reasonable cause, and died in prison. Lamenting her husband's death, her mother became ill and died. After that, her elder sister looked after her, but during the recent disturbance, she was hit by a stray arrow and died. After the castle fell, [all her relatives] dispersed and no one looked after this daughter. If I abandon her, she will eventually die in this ditch." The widow tearfully lifted up the blind girl and carried her on her back to a thatched hut. After the disturbance the widow had lost everything and had no means to raise the blind girl. But she could not leave her alone in the ditch. She brought some rice gruel to the girl and fed her little by little, saying to her, "Your parents suddenly died in adverse circumstances and your sister was hit by a stray arrow during the recent unrest, and also died. Since I felt sorry for you, I brought you here to look after you." As soon as the blind girl heard this, she grieved and cried day and night without taking any food, and then died. The grieving widow greatly pitied her, gathered firewood, and with half-burnt sticks cremated the deceased girl. The widow found two *ryō* of gold attached to the girl's sash. She took the money to a priest, who performed a Buddhist service for the girl. The widow donated the rest of the money to the [temple]. About ten days later, the widow found ten *ryō* of gold inside her hut.

When Shingen heard about the widow, he said, "It is quite rare to see a kind-hearted woman in today's world. Despite being poor, she tried to help a blind girl. And then she found the gold. Without keeping the gold for herself, she donated it to the Buddhist Way. She is a

....

1131. See *OT,* 8-2, n.7.

1132. The twenty-fifth chapter of the *Lotus Sutra* extols the merits of Bodhisattva Kannon.

1133. Miura Uemon, known for his talent at amassing wealth, served Imagawa Ujizane.

very honest woman and comparable to Aoto Saemon.[1134] She found ten *ryō* of gold as a gift from merciful heaven. If government officials, the magistrate, and the chief of staff[1135] arrest her because of the gold, they should definitely be afraid of heaven's punishment." Saying this, Shingen built a new house and gave it to the widow. Thanks to her virtuous deeds, the widow lived more comfortably for the remainder of her days.

Thus in this life, when people are prosperous and have gold and silver, they should be honest, polite, and have a sense of obligation. But when they become degraded, they lack manners, abandon their sense of obligation, and are selfish and greedy, wishing only for their own benefit. That is the tendency of people in general. But in a situation where her house was burned down, she lost her property, and she became so poor that she could not support herself for even one day, the merciful widow took care of the blind girl. Even after the girl was dead, instead of abandoning the corpse she gathered some firewood, cremated her, and offered a Buddhist service with the money she found. This was done for the sake of the deceased girl and not for herself. Who would not be impressed by her deeds?

So I record her deeds here as an example to educate people in the future. If people today forget righteousness when they see profit for themselves, and commit evil acts to benefit only themselves, do we not call them sinners compared to this widow?[1136]

12-6 The Fight between the Big Rocks

Nagao Kenshin lived in Kasugayama Castle[1137] in Etsu Province. Two huge rocks were in the castle before Kenshin died.

One evening the rocks suddenly jumped up into the air and moved around. Suspicious spectators wondered as the rocks rolled down to

---

1134. Aoto Saemon served as a recorder of administrative affairs for the Kamakura government and was known for his honesty.

1135. The *bugyō* 奉行 and *tōnin* 頭人 were Muromachi government officials who took care of local administrative affairs, including minor lawsuits.

1136. The story is based on *Kayatei-kayakuwa* 茅亭客話, 庚子歳天兵討益部賊云々. Asai faithfully follows the original story of a blind orphan and a widow and narrates a didactic tale.

1137. On Mount Kasuga, in present-day Nakayashiki, Jōetsu-shi, Niigata-ken.

a particular spot and fought each other. Soon the rocks leapt up and knocked at each other. The rocks were gigantic and people did not know why they were fighting. They thought it most extraordinary and could do nothing. The rocks fought each other until late into the night. Fragments and splinters from the fighting rocks flew through the air like hail. Finally they were crushed into pieces and the fighting ended.

On the following morning, people spotted bloodstains splattered on the ground where the two rocks had fought. People wondered and became more suspicious. Meanwhile, Kenshin fell ill and passed away. After that, the [Uesugi] brothers[1138] fought against each other. There were battles between the main keep and the castle's second station. In retrospect, people assumed that the fight between the two rocks was an omen of the fight between the two brothers.[1139]

13-1 The Tengu that Lived in a Tower

In the fourth month of the fifth year of Kanshō [1464] a *nō* performance[1140] was held at the river beach of Tadasu, northeast of the capital.[1141] Many *nō* actors, including Master Kanze Onami[1142] and his son Matasaburō, participated along with musicians.

Since it was a rare performance, all the people in the capital, including the upper and the lower classes, gathered like ants and were arrayed like stars to watch the performances. Even the shogun families set up special galleries three times during the performance, and gave silk kimonos, gold, and silver [as gifts for the special occasion] to

....

1138. The fighting was between Uesugi Kagekatsu, a protégé of Kenshin, and Kenshin's adopted son, Kagetora. Kagekatsu won the fight and Kagetora committed suicide in 1579.

1139. The story is based on *Shuih*, 後超石李竜時云々. Asai narrates a story with omens of Kenshin's death and his heirs fighting over the inheritance.

1140. *Nō* performances (*kanjin sarugaku* 勧進猿楽) were held to solicit donations for repairing bridges, temples, and shrines. The one mentioned in the text was held on three days (the fifth, seventh, and tenth of the fourth month) to repair Kuramadera Temple (*Honchō shōgunki* 本朝将軍記, 9).

1141. Various events and entertainment were held on the beach where the Kamo and Takano Rivers meet, in present-day Shimogamo, Sakyō-ku, Kyoto-shi.

1142. Kanze Saburō Motoshige, a nephew of Master Zeami (1363–1443), was a *nō* expert during the reign of Shogun Ashikaga Yoshimasa.

minor and major *daimyō*.[1143] Each day gifts piled up like a mountain.

One day when the shogun was absent, all the *daimyō* were enjoying their most refined courtesies.[1144] Young people sat in the galleries with their family crests on the curtains, while common spectators fought each other for seats on the lawn. Then the dressing room curtain opened and an actor with a *sanbasō*[1145] mask appeared and slowly walked on the *hashigakari*[1146] to the stage. While everyone was quietly watching, suddenly a fire broke out at the eastern end of the gallery. Soon a gust of wind caused over one hundred *ken* of galleries to catch fire. Because it was so sudden, people could not move the standing screen, *misu*,[1147]

....

1143. In the Edo period, those with fiefs of more than ten thousand *koku* belonged to and directly served the shogun, and were called *daimyō* 大名. Those with smaller fiefs were called *hatamoto* and *gokenin*.

1144. *Fūryū* 風流, tasteful courtesies including refinement in dining, clothing, and residence, were highly appreciated by wealthy merchants in the Edo period. *Fūryūjin*, "a person of taste," is still a popularly used term.

1145. 三番叟.

1146. The walkway or passage connecting the dressing room to the stage in a *nō* performance.

1147. Outer screen.

warigo,[1148] and other gifts for the occasion. As soon as the fire spread to the stage and dressing rooms, everyone in the audience tried to escape. But the hedges were so dense that not a single mouse could come in or out. So the confused men, women, and children knocked each other down. Soon heads and limbs were broken from the stampede, while hair and kimonos were on fire. Some were burned to death. Finally someone bravely broke through the hedge and many people came out of the compound.

After the fire died out, the shogun heard of the incident and ordered all the *daimyō* to repair and restore the galleries, including the stage. People were very amazed by how much the *daimyōs* accomplished overnight. But the commoners, including the women and children, did not appear at the second day's performance because they were very disturbed by the previous day's fire. However, the newly repaired galleries were happily crowded with all the *daimyō* of various provinces accompanied by their servants of high and low rank. There were no arguments or disputes over the [fire of the previous day] and the *nō* performance proceeded smoothly.

However, fourteen or fifteen children of townsmen were missing in the capital since the night of the fire. During the confusion, they escaped from the compound and lost their way in the Higashiyama, Kitayama, and Kamigamo[1149] areas. Soon all of them except one were found and returned home. Twelve-year-old Jirō, the son of a merchant of Imadegawa in northern Kyoto, was still missing. In vain, his parents hired many people to search for him in the mountains and temples. Twenty days later, the boy was finally found. He was standing stupefied at Kaguraoka[1150] in Yoshida in Higashiyama. He just sat for four or five days at home without taking any food, only drinking hot and cold water.

When Jirō finally regained himself, he began to speak. "I saw a monk of fifty years at the river beach of Tadasu. He said to me, 'If you want to see the *nō* performance, hang onto my sleeve. Don't say anything.' As soon as I clung to his left sleeve, he and I jumped over the

1148. Wooden containers for food.

1149. The neighborhood of Kamigamo Shrine, north of Funaoka Hill. Higashiyama, the eastern part of Kyoto, is named for Mount Higashi. Yasaka Shrine was at the foot of Mount Higashi. Kitayama refers to an area north of Kyoto, near the Nunaoka Hills.

1150. East of the Kamo River, near Yoshida Shrine, in present-day Sakyō-ku, Kyoto-shi.

hedge and climbed on a certain *daimyō's* gallery. The *daimyō* and his attendants did not see us and said nothing. The monk asked himself, 'What shall I eat?' and took some sake, fish, and fruits, and ate them. But the people around us did not notice and said nothing. When the monk looked around and saw the arrogant looks of the people in the many galleries surrounded by curtains with individual family crests, he said to himself, 'How disgusting to see those unworthy [people] with their beards stuck up, proudly showing off their taste by twitching their noses.' [Then he asked me,] 'Do you want to see them upset? I will show you them confused and upset.' Saying this, the monk held me and jumped up to the roof of the stage and chanted something. Suddenly a fire appeared in the eastern galleries. It was fanned by a gust of wind and then more than one hundred *ken* of galleries caught fire. Meanwhile, the people were very confused and upset and they were injuring themselves. Many of them died. When the stage and dressing rooms had burned down, the monk took me out to the river beach and said, 'Look at them!' He clapped his hands and laughed. 'I enjoyed it so much. Now come to my place,' said the monk as he took me to the nine-storied tower of Hōshōji.[1151] Inside his room [on the tower's top floor], I saw nothing but some hand-bells, *shakujo*, and *dokko*[1152] placed in front of a fearsome-looking image of a Buddha with wings.

"One day, he left me in his room and went down the tower alone disguised as a monk. On the street, sometimes he lowered his head at someone and other times he hit the head of a passerby, spat in someone's face, or pushed a man from behind and made him fall. But no one saw or noticed him doing these pranks. At one time, the monk grabbed the necks and topknots of two men and pulled them together. The surprised men drew their swords and slashed each other bloody. Many days passed in this manner.

"Once the monk went to watch fireflies on Seta Bridge[1153] in Ōmi.

....

1151. 法勝寺, a temple of the Tendai sect, in Okazaki, Sakyō-ku, Kyoto-shi.

1152. *Shakujō,* a walking stick with a lead top, wooden middle, and horn bottom, which makes metallic sounds when shaken. *Shakujō* and *dokko* are ritual objects in the Shingon sect of Buddhism.

1153. In present-day Seta, Otsu-shi, Shiga-ken. The bridge was famous for its fireflies.

He also took me to see the Kamo Festival and Matsuo Festival.[1154] When I asked him, 'What kind of a person was he that you lowered your head [to him] on the street?' he replied, 'He was very honest, merciful, and pious. Without any evil desires, the good gods and other heavenly gods are always with him to protect him. I bowed to him out of fear.' When I asked about the men who were raising their heads high, he said, 'Those raising their heads high usually accumulate wealth for themselves and look down on the poor and fools with their little knowledge. Among them are also those who boast of their meager talents. They keep their heads high and I feel hateful just looking at their faces. Those who I kicked in the back and knocked down were monks without any mercy or piety, who take the offerings of believers only to enrich themselves while boasting of their little knowledge [of the Way]. The two men who fought against each other were boastful about their military merits, so I had them injure each other. And those whose faces I spat on eat horses and cows. They also kill the dogs and chickens they keep at home. They think eating [animals is a mark of] prosperity, but I spat on their faces as I think they are filthy. Those who eat meat are often possessed by the gods of epidemics and are said to cause epidemics. I am afraid of all those who are honest and pious. We get into the bodies of those in higher positions when they are merciless, arrogant, and avaricious, and take their minds to make them into our family members.'[1155] The monk told me various other things that might happen in the future, but I can't speak about them now as they are related [politically] to this world. Then the monk said to me, 'Now you may go home.' I felt that I was coming down the tower, and don't remember anything after that." Thus Jirō concluded his story.

Thereafter everything happened as Jirō had narrated. Since then, a rumor spread that a *tengu* lived in the tower of Hōshōji. Later the temple was burned down during the Ōnin War.[1156]

....

1154. The Kamo Festival, or Aoimatsuri, is the most famous festival in Kyoto and is held in the middle of the fourth month. The Matsuo Festival, at Matsuo Shrine in Ukyō-ku, Kyoto-shi, also was held in the fourth month.

1155. The sentence suggests that those who are arrogant and avaricious become *tengu*.

1156. The story is based on *Dakkōki*, 博士上儒説. Asai introduces a *no* performance held in 1414 (*Sanshūmeisekishi* 山州名跡志).

13-2 A Ghost Fed a Baby with Her Milk

Many members of a farming family[1157] of Kazahaya District[1158] of Iyo Province died one after another, both children and adults. Eventually everyone in the family [who lived] in the village died except two brothers. This must have been an example of a consumption epidemic,[1159] which is said to have destroyed families. While the two brothers were grieving, the younger brother's wife also passed away. As he was living without his wife, their baby born in the previous spring cried and cried for milk. Seeing and listening to his baby crying from morning till night, the younger brother was so sad that his tears never dried. Thirty days after his wife was gone, she returned home. At first the younger bother was afraid of her. But since she visited him every night, he felt he could not ignore her. He became friendlier and spent nights talking intimately with her. Hearing this, the elder brother did not believe it and warned his younger brother, "The forty-nine days of *chūin*[1160] have not passed since your wife passed away.

Yet each night you invite a woman in and talk with her. This will bring shame not only to you but also to me for not having prevented you. You should not invite any woman in until at least a year after your wife's death."

The younger brother tearfully explained, "That is the spirit of my deceased wife coming here every night. In the beginning she knocked at the door, saying, 'I returned because I am so sad that my baby is hungry for milk.' When I opened the door, she held the baby and stroked its head while giving it milk. I was afraid of her in the beginning, but later we became intimate from talking each night. She leaves at dawn and returns every evening. She is the same and hasn't changed." The elder brother heard him and thought, "All the members of my family and the clan are dead except us two brothers. Surely a demon has fooled my brother [in order] to kill him.[1161] If that happens, it would be too late for regrets. Since

....

1157. The original Chinese version is about the Gimon of the Chou clan, a famous family lasting 13 generations.

1158. In present-day Nakashima-cho, Onsen-gun, Ehime-ken.

1159. Tuberculosis.

1160. The seven-week period of mourning after someone has died.

1161. The elder brother thinks that the clan enemy is trying to kill the last family members. In the Chinese story, the two brothers are imprisoned and die, thus putting an end to the whole family.

my brother would never be able to give up the demon appearing as his wife, I must kill her." Thus thinking and without telling his brother, the older brother brought a long sword and hid it by the gateway. At about the Hour of the Boar [around ten o'clock at night], someone opened the gate and entered. Instantly the brother charged and struck her down. "How sad!" she said raising her voice, and she went away.

Bloodstains were on the ground in the morning. The two brothers traced them to the grave of the younger brother's wife, where they found her lying dead by the grave. When they dug up the coffin, they found no body inside. So they buried the wife again, and the baby died too.

A while later the two brothers passed away one after the other, and the clan was wiped out completely.[1162]

13-3 A Snake Came out of a Lump

A farmer's wife of Nishigori District of Kawachi Province[1163] had a lump on the back of her neck. It was as small as a lotus seed in the beginning, but later grew as large as a chicken egg. Later it became as large as a jar that could hold three to four *shō*[1164] of liquid. Finally it grew as big as an earthen pot that could hold five *shō*. It was so heavy that the wife could not walk. When she stood up, someone had to hold it for her. But she had no pain. Sometimes, she even heard string music inside the lump, which consoled her. Later, on rainy and cloudy days, white smoke rose like threads out of the lump from thousands of tiny openings like needle points, and ascended into the sky.

All of the people in the household were afraid and said [to the husband], "If we keep her, she may bring us misfortune. She should be abandoned in a distant mountain or field." The wife tearfully begged her husband, "I know that everybody hates my disease. If I am abandoned, surely I will die. If my lump is cut open, I also will lose my life. If I am to die anyway, please cut it open and see what is inside." The husband thought it reasonable, obtained a sharp razor, and cut vertically to open the top of the lump. It did not bleed, but something

....

1162. The story is based on *Tetsuisan sōdan* 鉄囲山叢談, 河中有佻氏云々. Asai introduces a baby to make the story more poignant

1163. Near present-day Kawachi-Nagano-shi, Osaka-fu.

1164. One *shō* is about 1.8 liters.

jumped out of the white wound. There were five two-foot-long snakes, colored black, white, yellow, and blue. As soon as they were out, they crawled around the garden with their shiny scales. Everyone in the house was so surprised that they tried to hit and kill them. But the husband stopped them. Meanwhile all the snakes crawled into a deep, bottomless hole in the ground.

Soon an *azusa* medium[1165] was called in and he was asked about the situation. The medium said [in a trance], "Once this wife was very jealous of a young maidservant whom her husband loved, and she bit her neck. Since the wife's teeth were dyed black with *kane* liquid,[1166] the girl's wound on her neck became badly infected, and then she died. Due to her deep grievance, as revenge she was reborn as snakes living in the wife's neck to cause her misfortune. Even though they were taken out, the [evil spirit] will take the wife's life to get revenge." Someone off to the side listening to the medium said, "That happened a long time ago. Please calm her down. We will invite a priest to appease the maid's spirit." The medium quickly said, "The grudge of the maid was so strong that it would not be forgotten no matter how many times she was reborn. But you speak of 'appeasing the deceased's soul and spirit.' That sounds hopeful. The spirit might be induced to forgive. There is hope. Should we try to realize it?" The one sitting to the side told the medium, "Yes, we should try whatever is necessary. Quickly tell [the maid's spirit] that." The medium nodded and while shedding tears said, "We know that the *Lotus Sutra* has been the most important in this life. Please [invite a priest], have him make a copy of it for a day to appease and console the deceased's spirit, and apply *kotōrui*[1167] to the wife's wound." After saying this, the medium left. So the wife's family members followed the medium's instructions for consoling the spirit, invited a priest, and had him copy the *Lotus Sutra* for one day. After that, the wife felt cool. *Kotōrui* was found and applied to the wound. The wife finally was cured. Since then, it was said that she left behind her feelings of jealousy.[1168]

....

1165. *Azusa* mediums made predictions to the sound of the *azusa* bow.

1166. Married women used to dye their teeth black with *kane* or *ohaguro* dye made of vinegar and sake mixed with pieces of iron in order to show their married status and to prevent cavities.

1167. *Kotōrui* 胡桐涙, "tears of the *kotō* tree"; that is, the tree's sap.

1168. The story is based on the Chinese *Ishitsushi* 異疾志, 勹俊朝妻. Asai changes the long-handed monkey into the snakes in the lump to teach the wife the Buddhist lesson that jealous people will be reborn as snakes.

13-4 Warding Off an Epidemic

During the Hōtoku era,[1169] the daughter of Lieutenant General Nakayama Chikamichi[1170] lived in Nishiyama[1171] as a nun. She contracted a terminal disease called *rōsai*[1172] and gradually lost her health from occasional fevers and violent coughing.

It was said that the disease is caused by an insect inside one's body. The insect's form was not yet identified. Neither medicine nor acupuncture and *moxa* treatments were effective. Nine out of ten patients died. The insect was called *denshichū,* the transmitting insect.[1173] If one family member died of this disease, the whole family and clan would be destroyed. When three patients died of the disease, the insect was said to stand up and walk in the form of a human being or of a demon with feet, hands, eyes, ears, and a nose.

As time passed, the nun's illness advanced. She became unconscious and was ready to die. Her younger sister was looking after her. [One day] an insect like a white fly leapt out of the nun's body and trailed a white thread through the air. It went into the sleeve of the younger sister and disappeared. She shook her sleeve but could not find it.

That evening the nun died. After that, the younger sister fell sick with the same symptoms as the nun. All her family members grieved and gave her all kinds of treatments in vain. While grieving, [one of the family members] said, "No medicine will work. We should ask for the power of the Buddhas and gods." So [the family members] made an image of Yakushi Buddha[1174] out of sandalwood. They especially prayed to the Gozu Deva King of Gion,[1175] saying, "Please make her

....

1169. 1449–1452.

1170. Fujiwara Norichika (1416–1461) served Shogun Ashikaga Yoshimasa (*Honchō shōgunki,* 9, Minamoto Yoshimasa).

1171. The mountainous area in the western part of present-day Kyoto.

1172. Possibly tuberculosis.

1173. 伝巳虫.

1174. Yakushi Buddha is known for curing illness.

1175. The Gion area in Kyoto is famous for Yasaka Shrine, whose principal image (*honji*) is Yakushi Buddha and transformed image (*suijaku*) is Prince Susanoo. In China, the transformed image is often regarded as Gozu Tennō, the Deva King, with the head of a cow or horse (*Dekisaikyomiyage,* 出来斎京土産, 3 祇園). The *suijaku* 垂迹 is the deity form in which the Buddha appears to help the people. The idea shows how Buddhism assimilated to local deity cults. In this case, the Yakushi Buddha is transformed into the Gozu Deva King.

well." One evening while they were praying and lamenting, the patient dreamed of a stranger who said to her, "Tomorrow a monk dressed in a dark grey kimono with a crimson robe will visit you begging for food. Ask him about your disease." Then she woke up.

The following morning, a monk of fifty who looked very upright from [following] the precepts quietly walked inside the gateway and began to perform zuda[1176] by shaking his shakujō.[1177] When he was invited inside, [the sister] said to him, "I had a revelation in my dream. Please cure my illness." The monk said, "Keeping the precepts, I am devoted to the practices of a traveling ascetic. I am not interested in taking impure foods,[1178] but only in pure zuda. So I will not do what a miko[1179] would do." But [the sister] insisted and asked him, "I understand that a greatly merciful Buddhist monk would help others while forgetting himself. If you save one person, that would make many people happy. Wouldn't that create great merit for you? Besides, I am asking you because of my dream." With such lamenting and beseeching, the monk could not refuse her request. He finally said to her, "Well, if you insist so much. Bring me a roll of white silk. I will try to cure your illness using it."

"That would be easy." As soon as the silk was brought in and offered to the monk, he received it and left. When he was asked about his temple, he replied vaguely, "It is somewhere in the Gion area."

That night the princess [sister] dreamed of a Buddhist image coming into the gateway accompanied by the twelve beneficent deities. When the twelve deities stroked her body from head to foot with a tag, something like a white thread came out of her body and rose into the sky, and she awoke. She felt very refreshed and cool with a good appetite. Her head felt very light, different from previous days.

On the following day, the monk came and gave her the silk roll on which something was drawn, and he left. Feeling strange, she opened the roll and found that an image of Yakushi Buddha was drawn in ink on the silk. She hung the image in front of her pillow and offered

....

1176. 頭陀, a Buddhist practice to eliminate desires arising from daily activities concerning food, clothing, and residence.

1177. See OT, 13-1, n.13.

1178. Fujōgeku 不浄下口, an impure way for a monk to obtain food by lowering his chin to farm and raise food.

1179. 神子, a medium that believes in and prays to the gods to acquire their favor.

homage to the image by burning incense in the morning and evening. Soon her illness was cured and she made the image her family's heirloom This was most extraordinary. The monk said that he came from the Gion area but no one knew about him. So he must have been the Gozu Deva King, who was a transformation of Yakushi Buddha. People said that Buddhist power and an ascetic [monk's] faith never fail to prove beneficial.[1180]

13-5 Zuiten's Strength

Zuiten, an ascetic[1181] of Dentsūin Temple in Koishikawa[1182] in Bu Province, was a native of Bō Province. After taking the tonsure when young, he came to Koishikawa to study. But since he was too poor to afford his meals, he had to travel to beg alms in the provinces of Kō and Shin, and in the two additional provinces of Kōzuke and Shimotsuke.[1183] He could not devote himself to studies and debates. He was physically very strong and none of the monks studying in the *danrin*[1184] could match his strength. So the monks who were studying called him by the strange name of Myōjōza.

Once in China the Zen Master Shinshū[1185] had a disciple called Myōjōza, who also was strong. When Master Enō[1186] of the Sixth Master went to Daiyūrei,[1187] Myōjōza chased him to take back the robe that had been given to his master, Shinshū.[1188] Enō placed the robe on a rock. Myōjōza tried to take it but it was as heavy as a mountain and

---

1180. The story is based on *Ishitsushi* 異疾志, 除明府. Asai incorporates the deity of Yasaka Shrine in Gion who wards off epidemics.

1181. *Shoke* 所化, an ascetic practicing the Way with a teacher.

1182. In present-day Bunkyō-ku, Tokyo-shi. The temple was founded by Priest Ryōyo of the Pure Land school in 1390–1394.

1183. In the southern part of present-day Chiba Prefecture.

1184. See *OT*, 10-6, n.4.

1185. Zen Master Shinshu 神秀禅師 was a high-ranking disciple of the Fifth Master Kōnin 弘忍 in Tang China.

1186. Master Enō made important contributions to the development of Zen Buddhism in Tang China.

1187. The southern part of Daiyūken, in Kōseishō Province.

1188. A robe is given to the successor of a sect or school. Myōjōza tried to take back the robe that had been given to his master Shinshū.

even he could not lift it. Enō said to him, "This robe is meant for those with strong faith, not those who only have physical strength." Myōjōza immediately understood. So being physically strong but weak in [Buddhist] studies, Zuiten was scornfully called Myōjōza.

One time, when Zuiten was walking in the mountains of Shin Province, he met a thief. He ran as fast as he could but the thief did not stop chasing him. Finally Zuiten bent a pine tree along the roadside and rested on it. There the thief finally caught up with him. He said to the thief, "I'm breathless from running away from you, so I am resting. I will give you all the money I have. Please spare my life. Why don't you sit on this tree and rest for a while?" The thief relaxed for a moment and sat down on the tree. When Zuiten got up, the tree sprang up to its original straight form. The thief was catapulted down into the valley. He landed on a rock, where he smashed his head and died. Such was the great strength of the monk Zuiten. Makara Jūrōemon, who served the Asakura clan,[1189] was another strong man.[1190] When Zuiten heard that Makara was the strongest man in the northern area, Zuiten went to challenge him. When he arrived at Makara's house, Zuiten stood on the veranda while Makara stood at the threshold. They grabbed each other's hands and tried to pull each other up. Zuiten did not move. Meanwhile a portion of the veranda's floorboards splintered while the threshold was broken to bits. The spectators were all amazed at their evenly matched strength.

Another time Zuiten attended a debate [on a treatise] and could not answer a question. The monk scornfully said to him, "This competition is [won] by studying, not by physical strength. Now Myōjōza Zuiten has revealed his true nature." Zuiten was so embarrassed that his face turned red. Feeling so ashamed, on the following day from morning to evening, he walked around the town practicing shokehachi,[1191] but the people paid no attention to him. The angry Zuiten said to himself, "Being a useless monk, I might as well wait for a chance and become a layperson," and threw the begging bowl on the ground, tore his priestly robes, and threw them into the river. He

---

1189. Asakura Takakage (1428–1481) unified the Echizen area but Asakura Yoshikage (1533–1573) was defeated by Nobunaga.

1190. Makara was famous for using a five-foot-three-inch-long sword. He earned great glory in the Battle of Anegawa (*Shinchōki*, 3).

1191. 所化鉢, begging for alms.

went to Echizen, worked under Makara, and finally died in the Battle of Anegawa.[1192]

Afraid of sinning while living as a layperson, Zuiten never ignored recitation of Amida Buddha's name. At his last moments, something like a white cloud came out of his mouth and ascended into the western sky. Since it occurred on a busy battlefield, only a few men saw it happen and were able to recount it later.[1193]

13-6 A Lump of Lice

A merchant lived in Morokata in Hyūga Province.[1194] One day a part of his lower back became hot with fever. Twenty days later, the fever and itchiness were gone. This part of his back was swollen like a concave tray turned upside-down. It was not painful but became terribly itchy as it got larger. It became so itchy that the merchant lost his appetite and was reduced to skin and bones. Medical men from all over, including surgeons and doctors for internal medicine examined him. They gave him all kinds of medicine to take orally and ointment to apply to the lump, but in vain. An expert surgeon called Chakuteruzu[1195] came on a *nanban*[1196] merchant ship and saw the merchant's condition. He said, "This is such an unusual illness that not many people know about it. It is called *shitsuryu,* which is caused by lice born between the skin and flesh. I will cure it." Saying this, Chakuteruzu bound the lump with a cord and applied medicine to it. He continued his explanation, saying, "People say that lice born during the night increase their number from three to five *to*[1197] as they fill the victim's clothing and consume the blood and flesh. The victim suffers unbearable pain and itching. But the lice remain only with the victim and do not bother others. This happens occasionally and doctors know the treatment. However, in this case, the lice are under the

---

1192. Oda and Tokugawa defeated Asakura and Asai at the Battle of Anegawa in the Shiga Prefecture in 1570 (*Shinchōki,* 3).

1193. The story is based on *Sumikonronden,* 李摩雲. Asai tells a story about the strong Japanese monk Zuiten.

1194. In present-day Miyazaki-ken.

1195. Unidentified.

1196. 南蛮, "southern barbarian."

1197. One *to* is about 18 liters.

skin and in the flesh, and barely visible to anyone. [My medicine] will prove to be effective this very evening."

That night the swollen lump burst open, and a *to* of lice came out. They were red and looked like large sesame seeds with feet and could crawl well. The patient felt his body become lighter. There was a small hole after the lice came out and more lice occasionally crawled out. Their number was countless. Chakuteruzu repeated, "There is no proper way to treat the lump to cure this disease [except] to burn a hundred-year-old *sukigushi*,[1198] mix the ashes with yellow dragon water,[1199] and apply it to the wound. No other treatment will work. I have a little of this medicine with me and would not regret its loss." Saying this, he applied one spoonful of the medicine to the wound. Just days later, the patient was cured.[1200]

13-7 A Demon in the Mountain

Lieutenant Ihee Koishi was a warrior of Tsu Province.[1201] In the eleventh month of the fifth year of Tenshō [1577] he was confined in the castle of Katoka in Kawachi Province. Because of the evil deeds of the castellan, Matsunaga,[1202] the attacking army was winning and was in a victorious mood and [had high] spirits. Thinking that the castle would not hold any longer, at night Koishi secretly left the castle. He joined his pregnant wife, who was hiding at a place called Yuge.[1203] That night, the couple passed through the Tatsuta Highway[1204] heading to Yamato Province.

Heavily pregnant and due to deliver that month, the wife had a hard time walking. Plodding along, the couple barely reached the pass. They rested a half *chō's* distance from the mountain's public path, as they were afraid of the soldiers chasing them. Then they heard a woman's

....

1198. A comb with small teeth used for removing dirt from the body.

1199. Unidentified. *Kōryusui ōryū* means "yellow dragon."

1200. The story is based on *Ishitsushi*, 虱瘤. Asai has changed the name of the doctor. A similar story appears in *Honzōkōmoku*, 40 人虱.

1201. *The suburb of Osaka.*

1202. Matsunaga Hisahide.

1203. Present-day Yao City in Osaka.

1204. An old highway connecting Osaka to Nara.

voice crying behind them and discovered it was a young maid who had served the wife for a long time. She was following them, tripping and stumbling along. She finally climbed up to the pass and caught up with her mistress. The couple had left her behind, afraid of the soldiers from the castle that were chasing them. When they said to her, "We are still here," and felt appreciative of her [loyal] heart, the girl seemed happy to see them. She tearfully explained, "I was thinking the whole way that I would follow you to the bottom of the sea to serve you, but you heartlessly left me behind, and the two of you tried to escape alone. Since I didn't know what to do, I just followed you." Greatly moved by her appeal, the couple began to depend on her, and decided to rest with her.

That night, the wife went into labor and had an easy delivery. It happened on a night when there was no moon and it was very dark. The husband could not do anything, but the young maid worked very hard looking after the mistress. "Without her, how would we have done anything? We are truly glad that she came after us. We should keep her in the future, as her heart is loyal to us. Whether it is a man or woman, such a servant, who thinks of her master and mistress, is most desirable." Thus thinking, the couple felt most appreciative of the maid.

Now the wife was resting and leaned against a tree while the maid held the baby to her bosom. Facing each other, the three decided, "In the morning, we will look for a house in the mountains and quietly rest there."

Having nothing else with which to celebrate the child's birth, the husband took out a rice ball from a pocket at his waist and gave it to his wife to comfort her. The wife, still leaning against a tree, carefully looked at the maid who was now licking the baby with her tongue. Feeling strange, the wife kept watching her maid, whose mouth got bigger and opened ear to ear. She now put the baby's head into her mouth and began to eat it. When she finished eating the baby's shoulder and right arm, the wife silently woke her sleeping husband. Koishi woke up and saw the situation, stealthily drew his sword, and tried to attack the maid. The maid bounced like a ball, jumped up to the treetops, and immediately changed herself into a fearsome demon. It jumped down to the ground, stood on a rock ten *ken* away from Koichi, and continued to eat the baby's legs and feet. Koishi ran and tried to slay it. In vain he swung his sword, as if dreaming and

chasing [the demon's] shadow. He chased the demon for a while as it finished eating the baby. It moved like a butterfly or dragonfly and finally leapt into the air and disappeared. The helpless Koishi returned to the tree to find that his wife was gone. He called her repeatedly but heard no reply. He did not know where she was taken. Koishi shed tears of blood and sought her in the strange mountain. The night already had turned to dawn when he finally found her head sitting on a rock three *chō* away from the public path. He did not know who had killed her. Seeing her head, Koishi felt enormous grief and tearfully buried the head at that spot. Then he visited a relative in Ōtani in the southern part of Kōriyama in Yamato[1205] and confined himself there for a while. He was feeling that this life was so futile that he began to think of his future life, and decided to renounce this life. He then went to the foot of Mount Kōya,[1206] sequestered himself at a place called Shinbessho,[1207] and observed the precepts. He spent months and years practicing only noble deeds. His whereabouts later became unknown.[1208]

13-8 The Horses that Spoke

In 1489, Junior First Ranked Shogun Yoshiteru[1209] was attacking Sasaki Takayori.[1210] He led his army to Go Province and set up his camp at Magari Village in Kurimoto District.[1211] The shogun was ailing and passed away on the twenty-sixth day of the month.

The night before the [shogun's] demise, an *ashige*[1212] horse in the second of the stable's[1213] fifteen stalls spoke like a human to the horse

....

1205. Present-day Yamaichi, Yamato-gun, Nara-ken.

1206. Kongōbuji, a temple at the foot of Mount Kōya.

1207. Entsūji, a temple on Mount Kōya, in present-day Izu-gun, Wakayama-ken.

1208. Similar stories appear in *Sorori monogatari* 曽呂利物語, 4-6 and *Tonoigusa* 宿直句草, 2-4. The oldest story about a baby being eaten appears in *Konjaku monogatari*, 27-15.

1209. See *OT*, 7-7, n.1.

1210. Sasaki Takayori, or Rokkaku Takayori (d. 1520), controlled the southern part of Ōmi Province and often was in opposition to the shogun.

1211. In present-day Kurimogo-gun, Shiga-ken.

1212. White with black or brown spots.

1213. Referring to a stable housing horses that were used in battle.

in an adjacent stall, saying, "He won't last [much] longer." The light brown[1214] horse in the next stall replied, "How sad!"

The grooms and other servants [who were gathered] in front of the stables heard the horses' conversation and were extremely frightened by it. The shogun passed away the following day. This was truly extraordinary.[1215]

13-9 Talking of the Strange[1216]
Brings the Strange

Since olden times, it has been said that something strange and frightening happens when people gather and tell the one hundred strange tales. There are some rules for telling the *hyaku-monogatari*.[1217]

When participants [in this event] gather on a dark moonless night, they set up an *andon*[1218] that is covered with blue paper and has one hundred lit wicks. One flame is extinguished as each story is finished. The room gradually becomes dark as each flame is extinguished. The atmosphere becomes gruesome in the shadowy blue light. As they continue to tell strange tales, something strange is bound to happen.

One night, five people all dressed in blue kimonos gathered in the area of Shimogyō, the lower part of the capital, and said to each other, "Let's tell the one hundred tales!" Following the rules, they lit the *andon* and began telling stories. Sixty to seventy stories were narrated. It was the season of the twelfth moon, a time of strong winds mixed with snow and usually cold. The people trembled from the cold. Out the windows they saw lights flickering like thousands of fireflies. Then the lights came into the room and gathered like a ball or a round mirror. Sometimes they broke and scattered, changed from color to white, gathered together like a five-foot [white] ball, and stuck to the ceiling. Next they crashed to the *tatami* floor sounding like thunder and then disappeared. Some of the participants collapsed and lost

....

1214. Black with a brownish-white tail.

1215. The story is a typical Japanese Buddhist tale in which animals speaking like humans can be interpreted as an ill omen. Examples include *Katakana-hon Ingamonogatari* 片仮名本因果物語, 2-13 and *Kanninki* 堪忍記, 5-19:7.

1216. *Kai* 怪, strange or unfathomable; creepy or frightening.

1217. 百物語.

1218. 行灯, a paper lantern with a wick inside often placed on a stand with legs.

consciousness. They later revived when [other] people in the house came to help them. Then they recovered as if nothing had happened.

A proverb says, "People should not talk about people during broad daylight. If they do, something harmful happens. They should not talk about demons, otherwise the demons will cause something strange." This must have happened as in the saying. Without completing all one hundred, these tales [of *Otogibōko*] are now finished.[1219]

1219. The story is based on *Ryūjōroku* 竜城録 夜座談鬼而怪至. Asai introduces the Japanese custom of telling the *hyaku-monogatari*. His last remark, "Without completing all one hundred, these tales are now finished," provides a clever conclusion and reflects the form or pattern of *kaidanshu* 怪談集, a collection of strange tales.

....

SELECTED BIBLIOGRAPHY

Unless otherwise stated, all Japanese language works were published in Tokyo.

Primary Sources

Kenji Sakai, *Kōyōgunkan* 甲陽軍鑑. Benseisha, 1979.

Kokinwakashū 古今和歌集, in *Nihon koten bungaku zenshū*, 7. Shogakukan, 1971.

Matsuda Osamu, Watanabe Morikuni, and Hanada Fujio, *Otogibōko* 伽婢子, in *Shin Nihon koten bungaku taikei*, 75. Iwanami Shoten, 2001.

Noma Kōshin, *Otogi monogatari* 御伽物語. Koten Bunko, 1950.

Sentōshinwa kukai 剪燈新和, in *Shin Nihon koten bungaku taikei*, 75. Iwanami Shoten, 2001.

Shinkokinwakashū 新古今和歌集, in *Nihon koten bungaku zenshū*, 26. Shogakukan, 1974.

Shūiwakashū 拾遺和歌集, in *Iwanami bunko*, 105. Iwanami Shoten, 1938.

Sugimoto Tsutomu, ed., *Honzō kōmoku keimō* 本草綱目啓蒙. Waseda Daigaku Shuppanbu, 1986.

Takahiro Okuno, *Shinchōkōki* 信長公記. Kadokawa Shoten, 1969.

Toshiyori zuinō 俊頼髄脳, in *Nihon kagaku taikei*. Kazama Shobō, 1969.

Wakanrōeishū 和漢朗詠集, in *Nihon koten bungaku taikei*, 73. Iwanami Shoten, 1955.

Wakan sansaizue 和漢三歳図絵. Tokyo Bijutsu, 1970.

Secondary Sources:

Brower, Robert H., and Earl Miner, *Japanese Court Poetry*. Stanford: Stanford University Press, 1967.

Callahan, Caryl A., *Tales of Samurai Honor*, in *Monumenta Nipponica*. Tokyo: Sophia University Press, 1983.

Craig, Teruko, *Musui's Story*. Tuscon: University of Arizona Press, 1988.
Dykstra, Yoshiko, *The Konjaku Tales*, 1–6, Intercultural Research Institute mono-
graph series 25. Osaka: Kansai Gaidai University, 1998–2003.
——, *Miraculous Tales of the Lotus Sutra from Ancient Japan*. Honolulu: University of
Hawai'i Press, 1987.
——, "Shintō Tales," *Journal of Intercultural Studies* 5 (1978): 67–88.
——, "Tales of the Compassionate Kannon: The *Hasedera Kannon Genki*," *Monu-
menta Nipponica* 31, no. 2 (1976): 113–143.
Fujioka Sakutarō, *Kamakura Muromachi jidai bungakushi*. Ōkura Shoten, 1915.
Hōjō Hideo, *Shinshū Asai Ryōi*. Kasama Shoin, 1965.
Inagaki Shisei, *Edo seikatsu jiten*. Seiabō, 1963.
Lane, Richard, "The Beginnings of the Modern Japanese Novel: *Kana-zōshi*,
1600–1682," *Harvard Journal of Asiatic Studies* 20 (1957): 644–701.
Mitamura Engyo, *Buke no seikatsu*. Seiabō, 1959.
Mori, Maryellen Toman, trans., *The Peony Lantern*. Hollywood: Highmoonoon,
2000.
Nagai Yoshinori, *Nihon Bukkyō bungaku kenkyū*. Koten Bunko, 1957.
Nishio Kōchi, *Chūsei setsuwa bungakuron*. Shima Shobō, 1963.
Noma Kōshin, *Ryōi tsuiseki*. Kasama Shoin, 1965.
Putzar, Edward, "Inu Makura: The Dog Pillow," *Harvard Journal of Asiatic Studies* 28
(1968): 98–113.
Rucinski, Jack, "A Japanese Burlesque: *Nise monogatari*," *Monumenta Nipponica* 30
(1975): 39–62.
Shirane Haruo, *Early Modern Japanese Literature*. New York: Columbia University
Press, 2002.
Wada Kyōko, *Otogibōko*. Perikansha, 1995.